The Dark Triad of Personality in Personnel Selection

In loving memory of Erika Schwarzinger

The Dark Triad of Personality in Personnel Selection

Dominik Schwarzinger

hogrefe

Library of Congress Cataloging in Publication information for the print version of this book is available via the Library of Congress Marc Database under the Library of Congress Control Number 2022948271

Library and Archives Canada Cataloguing in Publication

Title: The dark triad of personality in personnel selection / Dominik Schwarzinger.
Other titles: Die Dunkle Triade der Persönlichkeit in der Personalauswahl. English
Names: Schwarzinger, Dominik, 1983- author.
Description: The present volume is a translation of D. Schwarzinger: Die Dunkle Triade der Persönlichkeit in der Personalauswahl, published under license from Hogrefe Verlag GmbH & Co. KG, Göttingen, Germany. © 2020 by Hogrefe Verlag GmbH & Co. KG. | Includes bibliographical references.
Identifiers: Canadiana (print) 2022045180X | Canadiana (ebook) 20220451834 | ISBN 9780889376182 (softcover) | ISBN 9781616766184 (PDF) | ISBN 9781613346181 (EPUB)
Subjects: LCSH: Psychology, Industrial. | LCSH: Employee selection—Psychological aspects. | LCSH: Psychology, Pathological. | LCSH: Machiavellianism (Psychology) | LCSH: Narcissism.
Classification: LCC HF5548.8 .S39 2023 | DDC 158.7—dc23

www.hogrefe.com

The present volume is a translation of D. Schwarzinger: Die Dunkle Triade der Persönlichkeit in der Personalauswahl, published under license from Hogrefe Verlag GmbH & Co. KG, Göttingen, Germany.
© 2020 by Hogrefe Verlag GmbH & Co. KG

PUBLISHING OFFICES

USA:	Hogrefe Publishing Corporation, 44 Merrimac Street, Suite 207, Newburyport, MA 01950 Phone (978) 255 3700; E-mail customersupport@hogrefe.com
EUROPE:	Hogrefe Publishing GmbH, Merkelstr. 3, 37085 Göttingen, Germany Phone +49 551 99950 0, Fax +49 551 99950 111; E-mail publishing@hogrefe.com

SALES & DISTRIBUTION

USA:	Hogrefe Publishing, Customer Services Department, 30 Amberwood Parkway, Ashland, OH 44805 Phone (800) 228 3749, Fax (419) 281 6883; E-mail customersupport@hogrefe.com
UK:	Hogrefe Publishing, c/o Marston Book Services Ltd., 160 Eastern Ave., Milton Park, Abingdon, OX14 4SB Phone +44 1235 465577, Fax +44 1235 465556; E-mail direct.orders@marston.co.uk
EUROPE:	Hogrefe Publishing, Merkelstr. 3, 37085 Göttingen, Germany Phone +49 551 99950 0, Fax +49 551 99950 111; E-mail publishing@hogrefe.com

OTHER OFFICES

CANADA:	Hogrefe Publishing Corporation, 82 Laird Drive, East York, Ontario M4G 3V1
SWITZERLAND:	Hogrefe Publishing, Länggass-Strasse 76, 3012 Bern

Printed and bound in Germany

ISBN 978-0-88937-618-2 (print) • ISBN 978-1-61676-618-4 (PDF) • ISBN 978-1-61334-618-1 (EPUB)
http://doi.org/10.1027/00618-000

Contents

Preface

In recent years, three classics of psychology have once again gained greater scientific and, above all, public recognition – narcissism, Machiavellianism, and psychopathy. Under the appealing title of the "Dark Triad of Personality" (Paulhus & Williams, 2002), they are increasingly being considered in many different areas, from couple psychology to management research. Just a few years have seen the compilation of an enormous breadth of knowledge about the Dark Triad. Currently, however, a growing number of critical voices are complaining that the depth and stringency of some research have been partly neglected; this hinders scientific progress, often creates misunderstandings, and may ultimately pose considerable risks, especially for applied purposes.

This book discusses the *Dark Triad of Personality in Personnel Selection,* an applied field that is not only highly regulated legally and professionally, but that, because of its significance for both individuals and organizations, also requires a special sense of proportion and quality, not at least for reasons of professional ethics. The following text addresses all relevant aspects for such an application, evaluates the current state of research, and provides practitioners with a solid basis for operative applications of the Dark Triad in the workplace.

There are many individuals and organizations without whom the present book would not have been possible; I can only honor the most important ones here. My greatest thank goes to Professor Heinz Schuler for many years of inspiration and collaboration; to the Hogrefe Publishing Group for the excellent cooperation on the present book project and the test TOP, especially Tanja Ulbricht and Sara Wellenzohn for the original German versions; to Lisa Bennett, Regina Pinks-Freybott, and Robert Dimbleby for the present English language adaptation; and, finally, to Anne Konz, on behalf of all readers, for her invaluable linguistic revisions and corrections to the manuscript.

Dominik Schwarzinger
Berlin, August 2022

1 Introduction

1.1 The Dark Triad of Personality – A Trending Topic in Organizational Psychology

The traits of narcissism, Machiavellianism, and subclinical psychopathy have become a big topic in psychological research since first considered together under the term Dark Triad of personality over the last two decades. We see this in the number and the breadth of content of scientific articles published on the Dark Triad. The initial work of Paulhus and Williams (2002), for example, has been cited several thousand times, and Muris et al. (2017) included almost 100 papers in their meta-analysis, each comprising all three Triad components. The vast majority of these papers have been published in recent years, thus witness to a nearly exponential increase in the number of articles (see Figure 1).

In 2019 – only 3 years after the editorial deadline of that meta-analysis and 17 years after the introduction of the Dark Triad – several hundred specific specialist publications had become available. The journal *Personality and Individual Differences* alone published more than 20 per year. A selection of the topics explored in these articles on the Triad illustrates the breadth of the burgeoning interest: number of children, intelligence, preferences for place of residence, academic misconduct, insomnia, violence in relationships, sporting activity, behavior in social media.

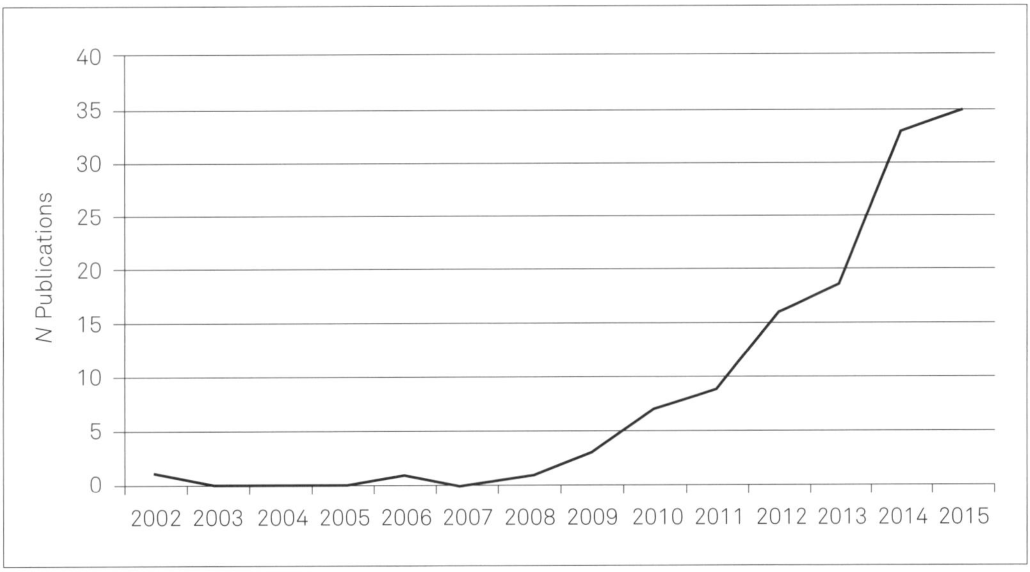

Figure 1. Publications on the Dark Triad since the creation of the term, based on a web-of-science search. Reprinted with permission from "The malevolent side of human nature: A meta-analysis and critical review of the literature on the Dark Triad (narcissism, Machiavellianism, and psychopathy)," by P. Muris, H. Merckelbach, H. Otgaar, & E. Meijer (2017), *Perspectives on Psychological Science*, 12, 185. © 2017 Sage.

The trend extends so far that several publications now contain considerable criticism (e.g., Adam, 2019; Miller et al., 2019). This criticism is leveled not so much toward the concept of the Dark Triad itself as toward how studies are conducted, such as the theoretical foundations and the measurement methods used – but above all toward how the multitude of findings was not cumulatively studied and integrated. In other words, these questions concern some of the very principles of serious scientific research. We can understand this criticism as being directed at both those undertaking the research and at the system that has generated and permitted an excessive number of such uncritically verified publications, all of which contributed to the current, partially confused state of the research on the Dark Triad.

This situation is something that occurs from time to time in various scientific fields, which the scientific community concerned is in the process of trying to rectify, and as a result is perhaps not such a serious matter. A comparatively greater problem, however, is that, before the above-mentioned corrections and without recourse to the admonitions of the relevant experts, the Dark Triad has also attracted overwhelming interest in disciplines related to psychology, such as business management and human resources research but above all in the popular scientific and general press. This interest has arisen primarily because of the impact the Dark Triad has on the working world, a research focus that has recently become increasingly important (e.g., Cohen, 2016; O'Boyle et al., 2012; Spain et al., 2014; Wille et al., 2013). The results of this research are readily adopted outside academia, in particular in online media of all types and quality, but also in the career sections of major daily and weekly newspapers. Indeed, there has been real hype about the impact of these features in professional life.

For example, we read articles with titles such as "The Dark Triad – Why Radically Ruthless People Get Ahead" which discuss narcissists and psychopaths in top management positions. The popular debate thus emphasizes the enhanced values of the Dark Triad as partly conducive to professional success, especially in leadership positions, whereas, according to the definition of the characteristics and the traditional colloquial use of the terms, they are primarily and predominantly associated with *negative* consequences for third parties. A fact that has been well proven empirically in the last few years.

Based on the previous scientific findings (or the media coverage?), it cannot surprise that employers would like to "detect, remove, punish, [or] retrain employees with these characteristics" (Jonason et al., 2014, p. 122). For the characteristic of psychopathy, there have been several calls for the use of screening measures to keep dangerous persons away from certain positions (Skeem et al., 2011). Several relevant authors explicitly refer to possible aptitude-diagnostic use, namely, personnel selection based on the Dark Triad (e.g., O'Boyle et al., 2012; Schyns, 2015; Wu & LeBreton, 2011) – which has now turned it an object of recent personnel psychology research.

Further research into the effects of the Dark Triad in the workplace is urgently needed if it is to be used not only for the accumulation of scientific knowledge and for public discussion, but also in everyday human resources work. To justify the actual operative use of the Dark Triad traits as a basis for personnel decisions, one must first be able to reliably predict criteria relevant to this purpose – and here the findings are far less clear than public reception would suggest. Luckily, based on data stemming from companies and professionals, there is now enough high-quality empirical work available to allow statements about the extent to which the use of the Dark Triad may be beneficial in personnel work – and for which purposes.

However, the applied use of narcissism, Machiavellianism, and psychopathy in aptitude diagnostics generates several potential problems, ranging from ethical considerations and professional-legal guidelines, to still unclarified theoretical issues and the basic psychometric demands on the standard test procedures used for this purpose. In contrast to the criteria relationships that have so far been the subject of most research, these questions are still largely unresolved, primarily because Triad research was not oriented toward work and organization from the beginning, and because a broader occupation with this matter has taken place only in the last 10 years. Above all, however, we have little experience in the organizational context concerning how the Dark Triad can be applied succesfully in practical personnel work, what reactions it provokes, and how valuable the results obtained really are. This book makes initial contributions to this and examines whether the hype about the Dark Triad of personality is justified from a personnel-psychological point of view.

1.2 Do We Need to Consider Dark Personality Traits in the Workplace?

The present focus on dark personality traits in work and organizational psychology arose mostly from the desire to identify features responsible for employees or executives "derailing" their careers – a risk some authors perceive for more than half of all managers (Dalal & Nolan, 2009). Based on expert estimates, Simonet et al. (2018) assume that the cost of a single "derailed" executive can run into the millions, making them costly and as we will see, also common.

In De Fruyt et al. (2013), 20% of the managers tested had a potential personality disorder. The authors make clear that every HR manager should deal with this issue, since 15% of the population (here: USA) display at least one personality disorder or its symptoms during their lifetime: Every HR manager thus inevitably encounters affected employees. This also demonstrates that the problem affects not only managers or employees from the higher hierarchical levels of an organization; on the contrary, the "dark side" of a person's personality (especially if one includes not only clinical disorders but also their much more widespread subclinical forms) is one of the main factors influencing deviant behavior at all levels and in all sectors of the economy (see Sections 2.2 and 4.1).

Although the study of dark personality traits is certainly relevant and not new, only in recent years has it attracted widespread interest in industrial and organizational psychology and management sciences (Harms & Spain, 2015). This even led to two special journal issues on the subject of dark personalities in the workplace (Murphy, 2014; Stephan, 2015). These show that a wide variety of mental disorders and more harmless abnormalities – and even excessive manifestations of actually positive characteristics, such as perfectionism – are usually negatively associated with job performance (e.g., McCord et al., 2014). Other studies also discuss the positive effects of dark characteristics, although these are not unequivocally the case and do not apply in the same way to all characteristics and occupations (e.g., Gaddis & Foster, 2015).

In summary, the literature recognizes the potential added value of looking at the dark side of personality while pointing out the unclear and sometimes contradictory state of research – especially for the practical application in personnel work – and the considerable limitations and risks that are still largely unexplained and often not researched. Jackson (2014) states that job-related research is appropriate for maladaptive personality traits in general, but that the step toward applying it to actual staffing decisions presents challenges that are anything but trivial. Harms and Spain (2015) see dark traits eventually becoming mainstream in research, while for the application of these traits in organizational practice unresolved questions remain regarding their theoretical foundation, primarily those that address the practical detection of dark personality traits.

Spain et al. (2014), for example, point out in their review that the most widely used inventories for measuring the Dark Triad have been criticized for their psychometric quality while also raising practical and even potentially legal problems, especially regarding their use in applied professional contexts. O'Boyle et al. (2012) see extreme limitations to the commonly used measures, which they describe as inadequate specifically for personnel selection. That drives their clear recommendation – shared they say by many other authors – that future research on the Dark Triad be concerned with better job-related measurement.

The great interest in the Dark Triad and its presumed aptitude-diagnostic benefits thus is juxtaposed against a multitude of unresolved questions concerning its actual usefulness and applicability for practical personnel assessment – first and foremost concerning the measurement methods to be employed for this purpose. The present book addresses these problems and closes the gaps in our knowledge regarding the Dark Triad in personnel selection. However, because of the great damage that accompanies these dark characteristics as well as the great opportunities offered by observing the dark side, I call for more efforts to be made – both in research and practice – to fully exploit the potential of these characteristics while also preventing serious mistakes from being made with dealing with other people (applicants). It is paramount in this pursuit that we do not switch to the dark side by displaying noncompliant behavior ourselves.

1.3 The Structure of This Book

As mentioned in the previous section, there is a need for further research on the effects of the Dark Triad of personality at the workplace along with considerable skepticism about its practical applicability, viz. the use of existing measurement methodology for purposes of personnel selection. The present book, therefore, aims to clarify the extent to which – and how – the Dark Triad may be applicable in operational personnel work. To this end, I present findings from the current literature that can be used to evaluate the basic aptitude-diagnostic usefulness of narcissism, Machiavellianism, and subclinical psychopathy as well as discuss the general conditions and requirements for their practical use, especially for personnel selection. I then present a test procedure to meet the requirements regarding legal and professional guidelines and practical applicability in the target field of an organization. Thus, like the "grand migration" (Furnham, Richards et al., 2013, p. 200) from the clinical to the subclinical sphere, this text attempts to establish a "small migration" (Schwarzinger, 2020, p. 13) of the Dark Triad from the subclinical to the sphere of work.

The necessary steps of this migration movement can be divided into two large blocks: the basics and practical application. Chapters 1 to 3 comprise the basics, Chapters 4 to 6 the practical application. Chapter 7 presents a conclusion with recommendations.

Following this Introduction, I present the basics for the main topic in Chapter 2, which is therefore kept rather concise. Section 2.1 concerns the status of personality structure research and the systems developed in clinical psychology. Regarding the former, I discuss the widely recognized Big Five and HEXACO models, and regarding clinical psychology, I primarily touch on the DSM system of the American Psychiatric Association (APA). Section 2.2 regards central findings on personnel-psychological applications of general personality traits and common conceptualizations of professional success and failure. Building on this, in Section 2.3 I deal with the concept of so-called dark personality traits, describing in more detail the background to the ever-growing occupation-related interest, the genesis of the term, and the characteristics it covers. In addition, I differentiate it from the DSM system and describe the new, alternative DSM-5 model for personality disorders.

Chapters 3 and 4 are devoted to the Dark Triad of personality. Section 3.1 provides an introduction to the historical development and the current state of research on the (isolated) consideration of the three characteristics of narcissism, Machiavellianism, and psychopathy. Section 3.2 describes selected (non-occupation-related) findings on the characteristics of the issues that have received the most attention in research. These findings serve to provide a basis for understanding the typical motivation and behavior of Dark Triad characteristic bearers, which is also important for developing an occupational understanding of these characteristics. Section 3.3 compares different views on the structure of the Dark Triad, typical analytical methods used in its study, and the methodological criticism formulated in recent years, especially concerning these aspects. It also distinguishes the Dark Triad components from each other and describes their respective characteristics.

Chapter 4 presents a wide range of evidence for the basic aptitude-diagnostic usefulness of the Dark Triad. Section 4.1 turns, first, to their relationships with counterproductive behavior in the workplace, whereas Section 4.2 regards their relationships with criteria of job performance and success as well as (destructive) leadership behavior. Section 4.3 discusses further aptitude-diagnostic fields of application of the Dark Triad as well as occupationally relevant correlates of interest in practical personnel work and career guidance.

Chapter 5 deals with the professional, legal, and ethical demands placed on the operational use of the Dark Triad. Section 5.1 concerns the various measurement approaches proposed so far for the Dark Triad and then evaluates them regarding their quality and usability in personnel practice. Building on this, Section 5.2 discusses the necessity of job-related measurement procedures and the professional and legal requirements for the use of such procedures in the context of applied aptitude diagnostics. Finally, Section 5.3 focuses on the viewpoint of the applicants and associated ethical aspects.

Chapter 6 provides an overview of the test procedure Dark Triad of Personality at Work (TOP; Schwarzinger & Schuler, 2016, 2019) as an example of an explicitly work-related inventory of the Dark Triad. Section 6.1 first summarizes the objectives of test development and describes the construction of the TOP, from the formulation of items to item analysis to the factorial exploration of the item material. Section 6.2 reports the results of the reliability and validity studies regarding the relationships to external variables, their effects on third parties, and measures of individual and collective performance and professional success. The final part of this chapter, Section 6.3, addresses questions about the practical use of the TOP, the legitimacy of its application against the background of professional formal and legal standards, and its acceptance by the test participants.

In a joint consideration of the theoretical work on the content and structure of the Triad, its measurement methodology and occupation-related findings, as well as the operative application requirements of legal and professional nature, Chapter 7 draws some conclusions and provides practical recommendations for the use of the Dark Triad of personality in both empirically researched (Section 7.1) and practically applied vocational-aptitude diagnostics (Section 7.2).

2 (Dark) Personality, Work Performance, and Professional Success

Before I explore the focal topic of the Dark Triad of personality in Chapter 3, I would like to devote this chapter to an overview of the different approaches to the question of what constitutes human personality in general, the dark side of personality, and the job-related application of "bright" and "dark" characteristics. Because of the breadth and depth of these lines of research, I do not claim completeness. Nevertheless, an overview of the commonly studied major personality traits and how they affect work performance as well as the concepts and classifications chosen in clinical psychology for the most common personality disorders is important as a basis for understanding the structure of the Dark Triad, its kinship relations, and previous profession-related findings.

In addition, I present various conceptualizations of job performance and job success, to define the criteria for assessing the aptitude-diagnostic suitability of personality traits and the Dark Triad.

2.1 From Physiognomy to the Five-Factor Model and the DSM-5

The study of the human personality looks back on a long and varied history that has failed to produce a singular and unambiguous system comparable to that of natural scientific theory, "not to mention [the absence of] a periodic table of the psychic elements" (Schuler, 2014a, p. 143). It is therefore not surprising that, through the ages, personality has been defined quite differently depending on the time and language background (Amelang & Bartussek, 1997). This ranges from early attempts to address differences in character traits from the "outside," that is, from someone's appearance or behavior, examples being Lersch's phenomenological personality theory and – already linked to aptitude-diagnostic expectations – Lavater's physiognomic interpretation of character (Schuler, 2014a); to investigations from the "inside," using modern neuroscientific or molecular genetic methods (see Asendorpf, 2009).

2.1.1 "Normal" Personality and Personality Disorders

Today, a multitude of personality theories still exist side by side. The most widespread and accepted view resulted from empirical research on personality using a trait-based approach to differentiate and classify personality by (empirically) reducing it to a few statistically independent dimensions. There is currently widespread agreement that human personality in the normal range can be described completely with varying degrees of expression on these broad dimensions – between three and seven depending on the author – which can be explained by fewer higher-order factors or can be divided into two central aspects and further subfacets (Guenole, 2014).

Research on hierachical models also managed finding two higher-order factors, designated alpha and beta (Digman, 1997) or stability and plasticity (DeYoung et al., 2002), and a general factor of personality (e.g., Erdle & Rushton, 2010; Musek, 2007) as well as confirming the usefulness of finer-grained subfacets (e.g., DeYoung et al., 2007) – especially for application-related questions. Below, I will come back to this approach in my treatment of the Dark Triad of personality. Neuroimaging or molecular genetic methods increasingly confirm the assumptions of the trait-based approach and point out specific differences for personality factors in brain anatomy (e.g., DeYoung et al., 2010).

The findings described, however, refer to the so-called "normal" area of personality. Although there are some connections between this area and mental disorders – and the latter are sometimes simply seen as extreme manifestations of human character traits (see Moscoso & Salgado, 2004) – classification schemes have emerged in clinical psychology which are virtually independent of this area. These include the *Diagnostic and Statistical Manual of Mental Disorders*, DSM for short (DSM-5; APA, 2013), and the *International Statistical Classification of Diseases and Related Health Problems*, ICD for short (ICD-11; WHO, 2019).

The ICD is much more broadly based on diseases in general, whereas the DSM focuses exclusively on mental diseases, which is why it can also map more disturbance patterns and more finely broken-down diagnostic criteria. The ICD-11, in the section on personality disorders check lists only general characteristics of the group (though, for example, neither narcissism nor psychopathy is further explained or their diagnostic criteria detailed). Section 3.1.1 of this volume provides some criteria for narcissistic personality disorder according to DSM-5 as an example of such a classification scheme. A diagnosis can be made, for example, using the *Structured Clinical Interview for DSM-5 Disorders* (SCID-5-CV; First et al., 2019). However, only persons with a corresponding license, such as psychotherapists, are authorized to officially diagnose and treat personality disorders.

In contrast to the dimensional view of distinctive traits outlined above, the DSM and the ICD agree in their focus on typical clinical profiles manifested by certain symptoms: a categorical model of mental disorders.

Yet, the domains of clinical and normal personality are not completely independent of each other, as evidenced in conceptual work, for example, on the Big Five and DSM disorders (Widiger et al., 2002) or on the meta-analytically confirmed correlation patterns for these domains (Samuel & Widiger, 2008a) as well as the shared latent dimensions of both sides and proposals for a common version under a hierarchical model (Markon et al., 2005). In the clinical field, the "phenomenological view" (or categorical view) is therefore increasingly being supplemented by a dimensional one (e.g., Eaton et al., 2011). This is why the DSM also includes an approach to a dimensional conceptualization of personality disorders in Part III of its latest version (DSM-5) – although the previous categories remain in the main part of the DSM-5.

In my reflections on dark personality traits in Section 2.3.1, I discuss the DSM-5 and the new dimensional approach contained therein in more detail. But first, I want to present a concise outline of the state of the art of research on normal personality traits and then (in Section 2.2) its possible applications in personnel psychology.

2.1.2 The Big Five and the Absence of Dark Factors

The so-called Five-Factor Model of Personality (FFM) by Costa and McCrae (1985) with its five broad bipolar dimensions (Neuroticism, Extraversion, Openness to Experience, Agreeableness, and Conscientiousness) is today generally accepted as a frame of reference. The synonym Big Five is also used for this model or its components (Goldberg, 1993). I discuss the development of this model in more detail in the following, as it is possibly one of the principal reasons for the long disregard of dark characteristics. The question is: Why are the dark traits not part of the classic, broad personality models such as the Big Five?

As early as 1933, Thurstone first reported on an FFM, and other well-known authors such as Cattell or the Guilfords found solutions like today's Big Five (Digman, 1996). A milestone in personality structure research was the lexical approach of Allport and Odbert (1936) to extract personality descriptions from a standard dictionary. On this basis, Cattell (1947) initially identified 35 trait clusters, which Fiske (1949) reduced to five factors (Wiggins & Trapnell, 1997). Tupes and Christal (1958, 1961) first found a clear and generalizable factor-solution in Cattell's variable clusters that consisted of five traits: enthusiasm/extraversion, tolerance, conscientiousness, emotional stability, and culture (Wiggins & Trapnell, 1997), which is why they are called the "true fathers" of the Big Five (Goldberg, 1993, p. 27). By the late 1980s and 1990s, there was a "near-consensus on the number and nature of the basic dimensions of personality differences" (Lee & Ashton, 2006, p. 182), and with the spread of the first inventory based on the five factors, the "hegemonic position" of the FFM was manifested (Schuler & Höft, 2006, p. 117).

But why are there no dark characteristics in such an elaborate model? Spain et al. (2014) attribute this to a lack of dark personality aspects in the lexical approach. According to Tellegen (1993), for example, evaluative descriptions such as "evil" were removed from the basic adjective list of Allport and Odbert (1936) that was later factor-analytically condensed into the Big Five (see also Saucier, 2019). That certain "negative" aspects are missing is shown by the fact that the inclusion of corresponding adjectives in new and independent lexical studies not only produced new extreme aspects of existing factors but also led to completely new ones that point in precisely this direction (see HEXACO, Ashton & Lee, 2008; Big-7, Waller & Zavala, 1993).

Of the other models under discussion, I would like to briefly discuss only that of Ashton and Lee (2008) in more detail (see box HEXACO model): Here, new lexical analyses (of seven European and Asian languages as well as in other language families of different origins) enabled to identify a factor that encompasses central aspects of dark personality traits (via their exact opposite).

HEXACO Model

In the HEXACO model of personality structure, the new factor Honesty-Humility is found as the sixth main dimension of personality, in addition to Emotionality, Extraversion, Agreeableness, Conscientiousness, and Openness to Experience.

Emotionality and Agreeableness are not direct equivalents of the FFM factors, merely their rotated variants; the factors Extraversion, Conscientiousness, and Openness to Experience of the HEXACO model, on the other hand, very closely resemble those of the

FFM (Lee & Ashton, 2006). Although the model thus does not simply represent a "Big Five +1" model, its central contribution lies in the new factor of Honesty-Humility or the "H-factor." In simple terms, this sixth factor represents a kind of opposite of those traits often associated with or subsumed under the Dark Triad, which is why Paulhus (2014) sees low values on the "H-factor" as a common core of the Dark Triad (see Section 3.3).

Lee et al. (2005, p. 182) examined and described the content of this new factor and its added value to the Big Five in predicting workplace delinquency as follows: "[Honesty-Humility] represents individual differences in a reluctance versus a willingness to exploit others, a tendency that is not adequately captured by any of the Big Five factors." As discussed below, precisely this tendency to exploit others for one's own benefit is a key characteristic of the Dark Triad. Further findings on the overall connection of the "H-factor" and the personality models presented with the Dark Triad may be found in Chapter 3. The next section deals with the criteria of professional success and their connections with "bright" personality traits.

2.2 Predicting Job Performance with Personality Traits

I now present common operationalizations of job performance and success because the connections of the Dark Triad with these criteria serve as the main justification for using narcissism, Machiavellianism, and psychopathy for aptitude diagnostics. I subsequently discuss findings on the validity of general personality factors for the prediction of these criteria.

2.2.1 Job Performance and Success

Job performance is one of the most researched criteria in industrial and organizational psychology, as reflected in the number of published articles on the subject (see Cascio & Aguinis, 2008). Job performance can be understood as a multidimensional concept that includes the total contribution of an individual to organizational success (Motowidlo, 2003). This makes instantly clear there is no single job performance, but rather it presents a construct consisting of many interconnected subaspects in a longer-term perspective, all of which contribute to the overall performance – and all of which are based on an overarching factor (Lohaus & Schuler, 2014; Viswesvaran et al., 2005). Attempts to measure job performance can therefore capture only individual aspects of the overall performance in each case; single performance criteria are deficient, i.e., they fail to capture all relevant parts of the total performance and are contaminated, having been exposed to influences unrelated to the actual performance of the person (Lohaus & Schuler, 2014).

To distinguish from actual work performance is *professional success*, the hallmark of which is not the contribution to the success of the organization, but the individual result (also beyond the concrete workplace). Especially in the case of dark personality traits do the differential relationships to these two criteria – individual success and the company's success – seem very likely. To measure success, we often use objective measures such as salary, salary increases, or promotions as criteria (Henslin, 2005), though these are deficient because in many occupations, and for many people, success cannot be validly measured in monetary terms or according to classical hierarchies. In addition, success at work can also be measured based on the purpose of the activity, one's own satisfaction with it, the feeling of personal fit with the workplace and the organization, or the concrete activity for one's own interests (Schuler, 2014a). Although research usually focuses on the relationship between different predictors and job performance, one can also consider subjective measures of success such as job satisfaction or career satisfaction. Both areas are interdependent but should be understood or measured as independent constructs (Henslin, 2005).

In addition to job satisfaction, (organizational) commitment is a second, important variable that describes value attitudes toward work. One measures the subjective perception of one's own task or job, the other one's perception of the fit and binding to the organization (Sanecka, 2013). Both thus represent indicators of a successful professional placement or development. I discuss various forms of measuring objective and subjective success and job performance again at the end of this section, but let us start here by introducing the most important aspects of the latter criterion.

A widespread differentiation of job performance is the classical one forwarded by Borman and Motowidlo (1993) into task performance and contextual performance. Task-related performance comprises the clearly describable or required performance at a workplace; contextual performance comprises such contributions toward colleagues, teams, or the organization which are often not formally required, i.e., are voluntary and do not serve the actual fulfillment of the job. A closely related or very similar concept, often used synonymously, is organizational citizenship behavior (OCB; Smith et al., 1983), which distinguished early on between behavior related to individuals, such as helping a colleague, and pro-organizational behavior, such as speaking positively about the company (Sackett et al., 2006).

Task- and contextual performance have a high, meta-analytically generalizable correlation and can, as described, be understood as components of the construct of general job performance. However, they must also be considered independently, at least in the peripheral areas. For example, we find a curvilinear effect such that too much commitment to others (from about half a standard deviation above average) leads to a decline in one's own task-related performance (Rubin et al., 2013).

Counterproductive Behavior in the Workplace

Counterproductive work behavior (CWB) is a concept that cannot be strictly counted as job performance but, on the contrary, describes behavior that decisively reduces or even negatively impacts a person's overall value to the organization. CWB comprises all intentional actions that are principally capable of causing damage to the organization or one of its members (Marcus & Schuler, 2004; Nerdinger, 2008). Although situation-specific factors and overall conditions also play a role here, the personality of an employee is central to the probability of their showing counterproductive behavior – theoretically explainable with specific Big Five profiles, low integrity, or lack of self-control (Marcus, 2000).

The latter approach to explaining counterproductive behavior represents a possible link to the Dark Triad, as it is also associated with a lack of self-control or impulsiveness (see Section 3.2.5). Gottfredson and Hirschi (1990) postulated low self-control as a cause of criminal acts in general and it is considered a driver of counterproductive behavior (Mussel, 2003). Lack of self-control was proposed as the first explicitly theoretical explanation for the CWB phenomenon, and it has since been empirically confirmed that the influence of this in-person variable is greater than that of situational conditions (Marcus & Schuler, 2004).

Bennett and Robinson (2000) demonstrated the great relevance of CWB for companies by compiling studies showing high levels of employee theft, absenteeism, drug abuse, and sexual harassment in the workplace. Apart from the resulting individual consequences for the victims, companies and the national economy suffer losses of billions each year as a result of each of these areas of counterproductive employee behavior (Marcus, 2000).

Like job performance, CWB is also assumed to have an underlying factor that can be broken down into different targets or victims or types of offenses (Marcus et al., 2016; Sackett, 2002). Well-known conceptualizations are the division into behaviors counterproductive toward the individual and toward the organization (Bennett & Robinson, 2000) and a comprehensive model by Gruys and Sackett (2003), which condenses CWB items from the literature into 66 individual behaviors on 11 facets.

Structurally, some authors see more evidence for hierarchical structures consisting of a general factor with two underlying factors or several facets, whereas others argue for the one-dimensionality of the feature. In any case, meta-analytical findings reveal high correlations while also confirming the advantages of considering the features separately (Berry, Ones, & Sackett, 2007; Dalal, 2005). Marcus et al. (2016) compared the different views: The best fit was provided by a bifactor model in which the CWBs simultaneously load on the 11 content scales and one of the three targets organization, another person, or own person.

OCB and CWB are negatively linked but are both independent concepts and not poles along a continuum, which can be determined by structural analyses, bivariate relationships, and relationships to external criteria (Sackett et al., 2006). Various authors have therefore proposed to distinguish at least three areas of job performance – task-related performance, OCB, and CWB (e.g., Dalal, 2005). Several methods of measurement can be used for these criteria of job performance and for job success, each with its own specific advantages and limitations (see Box 1).

Chapter 4 reports on the connections between the Dark Triad and task- and environment-related criteria of job performance, OCB and CWB, and various criteria of objective and subjective success, which were recorded with self- and other-assessments as well as objective measures. The work-related inventory for the Dark Triad presented in Chapter 6 (TOP) was also validated for all the criteria and measurement approaches mentioned. To provide a solid background for evaluating these findings, the following Section 2.2.2 provides an overview of the possibilities for predicting performance with bright or normal personality traits.

Box 1: Approaches to Recording the Criteria (Based on Lohaus and Schuler, 2014)

- Objective data have the advantage of clear definitions and measurability as well as low falsifiability. However, in most cases, they are highly deficient as they capture much too narrow a section of an activity, or they are contaminated if they are too broadly operationalized and a lot of external influences determine the performance criterion.
- With subjective performance assessments, the criterion deficiency can be countered by parallel consideration of a broader spectrum of aspects and the integration of aspects that cannot be observed objectively. However, they are potentially subject to greater judgment bias or conscious response behavior.
- Nevertheless, subjective assessments by supervisors, a classic form of performance assessment, are considered the method of choice in research on professional performance.
- External assessments by colleagues or managed employees are also useful, especially if the performance criteria such as leadership behavior can only be assessed by them.
- In addition, self-assessments are possible since the evaluators have the most comprehensive and long-term access to the criterion. Depending on the purpose, however, they show the highest distortion of the judgment of all subjective methods. Nevertheless, in particular counterproductive behavior is almost always captured by self-assessments, since many offenses are not even discovered in the first place or are not – or should not be – known to anyone else (on the faking of self-assessments, see also Section 5.1.1).

As many different measures and methods as possible should therefore be used to approach the hypothetical constructs of performance and success (Lohaus & Schuler, 2014).

2.2.2 Professional Aptitude Diagnostics with Personality Traits

As mentioned in Section 2.1, early attempts tried to find connections between various individual differences in personality traits and job-related behavior or effects. For example, one of the decisive investigations that contributed to the development of the Big Five was conducted in the US Air Force for aptitude-diagnostic purposes (see Tupes & Christal, 1958, 1961). Sackett et al. (2017) describe individual differences (and their application in the workplace, especially in personnel selection) as one of the central and most important practical issues in applied psychology over the last 100 years. One of the main areas of interest was individual differences in personality – understood as the stable characteristics people "bring" to work, for example.

According to Sackett et al. (2017), however, the evaluation of the use of personality for job-related questions resembles a "rollercoaster," characterized by four phases: After the original discovery of its basic usefulness, there followed a phase of increasing evidence of occupationally related correlates of personality from 1917 into the 1960s. After Guion and Gottier (1965) and Mischel (1968) denied the usefulness of personality tests for aptitude-diagnostic questions, research in this area subsequently collapsed, and not until 1991 was there a revival through conceptual and methodological developments, in particular, meta-analysis, to prove the usefulness of personality tests for the prognosis of occupational criteria. The present situation, since 2004, is characterized by the critical examination and refinement of our state of knowledge, i.e., theoretical-conceptual questions, the methodology of measurement, sources of judgment, and prognostic validity, in part also new factors such as the "H-factor" of the HEXACO model, and maladaptive aspects such as the Dark Triad (Sackett et al., 2017).

As diverse as they are, almost all of these research streams have one thing in common: They refer to the reference model FFM. For this reason, I present the validity of personality for the prediction of job performance using the example of FFM, and I also use this model as a frame of reference in the chapter on the Dark Triad (together with the HEXACO model).

Following the line of development shown above, one observes a decreasing interest in the job-related application of personality factors after "initially active use ... from 1973 onward" (Schuler & Höft, 2006, p. 119). The meta-analysis by Barrick and Mount (1991) and the subsequent second-order meta-analysis (Barrick et al., 2001) generalized the validity of the factor Conscientiousness, which has the highest criterion-related validity across all criteria and occupational groups. A few other relevant connections were found, for example, for Neuroticism, but no general validity was determined for all factors across all criteria and occupational groups (Schuler & Höft, 2006). Several recent meta-analyses come to similar conclusions, which is why Pelt et al. (2017) consider the Barrick et al. (2001) findings to be still valid and good estimates of the prognostic validity of personality factors.

In addition, other factors (such as the general factor of personality) and their underlying facet level were examined regarding the Big Five, whereby in some cases the superordinate general factor and individual facets show higher correlations to job performance than the individual Big Five dimensions. In a comparison of three hierarchical levels of personality – facets, global factors, and general factor – by Sitser et al. (2013), the general factor showed the highest and most consistent relationships to performance criteria; and meta-analytically, Pelt et al. (2017) also demonstrated higher predictive power for it than for a single Big Five factor to general job performance, the Big Five proved to have prognostic validity for other job performance and perception criteria, although they were also criticized for being too broad to predict specific professional behavior (see Schuler et al., 2014).

In summary, both subtle nuances and broad factors have proven to be useful predictors of human behavior at work. Which level of abstraction seems to be most suitable for personnel-psychological purposes depends on the criterion of interest, which is generally discussed under the term *bandwidth-fidelity dilemma* (Cronbach, 1990). This term describes the trade-off between a high bandwidth to enable the most comprehensive, broad prediction of job performance possible, and a very fine-toothed, accurate measurement for predicting specific aspects. Pelt et al. (2017) summarize the findings on this question: Broad constructs are generally preferable, they say, especially when predicting broad outcome variables such as occupational performance, whereas only very specific aspects can be better predicted by narrow facets. Ideally, the predictor and the criterion are well matched. Following the symmetry hypothesis (Cronbach & Gleser, 1965), Paunonen (1998) already proposed in principle an equivalence of the width of predictor and criterion for the greatest possible prognostic quality: coarse factors for general, broad, and more finely graded ones for specific, narrow criteria.

Compound Traits

An approach that deviates from the level of abstraction and also pursues the goal of high prognostic validity is the combination of different content areas that are best adapted to the respective criterion. Such scales, developed to achieve the highest possible predictive quality, are the *Criterion-Focused Occupational Personality Scales* (COPS), which represent a mixture of different definable properties, so-called compound traits; these are relevant in the workplace and were developed specifically for use in this context (Ones & Viswesvaran, 2001). COPS have shown superior practical suitability over clearly definable factors, such as the Big Five, for predicting occupational performance (Ones & Viswesvaran, 2001).

A prime example of COPS is integrity tests, usually questionnaires employed in personnel selection to identify individuals who are more likely to exhibit counterproductive behavior, for example, theft or substance consumption in the workplace. The term integrity was first used in the 1980s for this class of rather heterogeneous instruments in practical use since the 1920s (Sackett & Wanek, 1996). Integrity is thus not meant as a delimitable personality trait, and the tests are not based on any explicit theory. Only recently has there been a more intensive preoccupation in this respect (Berry, Sackett, & Wiemann, 2007). The meta-analysis by Ones et al. (1993) assigns general validity to integrity tests in predicting counterproductive behavior as well as predicting job performance across different criteria, predictors, and occupational groups. Schmidt and Hunter (1998) assigned the highest incremental validity to intelligence in predicting job performance for integrity test results because they are not correlated with cognitive performance (compared to, say, work samples). More recent meta-analyses (e.g., Van Iddekinge et al., 2012) confirmed their basic validity but estimated significantly lower values. Yet, the results cannot be compared, mainly because of the mostly proprietary data material of the analyses (integrity tests are almost exclusively commercially distributed). Thus, the actual amount of variance explained remains unclear, though the fundamental validity of integrity tests remains undisputed (Sackett et al., 2017).

Because of their design, compound traits and especially integrity tests have proven to be particularly suitable for aptitude-diagnostic applications. In terms of content, integrity represents in part the exact opposite of the dark-side personality traits, which in turn are conceptually considered compound traits (Dilchert et al., 2014). Dark content is too weakly represented in general personality models, which explains why there is a growing interest in researching the effects of dark traits in professional life, as they may represent useful additions to research on personality and job performance. For this reason, Section 2.3 deals with the description of the dark side of personality and its occupational application.

2.3 Dark Personality Traits as a New Approach in Personnel Psychology

Guenole (2014) notes that, in the field of work-related personality research, there have been no significant new developments since the establishment of the Big Five and the method of meta-analysis in the 1990s. According to Kaiser et al. (2015, p. 58), "Over the last several decades, the overwhelming majority of applied personality research has been based on the FFM, and therefore concerns the bright side." This is increasingly being recognized as a limitation, which explains the increased recent focus on dark personality traits.

The following section concerns the concept of dark-side personality traits, its conceptual genesis, and the current understanding of this group of traits. It clarifies which characteristics are included and how they can be distinguished from each other, the DSM-5 model, and general clinical perspectives. Further, it also explores why these traits are increasingly being considered from an occupational perspective and what the central findings for this field are, namely, whether consideration of the dark side of personality is fundamentally a beneficial and thus good approach to personnel psychology.

2.3.1 A General Taxonomy of Dark Personality in DSM-5?

Until recently, dark traits had received little attention in personality research. According to Spain et al. (2014), despite growing interest, no standard textbook contains a separate section on this topic. In the meantime, this has changed, and recently separate books were published on both the dark side of personality (Spain, 2019; Zeigler-Hill & Marcus, 2016) and the Dark Triad (Lyons, 2019). Nevertheless, various concepts are discussed in parallel under the term dark traits, so that there "... is the lack of a generally accepted taxonomy of dark personality traits" (Spain et al., 2014, p. 49).

This situation could change in the coming years due to the introduction of a new taxonomy of maladaptive personality traits in the DSM-5. Apart from the omission or changes to the naming of old disorders and the inclusion of many new ones, at first glance, the DSM-5 made no changes to the category of personality disorders relevant to the dark side. Indeed, all criteria for the disorders on Axis II of the predecessor DSM-IV remained unchanged and are listed in Part II in the section on personality disorders.

Conceptually more significant than the reorganization undertaken in DSM-5 (personality disorders are no longer listed under Axis II in DSM-5 because of the elimination of the so-called multiaxial system) is the development of a new approach to the diagnosis of personality disorders – the alternative DSM-5 model for personality disorders. Because of the complexity of the changes that would then be required in psychiatric practice, the authors did not consider completely replacing the original disorder types but included the model in Section III of DSM-5 to aid further research (see APA, 2013).

This model is a mixture of a dimensional and a categorical model and is therefore also referred to as a hybrid model (Zimmermann et al., 2015). This agrees with ongoing developments in clinical psychology, which is seeing a growing number of findings concerning the benefits of a dimensional view (e.g., Eaton et al., 2011; Krueger & Eaton, 2010; see also Section 2.1.1). A dimensional variable enables a "quantitative rather than a qualitative distinction between 'normal' and 'abnormal' personality" (Wille et al., 2013, p. 174), the characteristic is thus present – more or less pronounced – in every person. This is an essential prerequisite not only for measurability but above all for operational applicability in the (working) general population. Because this is an important question for practice, I deal with it in greater detail in Section 5.2.1.

Spain et al. (2014, p. 51) see the transition from DSM-IV to DSM-5 as a potential breakthrough in understanding the nature of dark personality. Guenole (2014, p. 86) states "the field of personality at work is now at a point reminiscent of the 1990s, where substantive developments in the field of personality are ready to be integrated to advance understanding of personality at work."

The model has a hybrid character because of its trait-based structure (a so-called maladaptive trait model) and the possibility to infer from that six of the existing categorical disorders (antisocial, avoidant, borderline, narcissistic, obsessive-compulsive, and schizotypal). The Personality Inventory for the DSM-5 Maladaptive Trait Model (PID-5; APA, 2013; Krueger et al., 2012) is available for basic assessment. Box 2 outlines the diagnostic procedure in a simplified way for better understanding.

Box 2: An Overview of the Alternative DSM-5 Model for Personality Disorders

- A personality disorder is diagnosed by examining the *functional level of* personality (Criterion A) and the five dark personality traits: *Antagonism, Psychoticism, Disinhibition, Negative Affectivity,* and *Detachment* (Criterion B), with a total of 25 facets of characteristics, i.e., a hierarchical, dimensional model (Zimmermann et al., 2015). These "maladaptive traits" are recorded using the *Personality Inventory for DSM-5* (PID-5).
- The assessment of the functional level of the personality is carried out regarding the areas of *self-(identity* and *direction)* and *interpersonal relationships (empathy* and *intimacy*) on a continuum (or five degrees of severity from no or minor impairment to extreme impairment). There must be at least one moderate impairment to make a diagnosis of a personality disorder (as further diagnostic features for a disorder, framework parameters such as *constancy, duration, possible alternative explanations (other mental disorder or physiological effects),* and *first occurrence* must also be considered as Criteria C through to G).
- For the initial diagnosis, the functionality of a person (Criterion A) and the specific combinations of aspects of the five dimensionally measured factors (Criterion B) can be used to draw conclusions about *borderline, avoidant, obsessive-compulsive, schizotypical, antisocial,* and *narcissistic personality disorders* (see APA, 2013).
- The new model thus represents a link between "normal" dimensional personality traits and categorical, official clinical disorders.

The hybrid nature marks the main conceptual difference regarding assessment between the alternative DSM-5 model and the Dark Triad of personality and the other research efforts on Axis II disorders that have so far been grouped together under the term dark side, as all these are purely dimensional in nature (Guenole, 2014). The significant difference between the dark traits (narcissism, Machiavellianism, and psychopathy) and the maladaptive trait model, on the other hand, is that they are specific mixtures of different aspects or narrow facets, i.e., compound traits. The maladaptive trait model, with its 5 factors and 25 subfactors, in contrast, has an empirically definable, hierarchical order like that of the FFM system. It is sometimes referred to as the negative equivalent of the Big Five (Marcus & Zeigler-Hill, 2015), and four of the five problematic personality trait domains are even explicitly assigned Big Five opposites in the DSM: (1) Negative Affectivity vs. Emotional Stability, (2) Detachment vs. Extraversion, (3) Antagonism vs. Agreeableness, (4) Disinhibition vs. Conscientiousness (see APA, 2013).

The use of these terms is problematic, however, because the Big Five poles already exist, for example, Neuroticism in the case of Emotional Stability, whose relationship and position to Negative Affectivity is thus unclear. On the other hand, for example, low Conscientiousness cannot be equated with the attributes of the antipole Disinhibition, such as Impulsivity or Irresponsibility. Dark qualities are not merely extreme versions or fringe areas of normal personality traits; rather, they broaden the focus beyond the ends of the normal continuum (Benson & Campbell, 2007) and not only by the mere extent of their expression but by their specific content. For example, maladaptive items of PID-5 for Neuroticism address suicide, those for Openness seeing things that are not real.

It has been repeatedly established that four factors show great similarity (Openness and Psychoticism, however, do not), but that a comparison at the facet level leads to both double attributions (aspects from Detachment to Neuroticism and Extraversion), and the individual relationships of the facets to an attributed factor are only partly present to a limited extent. For example, there is a low convergence of the Antagonism facets – the inclination to manipulation, dishonesty, and grandiosity – with low Agreeableness (Zimmermann et al., 2014). In terms of content, the Antagonism facets mentioned are closer to the H-factor of the HEXACO model, which has no equivalent in the Big Five (see Section 2.1).

The maladaptive trait model thus does not represent a dark one-to-one correspondence to the Big Five; nevertheless, it should be understood as a dimensionally conceived model of clearly delimitable factors. These dimensional factors or values become clinical categories after the translation of the initial diagnosis (presence of specific individual facets in connection with a limited functional level) into the six pathological characteristics. The dark characteristics are a combination of both – dimensionally measured, but mixed forms – and thus both the scales of the HDS (Hogan Development Survey; Hogan & Hogan, 2009) and the Dark Triad are so-called compound traits (Dilchert et al., 2014; see Section 2.2.2). For a better understanding, see Table 1, which presents the special features and possibilities of differentiating the various models listed here.

Table 1: Demarcation of the Different Dark Models

<table>
<tr><th></th><th>Single, definable factors (separate traits)</th><th>Combination of aspects (compound traits)</th></tr>
<tr><td rowspan="2">Dimensional</td><td rowspan="2">DSM-5 maladaptive trait model with 5 factors and 25 subfacets (test procedure: PID-5)</td><td>Dark properties (e.g., Dark Triad or Dark-Side Traits of the test procedure HDS with 11 scales)</td></tr>
<tr><td rowspan="2">Alternative DSM-5 model for personality disorders</td></tr>
<tr><td rowspan="2">Categorial</td><td rowspan="2"></td></tr>
<tr><td>DSM-5 Personality Disorders (DSM-IV Axis II; test procedure: SCID-5-PD)</td></tr>
</table>

2.3.2 Defining and Delimiting the Dark Properties

As I showed in the previous section, the first two defining characteristics of dark personality traits are them being compound traits and dimensionally measurable. The synonym subclinical is also used, which means only that it is a mitigated form of a clinical disorder. Such a manifestation is not so problematic as to affect daily life or functioning, which would be one aspect of the diagnosis of a clinical personality disorder but belongs to the normal personality (Spain et al., 2014; Wu & LeBreton, 2011). Therefore, the definition of Harms et al. (2011, p. 496) seems to be proper fitting:

Subclinical Personality Traits

"Subclinical traits represent a middle ground between normal personality traits, such as the Big Five, and clinical traits that are used to diagnose psychological pathologies."

While the alternative DSM-5 model for personality disorders (through the possibility of "translation") represents a process-based connection between the dimensional and the clinical-categorial view, dark traits are a clearly defined conceptual group between the normal and the clinical spheres: They require the dimensional measurement methodology of one sphere and represent content-related combinations of traits from the other.

The special properties of compound traits may also lie behind the attention they have received in recent years – is there possibly some special suitability of dark properties for aptitude-diagnostic questions? There are potentially both practical and predictive reasons for this: As mentioned above, dark traits are not integrated into existing personality inventories, which, on the one hand, allows completely new occupationally relevant aspects of personality to be recorded, and, on the other hand, compound traits have the advantage of already representing specific combinations of jointly effective traits (see Section 2.2). Last but not least, their use in the normal working population requires dimensional measurability and thus the largest possible differentiation from the diagnosis of genuine categorial disorders, since the latter is not legally permissible for personnel selection (see Wu & LeBreton, 2011, and Section 5.2). This dilemma has been solved for the dark characteristics by implementing a "grand migration" (Furnham, Richards et al., 2013, p. 200) from the clinical to the subclinical sphere. In contrast, the use of a measuring method from which personality disorders can be directly inferred, such as the PID-5, would represent a delicate balancing act (see Section 5.2).

Until recently, occupational and organizational psychologists did not consider the alternative DSM-5 model for personality disorders (Guenole, 2015; Spain et al., 2014). However, the factors and measurement approaches contained in the new DSM-5 should gain more attention in the future.

The following, therefore, discusses the compound characteristics under the designation of dark traits in more detail. To date, these classic dimensionally measured dark-side traits have been the clear focus of interest and have already spawned a wide range of findings – not the least because the Dark Triad of personality is attributed to them.

Studies on dark personality traits have focused on the Dark Triad (the traits narcissism, Machiavellianism, and psychopathy) and various concepts based on the DSM-IV Axis II categories (Spain et al., 2014). The Hogan Development Survey (HDS; Hogan & Hogan, 2009) has been used most widely. It measures dimensionally 11 of the DSM-IV Axis II personality disorders on separate scales (and subscales), which are euphemistic descriptions of their origins (Spain et al., 2014). Salgado took a very similar approach, using the term "dysfunctional" to measure all 14 categories of the DSM-IV with the Cuestionario de Estilos de Personalidad (CEP; Salgado, 2000). In line with Moscoso and Salgado (2004) and Hogan and Hogan (2001), Table 2 presents the DSM-IV Axis II disorders and their subclinical counterparts. Further, this overview also shows the classification of the Dark Triad according to Spain et al. (2014).

Table 2: DSM-IV Axis II Disorders, CEP, HDS, and Dark Triad Scales

DSM-IV (APA, 2000)	CEP (Salgado, 2000)	HDS (Hogan & Hogan, 2009)	Dark Triad (Spain et al., 2014)
Narcissistic PD	Egocentric	Bold	Narcissism
Paranoid PD	Suspicious	Skeptical	Machiavellianism?*
Avoidant PD	Shy	Cautious	
Passive-aggressive PD	Pessimistic	Leisurely	
Schizotypical PD	Eccentric	Imaginative	
Borderline PD	Ambivalent	Excitable	
Schizoid PD	Lone	Reserved	
Compulsive PD	Reliable	Diligent	
Histrionic PD	Cheerful	Colorful	
Antisocial PD	Risky	Mischievous	Psychopathy
Dependent PD	Submitted	Dutiful	
Sadistic PD	Assertive		
Depressed PD	Sad		
Self-defeated PD	Sufferer		

Note. PD = personality disorder; the terms in *italics* are research criteria that are not among the ten official diagnostic PDs of DSM-IV and DSM-5; * marked with question mark by the authors.

In addition to dark-side traits, various other terms are used as generic terms for the type of personality traits discussed in this chapter. Examples are aberrant personality (Gustafson & Ritzer, 1995), dysfunctional personality (Moscoso & Salgado, 2004), maladaptive personality (Wu & LeBreton, 2011) as well as the terms pathological, abnormal, and deviant, as mentioned by Guenole (2014). The publication by Zeigler-Hill and Marcus (2016), which deals specifically with the dark side of the personality, extends the term to include excessive expressions of positive or bright qualities such as perfectionism.

This follows the view that classification into the category "dark properties" can be based on the possible consequences, since there are no other formal criteria for them (see Marcus & Zeigler-Hill, 2015). The authors point out that, depending on the context or high level of expression, even the "brightest" property can have negative consequences (which is true). At the same time, they provide the reason why this key criterion is not ideal. It is well known that only the dose makes the poison (Paracelsus, 1538/1965), and if we apply this logic to drugs, for example, as at a given amount every drug becomes poisonous and in the present case, each personality trait would be a dark one. The level of expression or negative consequences associated only with high expressions therefore cannot be a defining characteristic of dark personality traits.

The term dysfunctional chosen by Moscoso and Salgado implies, like Wu and LeBreton's maladaptive, a negative evaluation of the properties and has therefore been criticized (Wille et al., 2013). Pathological and abnormal also implicitly imply an evaluation, as they have strong echoes of pathological disorders, with the latter, strictly speaking, detecting only a deviation from the norm. The terms aberrant and deviant also do not represent any additional specificity since they too describe only a deviation from the norm. Using these terms, however, removes the too narrow view of dysfunctionality, as dark side traits can lead to positive consequences for the person concerned, depending on the criteria and framework conditions (Wille et al., 2013).

Potentially positive aspects for the individual carrying the trait were repeatedly assumed for dark properties and in individual cases were empirically proven for the Dark Triad and the HDS scales. In addition to the obvious negative consequences, possible positive effects thus also belong to the definitional core of dark personality traits.

The view that dark is generally regarded as undesirable and light as desirable is outdated and oversimplified – all features may have their bright and their shady sides (Smith et al., 2018). For bright features, negative outcomes usually ensue at too high levels, often under the term "too much of a good thing" (Pierce & Aguinis, 2013); this makes them potentially problematic, but still not a dark feature.

Accordingly, neither an automatically negative consequence nor negative effects (in the case of exclusively high expressions) qualify as characteristically dark. Also, not all the candidates discussed share the characteristic of antagonism ("turning against others"), which many dark characteristics exhibit. On the contrary, the characteristics of the DSM tradition often refer to intraindividual problems, such as depression. Marcus and Zeigler-Hill (2015) further suggest that those traits associated with negative consequences even at moderate expression can be considered dark. This criterion also fails to express a clear distinction. Dark characteristics are dimensionally distributed: The values of a large proportion of a population lie around the mean value, so that in most cases moderate deviations from this value should not lead to negative consequences, especially not for third parties in the case of DSM-based characteristics, which relate to problems with oneself. They would therefore not be a dark characteristic.

The only other feature shared by all properties generally described as dark is their specific content. Whether this is adaptive according to the circumstances or has negative consequences, to what extent these consequences reflect strength, and whether they relate to oneself or to third parties are in practice highly significant questions – for the classification of the characteristics they have no initial significance. Only criteria that reveal *all* characteristics of the group regardless of situational conditions can serve this purpose. The Dark Triad, the HDS scales, and other candidates for the group, such as sadism (Chabrol et al., 2009), share the fact that their content describes negatively connoted, mostly hidden, dark sides of the human personality. While Neuroticism of the Big Five, for example, describes aspects of normal personality variation and items of corresponding procedures deal with everyday content, the dark facet Depressivity from PID5-BF deals with suicide.

I would like to use this example for an important and necessary remark regarding the consideration of dark characteristics in personnel work: Antagonistic dark-side traits of an employee, such as psychopathy, represent potential harm to others and should be reduced as part of responsible personnel selection (e.g., by recognizing and not hiring such applicants). On the other hand, people who suffer from increased manifestations of other dark personality traits, such as those based on the avoidant or dependent personality disorder, require our support and are therefore less a topic for personnel selection than for coaching or occupational health psychology, in extreme cases for consultation on and the provision of (external) professional help.

The final defining characteristic is thus the specific content that describes the dark sides of personality. The term dark side or dark-side personality traits has finally become established as a technical term through numerous publications by relevant authors such as Paulhus, the Hogans, and Salgado – presumably not the least because the special appeal the topic seems to have recently exerted on research is virtually analogous to the pop-cultural definition of the dark side in Lucas' Star Wars universe (Griffin & O'Leary-Kelly, 2004): the hidden, negative side, which nevertheless promises new, undreamt-of (individual) advantages. I also use the generic term dark-side traits here for the aforementioned characteristics and the Dark Triad. My focus is clearly on the last part of the term – traits – i.e., the individual, concrete characteristics. This limitation is important, because the dark side has spawned a whole series of further questions. (The term Dark Triad was even used by Perri and Brody (2011) in a publication from a different subject area to describe the alliance of organized crime, fraud, and terrorism.)

Many works have dealt with the dark side of management (Neider & Schriesheim, 2010) or the dark side of organizational behavior in general (Griffin & O'Leary-Kelly, 2004). The latter anthology combines several topics (some of which also fall under the generic term of counterproductive behavior) such as aggression and harassment at the workplace (e.g., Baron, 2004) but also includes behavior that deviates from classic CWB, such as destructive political behavior (e.g., Hall et al., 2004). The contributions collected there all refer to specific behaviors and their negative effects on the person and the organization, whereas the present book deals expressly with personality traits (which nevertheless clearly underlie several of the above-mentioned outcome variables). One difference thus lies in the definition of the functionality of dark side behaviors, the characteristics of which are negative consequences (Griffin & O'Leary-Kelly, 2004), whereas for dark-side traits also positive effects are discussed – at least for the carrier of the trait. I, therefore, propose the following definition of dark-side personality traits:

Dark-Side Personality Traits

Dark-side personality traits are dimensionally measured and normally distributed compound traits that involve negatively connoted aspects of human behavior or experience, but do not necessarily lead to negative consequences for oneself or third parties.

2.3.3 Dark Personality Traits in the Workplace

Interest in the effects of dark characteristics in the workplace is not new. Even in the early days of the study of personality in the 1920s and 1940s, inventories were used to measure maladaptive traits or identify problematic candidates or employees, primarily to prevent counterproductive behavior, which led to the line of research now known and growing under the name of integrity (Sackett et al., 2017). Explicitly dark characteristics have also been and are still used for aptitude-diagnostic purposes, for example, the Minnesota Multiphasic Personality Inventory (MMPI; Hathaway & McKinley, 1943) for the selection of police officers in the USA (Guenole et al., 2016) and in Austria (Federal Law Gazette of Republic of Austria – BGBl, II No. 400/2012; §14, 2).

Legal issues, discussed in more detail in Section 5.2, led to a decline in this field of research, and only since the 2010s did attention increase once again, for example, through the HDS, the Dark Triad, and the new DSM-5 model, which reconfirmed the relevance of dark-side traits in the workplace and explicitly supported their use in personnel selection (Guenole et al., 2016).

Except for the increasing occupation-related studies on the Dark Triad in recent years, discussed in detail in Chapter 4, almost all research on dark-side traits in the workplace is based on the work of the Hogans and colleagues and on the HDS, which was originally developed to predict managerial incompetence (Guenole, 2014). The 11 HDS scales are partly grouped into three dimensions according to Horney (1950): moving toward people, moving away from people, and moving against people. It is assumed that the negative effects of personality traits become particularly apparent in stressful situations at work, where cognitive resources are so stretched that impulses and implicit motives can no longer be adequately controlled (Hogan & Hogan, 2001).

In the following, I briefly present some of the central occupational findings for dark-side traits based on the DSM, primarily measured with the HDS. Validity for the HDS dimensions was shown in the prediction of several work-relevant questions, in part even beyond bright personality models (Spain et al., 2014). One main interest was leadership, corresponding to the original practical purpose of explaining managerial misconduct. The scales possess traditionally large differences. Some, such as Diligent, but also Bold (which represents narcissism) are sometimes positively associated with job performance or career development of managers over time, while others are usually negative, such as Skeptical (which is equated with Machiavellianism, see Table 2). In Harms et al. (2011), 11% to 17% of the variance in the development of leadership roles is attributed to dark factors. Kaiser et al. (2015) identified various behaviors for managers, for which too little or too much was considered problematic and connected them to dark characteristics – 16 of the 22 postulated connections were significant. These explanations of variance prove the practical relevance of dark-side traits for leadership behavior: According to their results, moderate values around the mean value are associated with optimal leadership behavior. Benson and Campbell (2007) demonstrated in part curvilinear relationships to leadership performance in assessments and supervisor evaluations. Any deviations from the mean value turn the relationship negative and not – as has often been found for curvilinear relationships – only those in the top quartile.

Gaddis and Foster (2015) did an extensive, worldwide meta-analysis of managers in which several dark-side traits were (mostly negatively) associated with a variety of performance criteria; for the overall performance assessment, only the Colorful scale also had positive effects. Furnham, Hyde et al. (2013) reported relationships of the HDS scales with performance indicators that had been subjectively collected with the Hogan Personality Inventory (HPI; Hogan & Hogan, 2007). These revealed largely negative relationships, primarily the Skeptical scale, but also positive ones, such as the Diligent, Colorful, and Bold scales. For example, the latter was positively associated with sales success. They conclude that the traits can also be beneficial, depending on the profession, for example, high values on the Diligent scale (as an expression of a slight "obsession") for quality-control activities. Based on Schneider's ASA theory (1987), Furnham, Hyde et al. (2014) assumed at the expressions of certain types of dark traits determine which occupational fields attract people (Attraction), which organizations they select (Selection), and in which organizations they ultimately remain as employees (Attrition).

In fact, an examination of employees in the UK found differences between the private and public sectors. Traits such as Cautious, Reserved, Diligent, and Dutiful are more pronounced in public organizations (originating in avoidant-insecure, schizoid, obsessive-compulsive, and dependent personality disorders, see Table 2). More pronounced in the private sector, on the other hand, are the antagonistic characteristics such as Bold, Skeptical, and Mischievous, which are the closest HDS equivalents of narcissism, Machiavellianism, and psychopathy. The Bold scale associated with narcissism and the Mischievous scale associated with psychopathy were also best suited to differentiate between public- and private-sector employees.

Moscoso and Salgado (2004) used DSM-IV Axis II disorders to study dysfunctional personality styles and job performance, too. Seven of the 14 dysfunctional styles surveyed in their study were related to performance indicators – the Shy, Sad, and Pessimistic styles (associated with Neuroticism) and the antagonistic Suspicious and Risky styles (most closely related to Machiavellianism and psychopathy) have a negative relationship with task and contextual performance as well as overall performance.

In addition to procedures based directly on the DSM categories, prototypical patterns or linear combinations of FFM facets have been proposed for the occupational diagnosis of dark characteristics (this approach is discussed in more detail in Section 5.2.1). Wille et al. (2013) showed that the so-called "aberrant trait compound" of the factor Narcissism is associated with the achievement of a hierarchically higher management position. Their study revealed that aberrant traits could also explain incremental variance to normal FFM dimensions in predicting various criteria of professional success, primarily subjective ones such as stress or job satisfaction. De Fruyt et al. (2009) showed that various dark traits captured with such a methodology are related to the final decision, the outcome of the interview, and other parts of the selection process – all negative except for obsessive-compulsive and histrionic. Simonet et al. (2018) too reported predominantly negative relationships of dark-side traits with the success criterion "leadership performance," while confirming that especially the interaction or the joint appearance of dark traits causes the concrete effects. For example, high values on Bold in combination with high values of Mischievous lead to the worst performance, whereas in the presence of low values of Mischievous, Bold does not show a negative relationship with leadership performance.

Harms and Spain (2015) concluded that dark personality traits can help explain job-related issues. Especially extremely high or low values influence leadership behavior or performance; a central condition seems to be how autonomous the activity is, i.e., one's scope of action. Depending on the activity and the corporate culture in question, specific characteristics can also have positive effects or better fit certain sectors.

As the explanations in this chapter show, dark-side personality traits are indeed a meaningful field of research for personnel psychology and especially for practical aptitude diagnostics. By depicting factors that have not yet been integrated into general personality models, they represent a theoretically sound extension of the range of characteristics under consideration. And they can (partially) clarify incremental variance of bright personality traits. By the HDS, they have now found their way from practice into scientific study.

Chapter 4 presents further occupational findings for dark-side traits, the focus being on those features that are most prominently represented in the literature in the last years – narcissism, Machiavellianism, and subclinical psychopathy (Paulhus & Williams, 2002) – but have only recently been considered in the occupational context, as the HDS has for two decades now. First, however, Chapter 3 presents the historical development and current conceptual understanding of the Dark Triad as well as selected nonoccupational findings from studies on the three traits under that umbrella term. There, I clarify both theoretically and practically significant questions about their structure and measurement methodology.

3 The Dark Triad of Personality

Paulhus and Williams (2002) coined the term Dark Triad of personality 20 years ago through their joint studies of the closely related characteristics narcissism, Machiavellianism, and (subclinical) psychopathy. As the explanations in the following Section 3.1 show, these personality traits have been researched in their current understanding separately from each other for about five decades (for narcissism considerably longer) and have rich research traditions in both clinical and social psychology. Currently, they are increasingly being considered and researched as a unit in various areas of psychology and related fields; Furnham and colleagues provide an overview in their review of 2013.

This great interest is also witnessed by the fact that two special issues of scientific journals have been published on dark characteristics. The *Journal of Abnormal Psychology* (2017, Volume 126, Issue 7) deals primarily with topics related to this subject area, such as the development of dark character traits from childhood on, impulsiveness and problematic behavior, crime, suicide, and the role of psychopathy in the Dark Triad. Interestingly, however, it also addresses the question relevant to aptitude diagnostics of the connection between an executive's Dark Triad characteristics and depression in their subordinates. A special issue of *Personality and Individual Differences* (2014, Volume 67) examines the relationships of the Dark Triad to personality models, empathy, violence, well-being, prosociality, and moral concepts as well as financial misconduct. In addition, it treats the connections of the Dark Triad to caretaking in the parent-child relationship, partner rivalry, sexual fantasies, religiosity, the "seven deadly sins," and behavior on Facebook.

Yet, as the overview shows, most of the now numerous findings on the Dark Triad in the most diverse areas of life are of limited relevance for clarifying the possibilities of professional aptitude diagnostics with narcissism, Machiavellianism, and psychopathy. Section 3.2 nevertheless presents, as a background for understanding the characteristics per se, some of the central findings on the Dark Triad regarding their relationships and effects in areas of life not related to work, focusing instead on differences and similarities between the characteristics. Chapter 4 reports the connections of the Dark Triad with variables relevant to aptitude diagnostics in detail.

But first, Section 3.3 clarifies the theoretical question central to a general assessment of the possible aptitude diagnostic applications of the Dark Triad, namely, what are its respective components and overlaps of its characteristics: What structure does the Dark Triad have and how can the single characteristics be validly measured?

3.1 A Short History of Narcissism, Machiavellianism, and Psychopathy

3.1.1 Narcissism

The term narcissism is often used – sometimes inflationary – in the general language and in the press. There, it has negative connotations, is simply understood as great self-indulgence and arrogance, and has thus undergone a change of meaning (Hartmann, 2006). The term narcissism was originally coined in 1898 for autoerotic tendencies, for which the British sexologist Havelock Ellis borrowed the name Nárkissos (lat. Narcissus) from Greek mythology. The German psychiatrist Paul Näcke used the term "Narcismus" in 1899 to describe sexual perversion (Raskin & Terry, 1988). Sigmund Freud first used "Narzißmus" in 1910 (Akhtar, 2006), and later in various uses ranging from sexual developmental stages to clinical-diagnostic categories (Raskin & Terry, 1988). Freud (1931, p. 511) also defined the term and already addresses the relationship to leadership – later to become a central object of narcissism research (see Section 4.3.1) – and possible negative effects:

> ... People of this type impress others as "personalities"; they are particularly suited to guiding others, to taking on the role of leaders, to giving new impulses to cultural development, or to damaging the existing.

I cannot discuss all of the different lines of development and points of view of the long and extensive history of research on narcissism in the field of depth psychology and clinical psychiatry. Instead, to enable an understanding of the effects of narcissism in professional life, i.e., within the "functional" general population, it is important to first clarify the current conceptual meaning of the characteristic.

Twenge and Campbell (2009) considered the trait up and coming because it is in tune with the zeitgeist – indeed we live in the age of pretension and experience a veritable epidemic of narcissism. Not only does the (US-American) culture virtually promote the value of self-admiration, but especially children are also taught a much more positive and uncritical attitude toward themselves in their upbringing. A whole industry is devoted to self-love. Further, many believe that narcissism is important in today's professional world. First and foremost, there has been a "shift in shared cultural values toward more narcissism and self-admiration" (p. 23).

Whether individuals are becoming increasingly narcissistic, on the other hand, is disputed among scientists. A meta-analysis shows that narcissism levels among American college students have risen from decade to decade since the 1970s, with particularly dramatic increases between 2000 and 2006 (Twenge et al., 2008). Yet other authors refute this claim (Donnellan et al., 2009; Trzesniewski et al., 2008), whereupon Twenge and Foster (2010) again showed a significant increase through analyses controlled for ethnicity. Their data in turn were criticized for lack of control for sex and age (Roberts et al., 2010). A recent study by Wetzel et al. (2017) concluded that in fact the values even decreased from 1990 to 2010. They checked for several influencing factors but only considered data from three universities, whereby the first dataset did not come from the same university as that of the other two points in time studied, something that Twenge and Campbell (2009) had earlier criticized.

As the conflicting results show, the apparent perception of collective change toward more narcissism at the individual level is much less well established. Nevertheless, based on their data, Twenge and Campbell (2008) assumed that employers must also be prepared to face steadily increasing numbers of employees with narcissistic aspirations.

Diamond (2006) also pointed out for the clinical area that increasing values for corresponding samples are not proven, and that it is nevertheless a commonplace that we live in the age of narcissism. DSM-5 (APA, 2013) also does not mention rising prevalence rates and includes narcissistic personality disorder in Part II, Personality Disorders, Cluster B.

While compiling the latest version of DSM-5, conceptual discussions took place about the basic type and classification of the disorders. As a result, narcissistic personality disorder was eventually included both as a categorical form and in Part III, where it can be described and diagnosed by the alternative DSM-5 model for personality disorders (see Section 2.1). The diagnosis includes a general description of the disorder and the presence of at least five of the specific criteria according to DSM. These criteria include some of the key aspects of narcissism literature and deal with the self-view of the person as such, also in comparison to other people, as well as their desires and typical behaviors to fulfill their needs (see APA, 2013).

One can diagnose narcissistic personality disorder with the alternative DSM-5 model for personality disorders, if in addition to specific limitations on the four functional levels (Criterion A: identity, self-direction, empathy, intimacy) the two problematic personality traits of grandiosity and attention-seeking (both facets of Antagonism) are present (Criterion B). Finally, narcissistic personality disorder is listed under "Other Specific Personality Disorders" (F 60.8) in the International Statistical Classification of Diseases and Related Health Problems (ICD-11; WHO, 2019). The prevalence rate in community studies lies between 0% and 6.2%; 50% to 75% of those diagnosed are male (see APA, 2013).

Colloquially, however, narcissism is not used to describe the mental illness of an individual, but rather, as explained above, a broadly distributed subclinical variant that characterizes *everyone* – albeit to a greater or lesser degree. The common understanding of narcissism thus describes a phenomenon that has also been researched under the term narcissism in the general population since the compilation of the *Narcissistic Personality Inventory* (NPI; Raskin & Hall, 1979).

The NPI does not diagnose the personality disorder in the sense of a "yes/no" statement; ideally, it should enable the measurement of the personality trait narcissism (Raskin & Hall, 1979) and thus place narcissism on a continuum (Samuel & Widiger, 2008b). Although abridged versions and other measures have been proposed, the NPI is still the gold standard of narcissism measurement used to accumulate most findings on narcissism (for a summary of the quality criteria of the procedure, see Section 5.2.2). In addition, above all the Bold scale of the HDS (Hogan & Hogan, 2009) and the Narcissism scale of the *California Psychological Inventory* (CPI; Gough & Bradley, 1992) are considered to detect narcissism, and results relating to these scales are described in publications as narcissism in terms of content – or even offset against each other in meta-analyses (see Grijalva et al., 2015). Early studies of the factor structure of the NPI by Emmons (1984) and Raskin and Terry (1988) found four to seven factors, whereas other authors suggest only two (see Ackerman et al., 2011). An elaborate series of studies by Ackerman et al. finally provided confirmation of a robust three-factor solution consisting of Leadership/Authority, Grandiose Exhibitionism, and Entitlement/Exploitativeness.

Regardless of the exact number of factors in the NPI, the central aspects of narcissism and narcissistic personality disorder (in character, not severity) remain the same: grandiosity, arrogance, authority, entitlement, and exploitation, and in all concepts and factor solutions, there is always a factor of leadership. Lack of empathy is not included in the NPI item material, but as both a diagnostic criterion of the disorder and the alternative DSM-5 model for personality disorders, there as part of the functional diagnosis. Vulnerable narcissism, which has become more prominent in depth psychology, is also hardly represented in the NPI and according to DSM is not an explicit criterion, though it is mentioned in both the diagnostic features of narcissistic personality disorder in Cluster B ("Vulnerability in self-esteem," "very sensitive to 'injury' from criticism or defeat," APA, 2013, p. 671) and in that of the alternative DSM-5 model for personality disorders ("variable and vulnerable self-esteem"; APA, 2013, p. 767); but even there it is not a diagnostic criterion.

This overview shows there is a long tradition of research on narcissism and narcissistic personality disorder. For further information on this topic, please refer to, among others, the handbook by Campbell and Miller (2011). In Chapter 4, I present a selection of the numerous findings for the typical behavior and experience of persons with elevated narcissism levels, especially related occupational effects, together with the other Dark Triad characteristics.

3.1.2 Machiavellianism

Machiavellianism is the part of the Dark Triad that is most briefly considered scientifically, and, contrary to its two counterparts, from the beginning it was understood exclusively as a dimensional personality trait. While Machiavellianism received greater attention until the 1980s (see Fehr et al., 1992), the construct has since received less broad and deep consideration than the other components of the Dark Triad, which is why there is no comparable research literature. The Fehr et al. overview article (1992) and the chapter by Jones and Paulhus (2009) provide good summaries and form the central basis of this section.

As with the NPI for narcissism, a procedure marked the beginning of Machiavellianism, and the findings obtained with it mark the core of its scientific consideration: the Likert-type Mach scale (IV), better known as the Mach IV (Christie & Geis, 1970). The contents of this scale, which comprises 20 items, were extracted primarily from the writings of Niccolò Machiavelli, who in one of his major works, *Il Principe* from 1513, analyses successful rulers and their style of politics. In addition to his views on the nature of man, these primarily regard the style of government he believed to be necessary to maintain power. Man is not to be trusted because he pursues his ambitions ungratefully and selfishly (Schröder, 2004). The ruler must – if he wants to maintain power – be prepared to use every conceivable strategy, including manipulation, lies, and flattery. The quintessence of his advice is "the end justifies the means" (Jones & Paulhus, 2009, p. 93).

The Mach IV has been continually developed since 1954, when a working group led by Christie and Geis was concerned with the character traits of people who exercise power over others, i.e., with leaders (Christie, 1970a). In the context of studies on manipulative personalities, they aimed to clarify whether there is a "corresponding personality syndrome" for such characteristics (Jones & Paulhus, 2009, p. 93). In the monograph *Studies in Machiavellianism* (Christie & Geis, 1970), they report on scale development and validation and describe the theoretical foundations as a relative lack of affect in interpersonal relationships, a lack of concern with conventional morality, a lack of gross psychopathology, and low ideological commitment.

Three aspects were drawn from this to create the Mach IV procedure: Tactics, Views, and Morality (Christie, 1970b), namely, by querying the attitudes toward these characteristics or their usefulness, not own actual behavior (Jones & Paulhus, 2009). Tactics describes the person's opinions on interpersonal behavior strategies, Views their (cynical) views on human nature, and Morality inquires about the acceptance of common moral concepts (Fehr et al., 1992; for a summary of the quality criteria of the procedure, see Section 5.2.2).

Machiavellians have cynical views of other people and of their own sociopolitical possibilities, which has been explained by an external locus of control (Jones & Paulhus, 2009). Special abilities were not found in terms of cognitive measures or the recognition of emotions, but the overall construct is associated with low empathy (Jones & Paulhus, 2009). Nevertheless, Machiavellians do not openly act aggressively or hostilely but, on the contrary, behave with emotional detachment; in conflict situations, they remain calm (Jones & Paulhus, 2009; see also Christie & Geis, 1970). Machiavellians seem to be more inclined to and better at various forms of manipulation, such as persuasion, self-revelation, ingratiation, certain so-called impression management tactics, lies, and deception. Yet, an important factor influencing this remains the situation (Fehr et al., 1992; Jones & Paulhus, 2009).

In conclusion to various experimental studies, Geis and Christie (1970, p. 312) state: "High Machs manipulate more, win more, are persuaded less, persuade others more and otherwise differ significantly from low Machs." This is especially the case when three factors are present: the possibility of improvisation, direct contact, and affective "distractors," which influence the performance (of the opponent) (Fehr et al., 1992). Geis and Christie (1970, p. 285) describe this emotional distancing as the "cool syndrome." Differences in behavior and results can largely be explained by the cool detachment of the Machiavellian, who can concentrate on the situation and develop the best strategy for victory – unimpressed by external influences.

Core Characteristics of Machiavellianism

The core characteristics of the construct can be seen in a cynical view of other people, reckless strategic behavior as well as emotional distance and detachment (see Jones & Paulhus, 2009).

In response to criticism of the psychometric quality of the Mach IV (see Jones & Paulhus, 2009), various other Machiavellianism personality tests have been proposed, including the Machiavellian Personality Scale (MPS; Dahling et al., 2009), the Trimmed-MACH (Rauthmann, 2013), Mach V and Mach VI (Jones & Paulhus, 2009), and the occupational Machiavellian personality scale OMS (Kessler et al., 2010). However, these methods have not received huge attention, so even in recent studies mostly the Mach IV is used.

The most widespread view of the structure of Mach IV is that of a two-factor solution consisting of Tactics and Views, which has been repeatedly found by factor analysis (see Fehr et al., 1992; Jones & Paulhus, 2009). Nevertheless, in research work, the Mach IV is used almost exclusively as a unidimensional scale, i.e., only the factor Machiavellianism is measured and reported. Theoretically, both factors must be present to explain Machiavellian behavior – the cynical view of third parties and the belief in the effectiveness of specific tactics to achieve goals (see Jones & Paulhus, 2009). More recent works also refer to the structure (e.g., Miller et al., 2017), raising the repeatedly discussed problem of a lack of means to differentiate between Machiavellianism and psychopathy (see McHoskey et al., 1998).

I discuss this in more detail in Section 3.3 in connection with the overlapping of Triad characteristics; further findings for Machiavellianism and especially its occupational implications are discussed in Chapter 4. But first, I present the third and most dangerous part of the Dark Triad – psychopathy.

3.1.3 Psychopathy

Like narcissism, the term psychopathy is used in different areas and with different meanings. Murderers, tricksters, serial offenders, but also psychologically conspicuous (but harmless) people as well as – recently more increasingly – supervisors and corporate leaders are called psychopaths (see Skeem et al., 2011).

The common use as a term for various kinds of "lunatics" stems from the actual meaning of the word, which is composed of psyche (Greek: soul) and pathos (Greek: illness), i.e., mental illness, which is why the term psychopathy has long been used to describe all sorts of personality disorders (Fiedler, 2001). The precursors of the phenomenon of psychopathy, discussed today as a severe antisocial disorder with frequently violent behavior, may be seen in the phenomenon of neglect, aggressiveness, and lack of consideration for fellow human beings, something Rush described as far back as 1812 as "moral alienation of mind" and Prichard in 1835 as "moral insanity." The term "psychopathic" was first used by the German psychiatrist Koch in 1891, but in contrast to today's usage, it was also applied to neuroses and cognitive impairments (Skeem et al., 2011).

The current scientific understanding of the term highlights at least one central difference to these early descriptions – the (apparent) mental health of the psychopath. The French psychiatrist Pinel emphasized this as early as 1809 in the first description of the (present-day) psychopathic construct as "manie sans délire" ("madness without delirium"); thus, psychopaths are in their right mind despite affective impairment and impulsive reaction (Basler, 2007). Since the first complete description of psychopathy in the seminal work *The Mask of Sanity* (Cleckley, 1941), it has therefore been discussed as a central feature that psychopaths are characterized by a façade of normality that does not indicate a disorder. Cleckley's monograph is considered the starting point of modern psychopathy research (Patrick, 2006b) and provided the basis for today's "gold standard" of measurement, the Psychopathy Checklist (PCL; Hare, 1980, 2003). The PCL focuses on the (predominant) antisocial and emotional-interpersonal aspects, whereas the few positive orientations of the psychopath described by Cleckley were not integrated (Patrick, 2006b).

Patrick explained the fact that psychopaths are not really "healthy" or "normal" (2006b) by locating a fundamental inner defect in the psychopath, which Cleckley sees in a deficit of emotional experience, analogous to semantic aphasia (a disorder of the meaning-related understanding of language). The defect of psychopaths "consists of an unawareness and a persistent lack of ability to become aware of what the most important experiences of life mean to others" (Cleckley, 1976, p. 371) – an assumption that could be confirmed decades later with neuroimaging techniques. Because of this limitation, the psychopath fails to develop a functioning conscience in socialization (Lykken, 2006) and lacks precisely those qualities that enable us to live in social harmony (Hare, 2005).

Skeem et al. (2011) see a combination of hereditary background and psychobiological effects (e.g., lack of social learning success because of lack of fear) as the most likely explanations for the development of psychopathy. Various neuroscientific and genetic studies have provided evidence of actual differences between psychopaths and nonpsychopaths; in particular, advancements in imaging techniques over the past decade have enabled enormous progress to be made in this area (Spezzaferri et al., 2017).

A main brain anatomical feature of psychopaths is assumed to lie in a reduced size of the amygdala in the limbic system or its dysfunction, namely, reduced activity in processing emotional stimuli (Spezzaferri et al., 2017). In addition, limitations in the structure and functionality of various areas of the prefrontal cortex have been proven meta-analytically (Yang & Raine, 2009), where larger volumes of the medial orbitofrontal and reduced activity of the dorsolateral prefrontal cortex were found in psychopaths (Korponay et al., 2017). Glenn et al. (2010) examined the volume of the corpus striatum, a subcortical region that plays a basal function in motivational, emotional, and cognitive processes and is associated with reward-seeking and impulsiveness and found structural differences and higher volumes that might be responsible for typical deficits in psychopaths.

However, it is not the peculiarities of individual areas, but rather the specific connection between different areas of the limbic system and the prefrontal cortex that, together with neurochemical aspects, lead to the specific experience and behavior of the psychopath (Spezzaferri et al., 2017). In this regard, deviations in neurotransmitters such as GABA, serotonin, and dopamine as well as monoamine oxidases (MAO), and hormones are discussed (Spezzaferri et al., 2017; Tikkanen et al., 2011; Yildirim & Derksen, 2013).

Yang et al. (2010) compared a nonpsychopathic control group with "successful" psychopaths (understood to be who have not yet been convicted) and with "unsuccessful" psychopaths (understood to be those who have already been previously convicted; in the respective self-reports, both psychopathy groups reported the same number of crimes committed, so the conviction alone is the measure of failure). Only the unsuccessful psychopaths had different, mostly lower volumes of different regions of the prefrontal cortex, whereas the successful psychopaths did not differ from the control group. Only in the "unsuccessful" psychopaths was the gray mass also less dense, and their amygdala was 20% to 26% smaller than in the control group, depending on the region. The surface structure of the amygdala also differed in the unsuccessful psychopaths and showed clear deformations in various places. The changes found affect parts of the brain that are associated with the processing of fear and fear-conditioned learning. These very same parts could therefore lead to increased risk behavior and an associated higher probability of being caught and sentenced. In general, this limitation, through a lack of learning in socialization, can also lead to less moral development and the development of psychopathy (Yang et al., 2010).

Psychopathy is to a certain extent hereditary: Estimates range from 30% to 53% (Bezdjian et al., 2011) and are strongest for the affective factor (Dhanani et al., 2017), although socialization aspects and the concrete interaction of both areas also play a role (Hicks et al., 2012). Men traditionally have higher scores in psychopathy than women (see Colins et al., 2017). Babiak et al. (2010), using PCL data, found a rate of over 3% psychopaths among top managers – compared to less than 1% in the general population a clear overrepresentation. Dutton (2012) sees CEOs as the occupational group with the highest proportion of psychopaths.

Although psychopathy has been widely researched using highly elaborate procedures and is considered a recognized, clearly defined disorder, it has not been explicitly included in the official diagnostic systems, where related disorders are found under the name of Dissocial Personality Disorder (in ICD) or Antisocial Personality Disorder (ASPD; in DSM). However, these differ from psychopathy because they primarily include the (observable) antisocial behavior and criminal effects but not all specific personality traits of psychopathy, especially not the interpersonal aspects. Hare, therefore, regards the ASPD as a minimum diagnosis, evident in over 80% of all imprisoned criminals, although only 15% of them can truly be classified as psychopaths, and especially "healthy or successful" psychopaths do not meet the criteria of an ASPD (Hare, 2005). Accordingly, although a large proportion of (imprisoned) psychopaths could be diagnosed with ASPD, only about 5% of prisoners diagnosed with ASPD could be categorized as psychopaths (Ogloff et al., 2016). According to Hare, the DSM should therefore include psychopathy as a separate diagnosis, as it conceptually differs from ASPD (Hare, 1996).

Although the current DSM working group decided to stick with observable behaviors and not to include psychopathy as an independent disorder in the new DSM-5, it is mentioned in the context of the ASPD diagnosis and in Part III of the alternative DSM-5 model for personality disorders, which list differential diagnostic aspects. The DSM-5 definition states that ASPD is also referred to as psychopathy, sociopathy, or dissocial personality disorder (APA, 2013, p. 659), but its focus clearly lies on the visible behaviors and social adaptation disorders. However, it also lists several other psychopathic characteristics such as excessive self-esteem, lack of empathy, or superficial charm, and states that these "are features that have been commonly included in traditional conceptions of psychopathy" (p. 660). The alternative DSM-5 model for personality disorders allows an additional coding of the ASPD to be used to determine whether there is a "distinct variant often termed *psychopathy* (or 'primary' psychopathy)" (p. 765). Psychopathy is also characterized by a low level of anxiety and social withdrawal and attention-seeking. Low anxiety, on the other hand, is not a diagnostic criterion of ASPD (see APA, 2013).

At the latest since the publication of the current version of PCL (Hare, 2003), the view of psychopathy that has prevailed is that of a superior factor psychopathy and four underlying factors: a deceptive interpersonal style (Interpersonal), affective deficits/emotional coldness (Affective), an impulsive, responsible, and aimless lifestyle (Lifestyle) and a criminal, antisocial history (Antisocial).

A factorial structure like that of PCL has also been demonstrated for self-reports (Lilienfeld & Fowler, 2006), first and foremost, the Self-Report Psychopathy Scale (SRP; Hare, 1985), for which the factor structure could also be confirmed in the general population (Williams et al., 2007). The method allows for a subclinical measurement of psychopathy, since the developmental and target samples are taken from the general population and the questionnaire generates continuously distributed, dimensional data. In general, subclinical psychopathy usually means only those values that have been collected via self-reports.

The self-report version is available in its current version as SRP 4 (Paulhus et al., 2016). There is also a job-related psychopathy scale that maps the four factors according to Hare – the B-scan (Mathieu et al., 2013). I discuss the procedure and its quality criteria further in Section 5.2.2.

The Kiel Psychopathy Inventory (KPI) by Köhler et al. (in preparation) also represents a self-report measure for mapping the complete contents of psychopathy according to the Hare model. In validation studies, it demonstrated its suitability for research in the general population, making a dimensional measurement of psychopathy possible (Heinzen et al., 2014). The Psychopathic Personality Inventory (PPI; Lilienfeld & Andrews, 1996) has a slightly different structure: There, the subscales Blame Externalization, Rebellious Nonconformity, Stress Immunity, Social Influence, Cold-Heartedness, Machiavellian Egocentricity, Carefree Nonplanfulness, and Fearlessness are condensed into either two or three factors. While extracting Cold-Heartedness as an independent factor is being discussed, the other two are clearly distinguishable factors and central characteristics of psychopathy: Fearless Dominance and Self-Centered Impulsivity. This structure corresponds to the classical view of psychopathy:

Primary and Secondary Psychopathy

The first version of PCL (Hare, 1980) consists of a general factor psychopathy, later a two-factor structure was adopted – *Primary* and *Secondary Psychopathy*, which were described as „selfish, cold-hearted and ruthless exploitation of others“ and „chronically unstable and antisocial lifestyle“ (Harpur et al., 1988) and have been recorded separately since the revised version of PCL of 1991.

Other authors prefer a hierarchical structure with a global psychopathy factor based on three factors: Arrogant and Deceitful Interpersonal Style, Deficient Affective Experience, and Impulsive and Irresponsible Behavioral Style (Cooke & Michie, 2001). As a theoretical rationale, they argue that antisocial behavior is a consequence of psychopathy and not part of it. They propose to exclude the "antisocial" items and provide empirical support for their thesis that the model is better suited for further research on psychopathy because it "brings personality back to the heart of this personality disorder" (Cooke et al., 2006, p. 99).

Hare (2003) proposes the four-factor model, which roughly corresponds to the Cooke and Michie solution plus the antisocial factor. The complete exclusion of this aspect and thus of about one-third of the actual PCL items has been criticized from a theoretical point of view, as the items of the antisocial facet are important markers of psychopathic personality and definitional parts of psychopathy (Hare & Neumann, 2006; Williams et al., 2007).

Cooke et al. (2007), in turn, criticize this approach as tautology and call it above all a conceptual discussion of what is to be counted as part of the construct. Using comprehensive theoretical considerations and comparisons of confirmatory solutions for different models, they provide evidence for the advantage of a three-factor model. The assumption that crime is a defining part of psychopathy, which is often wrongly equated with PCL, is wrong; rather, it should be understood as its (frequent) correlate (Skeem & Cooke, 2010).

In study of psychopathy for aptitude-diagnostic purposes, the exclusively personality-based approach is preferred, albeit for another, purely practical reason: Severely criminal, antisocial behavior has little prevalence in the working general population and is, therefore, less relevant in professional life, while at the same time the retrieval and collection of information relevant to criminal law is subject to very narrow limits in the application context – not the least those of applicant acceptance (see Section 5.3).

Hare provides a good overview of psychopathy (e.g., 2005), Hervé and Yuille (2007) and above all the handbook on the subject by Patrick (2006a, 2018a) give more in-depth information. The second edition of the *Handbook of Psychopathy* complements (rather than replaces) the first one with new insights gained since its first publication. Among other things, it presents in detail the developments through DSM-5 and the dimensional view as well as the genetic, neurochemical, and brain-anatomical foundations of psychopathy, which are only briefly touched upon here (Patrick, 2018b, p. xi).

Following this separate presentation of the historical development and our current understanding of the concepts of narcissism, Machiavellianism, and psychopathy, the next section presents the findings made during the joint investigation of these characteristics under the generic term Dark Triad of personality.

3.2 Selected Findings of the Joint Consideration of the Characteristics

This section presents nonoccupational findings on those issues that have received the most attention in the research tradition on the Dark Triad and that are important for understanding the typical experience and behavior of people with elevated levels of narcissism, Machiavellianism, and psychopathy, especially their effects in the workplace. These issues include their (evolutionary) biological development and differences in this respect, emotional deficits and moral concepts associated with the Triad, their place in general personality models, and their relationship to cognitive characteristics, as well as interpersonal life and behavior styles associated with the Triad, including above all antisocial behavior.

I pay particular attention to differences *between* the characteristics, because, apart from some common features of the Dark Triad, all three have specific proportions that are responsible for differential relationships to external criteria and are therefore described as "overlapping but distinct constructs" (Paulhus & Williams, 2002, p. 556).

For this reason, Furnham, Richards et al. (2014, p. 119) consider it a "theoretical impossibility" for a person to exhibit all three characteristics to the full extent or a similar degree. To support this view, they cite the example of impulse control, which Machiavellians possess (to a certain extent), whereas "real" psychopaths lack almost completely – such a basic trait could not be exhibited and not exhibited at the same time.

3.2.1 (Evolutionary) Biological Aspects

Fundamental differences between the Triad traits are suggested by twin studies in which both narcissism and psychopathy were found to have medium to strong hereditary components. This contrasts with significantly fewer genetic influences for Machiavellianism, for which alone shared environmental factors play a role (Vernon et al., 2008), i.e., those that contribute to similarities in traits, such as the same upbringing because of the same parental home in the case of siblings. The hereditary portion of the Dark Triad thus lies within the range of that of "normal" personality traits (Schuler, 2014a). One study traced differences between narcissism and psychopathy back completely to genetic and nonshared environmental factors (Veselka et al., 2011), namely, those that contribute to differences in the trait, such as independently made life experiences.

Jonason et al. (2016) investigated which typical environmental conditions may be related to or contribute to the development of the Dark Triad. They found that primarily uncertainty or imponderability in childhood, but also a harsh or stressful childhood are associated with high Triad values. For the individual criteria, they found differences between the characteristics in some cases. Narcissism was related to a better socioeconomic status as a child and a childhood considered privileged, while psychopathy was more related to insecure, harsh conditions. The strength of the expression of the characteristics weakens with adolescence, perhaps because of increasing impulse control through the development of prefrontal cortex functionality (De Clerq et al., 2017).

A consistent finding is the higher incidence of the Dark Triad in men (e.g., Chabrol et al., 2009; Jonason et al., 2010; Jonason et al., 2009; Paulhus & Williams, 2002). Muris et al. (2017) calculated a meta-analysis of gender differences and found that men generally have higher scores, especially in psychopathy, for which a significant gender difference remained even after controlling for shared variance.

The Triad characteristics of individuals seem to be identifiable in facial expressions: Subjects respond to faces of individuals with high levels of psychopathy and Machiavellianism with brain activity that signals lower confidence (Gordon & Platek, 2009). Holtzmann (2011) modeled typical Triad high-scorer faces regarding "craniofacial structures" using 112 data points in the face. Especially in female faces, assessors correctly assigned high and low values for all three features to the "face prototypes." There was also a tendency to show correlations between the faces and the personality test values, which, according to Holtzmann, could indicate a physiological mapping of phenotypes of the psychological Triad traits (which makes the Triad a potential object of research in "physiognomy," see Section 2.1). However, another study provided only clear evidence of the visibility of the trait in faces for narcissism (Shiramizu et al., 2019).

3.2.2 Emotional Deficits and Moral Concepts

A central aspect that is continually discussed in the context of the Dark Triad is the emotional coldness or lack of empathy of bearers of the traits. Thus, the Dark Triad is associated with various types of emotional limitations, such as lower overall empathy (e.g., Ali et al., 2009; Jonason et al., 2013), primarily with lower "affective" empathy, while "cognitive" empathy – the ability to recognize the emotional states of others – is generally not limited (Wai & Tiliopoulos, 2012). However, this relationship has feature-specific differences: In multiple regressions, psychopathy was negatively related to the degree of the "cognitive" empathy of perspective-taking as well as the "affective" empathy of empathic concern; narcissism was positively related to empathic fantasy and "personal distress" at the negative feelings of others (Jonason & Kroll, 2015).

Alexithymia (emotional blindness) has also been repeatedly linked to the Triad (e.g., Jonason & Krause, 2013): The ability to recognize feelings was positively related to narcissism and negatively related to Machiavellianism and psychopathy; this relationship could also be explained largely by common genetic and nonshared environmental conditions (Cairncross et al., 2013).

People with elevated values in Machiavellianism or psychopathy even react with positive affect to the sad faces of others (Ali et al., 2009). Wai and Tiliopoulos (2012) confirmed positive affect toward sad faces for narcissism, Machiavellianism, and primary psychopathy, and found negative affect toward happy faces. Individuals with elevated scores on two of the three Triad characteristics also show lower emotional expression themselves, though a positive relationship was found for narcissism (Lyons & Brockmann, 2017). Their low empathy results in less compassion for others; but this only applies to psychopathy, as narcissism was associated with higher compassion for others – at least according to self-description (Lee & Gibbons, 2017).

Twin studies revealed a lower "moral development" to the effect that there were positive connections between Machiavellianism and psychopathy and the lowest level of moral development according to Kohlberg (1984), and negative connections between psychopathy and the highest level (Campbell et al., 2009). The phenotypic correlations could not be explained by genetic foundations, but by correlated environmental conditions. Machiavellianism and psychopathy are associated with a less developed ability to make moral judgments, though narcissism was not. The relationship of psychopathy was completely moderated by perspective-taking ability (Williams et al., 2006). Psychopaths tend to engage in hobbies described as immoral, such as "ego-shooters," internet pornography, and computer hacking; Machiavellianism showed similar but weaker correlations; and narcissism was associated only with violent sports activities (Williams et al., 2001).

The Triad characteristics are associated with very conservative values or morals, for example, concerning illegal immigration, torture, environmental protection, and homosexuality (Arvan, 2013), and with prejudices against immigrants (Hodson et al., 2009). The Dark Triad characteristics are also associated with a greater willingness to commit or indulge in all seven deadly sins – anger, envy, gluttony, greed, lust, pride, sloth; only the latter is not associated with narcissism (Veselka et al., 2014).

3.2.3 Broad Personality Models

Apart from a shared core of low Agreeableness and low Honesty-Humility, which I discuss in more detail in Section 3.3, there are considerable differences between the Triad characteristics, even against the background of broad personality factors. Paulhus (2001, p. 228) describes narcissists as "disagreeable extraverts," and weakly positive relationships to Openness have been found; however, the latter and Extraversion are not related to Machiavellianism and psychopathy, both of which have a low degree of Conscientiousness, which is not true of narcissism (Furnham, Richards et al., 2013; Lee & Ashton, 2005; Paulhus & Williams, 2002). Neuroticism is negatively correlated with grandiose narcissism but positively correlated with secondary psychopathy (Miller et al., 2010); the Neuroticism facet of angry-hostility is positively correlated with all Triad components (DeShong et al., 2017).

O'Boyle et al. (2015) did a meta-analytical examination of the relationships of the Triad and the FFM (see Section 2.1.2) and found (besides the core of low Agreeableness) a corrected negative relationship of Machiavellianism with Conscientiousness (r=–.21) and a corrected positive one with Neuroticism (r=.09). Narcissism was positively associated with Extraversion (r=.40), Openness (r=.20), and Conscientiousness (r=.09), negatively associated with Neuroticism (r=–.16); psychopathy negatively associated with Conscientiousness (r=–.31) and weakly positively associated with Neuroticism (r=.05), Extraversion (r=.04), and Openness (r=.04). Vize et al. (2018) provided evidence for the positive relationship of narcissism with Extraversion and Openness and the negative relationship of

Machiavellianism and psychopathy with Conscientiousness. Also, Muris et al. (2017) confirmed a meta-analytically corrected positive relationship of narcissism with Extraversion (r=.31) and Openness (r=.15) and the negative relationship of Conscientiousness with psychopathy (r=–.27) and Machiavellianism (r=–.25). They also controlled for a shared variance of characteristics, showing that all relationships remained stable but resulted in a negative one of Machiavellianism with Extraversion (r=–.16) and a positive one of narcissism and Conscientiousness (r=.16). Kowalski et al. (2016) calculated a general factor of personality from the Big Five, the combined value of high Extraversion, Emotional Stability, Agreeableness, Openness, and Conscientiousness (see Musek, 2007), which was negatively associated with Machiavellianism and psychopathy but positively associated with narcissism. From comparisons of the Triad, the HDS, and the Big Five Douglas et al. (2012) concluded that the FFM does not allow a clear distinction to be made between the dark constructs.

Regarding the interpersonal circumplex (a circular model with basic dimensions of interpersonal behavior), the Triad is usually located in quadrant II – high agency (control, dominance, enforcement) and low communion (affiliation, community, care) (Furnham, Richards et al., 2013). Using several procedures that address different aspects regarding the axes of the circumplex, Dowgwillo and Pincus (2017) showed that there are clear differences between the level and direction of the characteristics, and that there are mean differences between the sexes but no structural differences.

Joint analyses of the Triad characteristics with the Supernumerary Personality Inventory (SPI; Paunonen, 2002) found correlations above all with the factors Seductiveness, Manipulativeness, Risk-Taking, and low Integrity (Veselka et al., 2012). The phenotypic correlations could be explained to a large extent by correlated genetic bases; in this study, too, nonshared environmental factors alone played a role in Machiavellianism.

Against the background of the alternative DSM-5 model for personality disorders (see Section 2.3.1), positive relationships of all Triad traits with Antagonism could be found; of Machiavellianism additionally with Negative Affectivity and Psychoticism, for psychopathy positive relationships with all domains of the maladaptive trait model (Grigoras & Wille, 2017). On a facet level, however, grandiosity was the only unifying aspect of the Triad. The maladaptive traits made a larger and incremental explanatory contribution to the Triad characteristics than the FFM factors, the main source of variance being Antagonism. However, the FFM explained a relatively larger part of the variance for psychopathy than the maladaptive trait model, here mainly through the factor Agreeableness. The meta-analysis by O'Boyle et al. (2015) also explained considerable variance in the Triad characteristics with the FFM, for psychopathy almost the entire variance.

3.2.4 Cognitive Skills and Related Characteristics

Regarding cognitive characteristics, differences between the Triad traits are present less between the concepts than between their measurement sources. Meta-analytically, the Triad characteristics themselves are independent of intelligence (O'Boyle et al., 2013), although it has been repeatedly assumed that intelligence could act as a moderating variable in the relationship between the Triad factors and outcome variables (see Muris et al., 2017; O'Boyle et al., 2012).

Narcissism is associated with highly positive assessments of one's own intelligence (Gabriel et al., 1994) and creativity, in pure self-assessment and measured with a biographical inventory to record creative behavior (Furnham, Hughes et al., 2013). Psychopathy and especially Machiavellianism, unlike narcissism, are not associated with an appreciation of one's own creativity and intelligence, and, contrary to corresponding self-assessments, also narcissists did not achieve better results on an intelligence test (Paulhus et al., 2001) and creativity tasks (Jonason et al., 2017). Regarding creativity, narcissists rated themselves positively and were at the same time considered less creative by others (Jonason, Abboud et al., 2017). Jonason et al. (2015) found narcissism and psychopathy to be associated with generally positive self-assessments of creativity.

Kapoor (2015) used implicit association measurement (IAT) to distinguish "positive creativity" associated with narcissism from "negative creativity" associated with psychopathy. In a task on creativity, psychopathy and Machiavellianism were correlated with potentially harmful uses of creative solutions, though none of the Triad characteristics were associated with a higher quantity of solutions, i.e., the fluidity of ideas. Accordingly, even slightly negative relationships for Machiavellianism and psychopathy were found with actual measures of divergent thinking (Dahmen-Wassenberg et al., 2016).

Despite only weak bivariate correlations to the three stages of the creative process – idea generation, idea promotion, and idea implementation – a positive correlation between narcissism and the externally assessed overall value of "innovative employee behavior" was found (Wisse et al., 2015); psychopathy did not correlate, Machiavellianism negatively. The connection for narcissism existed only if the supervisor was not a narcissist. Since the criterion "innovative behavior of the employee" was assessed by these very same superiors, employees may have been assessed as less creative for typically narcissistic motives, such as devaluing others in social comparison, or reasons of competition for attention from others (Wisse et al., 2015).

Regarding so-called emotional intelligence, Austin et al. (2007) found negative relationships for Machiavellianism using the Mayer-Salovey-Caruso Emotional Intelligence Test (MSCEIT; Mayer et al., 2002). Negative relationships exist for Machiavellianism and secondary psychopathy with the Trait Emotional Intelligence Questionnaire (TEIQue; Petrides & Furnham, 2006) (Ali et al., 2009). The same pattern (albeit with positive associations for narcissism) was shown in another study (Petrides et al., 2011), in which the relationships were attributed to common genetic influences and correlated nonshared environmental conditions. Vize, Lynam et al. (2018) in a meta-analytical study showed a negative correlation of Machiavellianism and psychopathy with emotional intelligence. A further meta-analysis (Miao et al., 2019) confirmed the negative relationships of Machiavellianism and psychopathy – both to the characteristic and to the "performance measure" of emotional intelligence. Narcissism, on the other hand, was not related in either study. Regarding socioemotional intelligence – as measured with a personality questionnaire and thus a concept that, like emotional intelligence, has little in common with intelligence as a measure of cognitive performance – even positive relationships were found for narcissism, negative ones for both partners (Nagler et al., 2014).

3.2.5 Interpersonal Behavior and Lifestyle

All Triad characteristics are associated (at different levels) with values such as "stimulation," "power," and "achievement," negatively with values such as "benevolence." In addition, they explain incremental variance in value types beyond the Big Five (Kajonius et al., 2015). They show connections to orientations and aspirations for money/consumption, sex, and power, and can also explain incremental variance in these values beyond the Big Five (Lee et al., 2013). Unsurprisingly, narcissism and psychopathy are positively related to the desire for or interest in fame, while Machiavellianism is negatively related (Southard & Zeigler-Hill, 2016).

The effects of the Triad are described as a socially aversive and particularly interpersonal problematic behavioral style (Lee & Ashton, 2005) or as a "short-term, agentic, exploitative social strategy" (Jonason & Webster, 2010, p. 420). All Triad characteristics, especially psychopathy, are correspondingly associated with a "fast life history strategy," characterized by low self-control, short sexual relationships, selfishness, and a focus on rapid reproductive success rather than long-term, stable parenthood – and this in several different cultures (Jonason et al., 2009; Jonason, Foster et al., 2017).

High scores on the Triad traits are associated with an increased likelihood of playing for money (Jones, 2014); if this entails punishment, only psychopathy was a predictor of playing with other people's money (and potentially losing it). For all Triad components and one underlying factor, relationships were demonstrated to sensation-seeking and impulsivity. Behavioral simulations did not show any relationship to risk behavior in a so-called "balloon pump experiment" (which the authors of the study said might have been too uninteresting for them); however, a combined value for the three characteristics (and only narcissism even in isolation) was associated with higher risk for gambling and lower delay discounting (temporal postponement of financial reward). Accordingly, participants with a correspondingly high level of Dark Triad traits preferred the option of receiving less money immediately over the option of receiving more in the future (Crysel et al., 2013). Malesza and Ostaszewski (2016) found similar results, stating that, while narcissism and psychopathy are related to self-reported measures of impulsiveness, Machiavellianism is not. In this study, psychopathy was associated with a stronger preference for immediate (but smaller) financial rewards. They conclude that, while Machiavellianism is not automatically associated with strong impulse control, it is at least associated with lower levels of impulsivity than narcissism and psychopathy. Narcissism is associated with a functional form of impulsivity, psychopathy with "dysfunctional" impulsivity, stemming from a lack of control self-regulation (Jones & Paulhus, 2011). The moderately pronounced impulse control of Machiavellians means the study revealed no relationship to the various forms of impulsivity. However, the latter finding was methodologically criticized and described as a misinterpretation; see my comments on partialing in Section 3.3.2.

Vize, Lynam et al. (2018) examined the relationship of the Triad to criteria of the broad categories of aggression, impulsiveness, and sensation-seeking/risk-taking and found all three characteristics positively associated with all categories, narcissism most strongly associated with aggression. Using standard procedures, such as the Mach IV as a measure of Machiavellianism, Jonason and Tost (2010) found psychopathy to be the only significant factor influencing lack of self-control in joint regression analyses of the characteristics. In contrast, the corresponding scale of the Dirty Dozen (Jonason & Webster, 2010) was associated with low self-control and the only significant predictor in the model. Depending on the procedure, this results in different relationships to self-control or, for the Dirty Dozen procedure, in relations that do not agree with the theory for Machiavellianism (see the criticism of Dirty Dozen in Section 5.2.2).

Mating

Jonason et al. (2009) sought the reason for the strategy of "impulsive short-term mating," which is more common among men than among women, in the higher degree of Triad characteristics among men, although they could clearly demonstrate this only for psychopathy. High scorers of all Triad characteristics generally set lower standards for their partners (in both the long and short term). Psychopaths, for example, do not value the kindness of partners in a long-term relationship, while narcissists value physical attractiveness and social status (Jonason et al., 2011). In line with the short-term nature of the relationships sought, all are interested in rather little "commitment" to the partner and not in romantic relationships. Narcissists most likely seek one-night stands, while psychopaths are more interested in pure (albeit permanently available) booty-call relationships (Jonason et al., 2012).

In terms of their sexual fantasies, the Dark Triad characteristics differ. What unites them all is the generally higher sexual desire, which is comparatively weak for Machiavellianism and strongest for psychopathy (Baughman, Jonason, Veselka et al., 2014). Semenyna et al. (2017) showed an interesting curvilinear connection between the Triad and general sexual openness (sociosexuality) in connection with the sexual orientation of women. Purely hetero- or homosexual women (the end poles of the continuum) show lower values on the Triad and a lower tendency to short-term, noncommittal sexual activity, whereas bisexual women (representing the midpoint of the continuum) show higher values on the Triad and sociosexuality.

Narcissism is perceived as less dark than the other two, although third parties rate all three rather less positively (Rauthmann & Kolar, 2012, 2013). Narcissists, on the other hand, have been shown to be perceived as more popular upon first acquaintance, precisely because of the facet that leads to decreasing popularity over time: exploitation/entitlement (Back et al., 2010). This is because narcissists are better judged on those cues that observers rate as positive, such as a neat appearance, charming facial expressions, or confident movements, and these are associated with higher values in exploitation/entitlement.

To win over potential partners, people with high Triad characteristics use specific tactics depending on the situation. In general, they all tend to use flattery, whereas only psychopathy is associated (in all situations) with the use of pressure or coercion, and Machiavellianism has no independent relationship to aggressive sexual tactics (Jones & Olderbak, 2014). Narcissism is associated only with coercion because of rejection after a costly date, which is in line with the findings of Bushman et al. (2003), who associate narcissism with sexual aggression after rejection. More generally, narcissists react with aggression to rejection or attacks on their ego, psychopaths to physical attacks (Jones & Paulhus, 2010).

Female narcissists have a higher overall, but also explicitly sexual competitiveness. Although this finding applies to the Triad in general, narcissism is the central influencing factor (Carter et al., 2015). To keep away or get rid of partners they have won – i.e., to avoid having to enter long-term romantic relationships and instead be able to make further short-term acquaintances – narcissists and Machiavellians alike primarily use specific strategies and concrete actions such as avoiding intimacy or even exerting violence against the partner. There is also a clear connection to psychopathy, but none to the milder behavior strategies (Jonason & Buss, 2012).

Health Aspects

Narcissism and Machiavellianism are mostly unrelated to self-assessed physical and mental health problems, while psychopathy is weakly related to poorer physical health and depression-related self-assessments. Among the objective measures of health hazards psychopathy was associated with general risk-taking, intravenous drug use, unprotected sex, and driving without a seat belt; psychopaths also have a lower life expectancy (Jonason et al., 2015).

Hudek-Knežević et al. (2016) examined the relationship to several diseases and conditions while controlling for sociodemographic characteristics and the Big Five and found that, on the whole, the Triad provided (little) additional explanation for several health indicators. Psychopathy was negatively associated with mood, more diseases, and unhealthy behavior; Machiavellianism was associated with worse mood, higher blood pressure, and weakly associated with less cancer; narcissism was associated with positive mood, healthier behavior, and fewer skin diseases. There is weak evidence that higher levels in the Dark Triad are associated with shorter monthly cycles and negative health outcomes for women, including more sexual diseases and miscarriages (Jonason & Lavertu, 2017).

It is questionable to what extent these correlative studies based on self-assessments contribute to our further understanding, especially of the more severe among the diseases mentioned. However, they do point to feature-specific differences in Triad properties, at least regarding risk behavior.

Differential effects are also apparent for different measures of life satisfaction and general well-being. Narcissism was positively, psychopathy negatively, Machiavellianism not correlated with these variables (Aghababei & Błachnio, 2015). Machiavellianism and secondary psychopathy were also negatively correlated with life satisfaction in another study (Ali & Chamorro-Premuzic, 2010), whereas primary and secondary psychopathy and Machiavellianism negatively correlated with commitment (in relationships), Machiavellianism negatively correlated with intimacy.

Antisocial Behavior

A form of behavior also associated with health consequences for the individual as well as with antisocial behavior toward competitors and ultimately even criminal aspects – and which should therefore serve as an introduction to the relevant section – is doping in sports. Nicholls et al. (2017) found that all Triad characteristics are associated with a more positive attitude toward doping. They explained nearly 30% of the variance in attitudes to it.

Moreover, people with high levels of a Triad component are generally convinced that they can cheat well, and this attitude is strongest for Machiavellianism (Giammarco et al.,

2013). All Triad components are associated with more frequent lies, both academic and relational; Machiavellianism was the only predictor here in joint analyses (Azizli et al., 2016). Narcissism is associated with unfounded lies and with lies for personal gain, Machiavellianism additionally with the number of people who are lied to, and "white lies," psychopathy most strongly with all the forms mentioned, but not with white lies. Psychopaths also rate their ability to lie the highest, but all persons with high levels of one of the Triad components produce positive values here. Machiavellians lie for intentions such as fraud, narcissists for goals such as increasing their popularity, and psychopaths for virtually all purposes, especially those associated with promiscuity. Psychopathy fully moderates the difference between the sexes in promiscuity-related lies (Jonason et al., 2014). However, none of the traits are associated with a better ability to recognize lies in others (Wissing & Reinhard, 2017), and none of the Triad components are associated with the self-assessment if others are believing their lies, although psychopaths are more likely to enjoy lying (Baughman, Jonason, Lyons et al., 2014) – they cheat even when there is a risk of being caught or punished, because of their fearlessness (see Section 3.1.3). Only at low risk did the other two Triad colleagues also tend to cheat (Jones & Paulhus, 2017). This relates to the finding, which is interesting for using the Dark Triad in the form of self-assessments in the occupational field, according to which Machiavellianism and psychopathy are negatively associated with (self-assessed) socially desirable response behavior, presumably because persons with high values of these characteristics are not afraid of the consequences (Kowalski et al., 2018).

Interpersonal manipulation is assumed to be one of the core characteristics of the Dark Triad (see Section 3.3) and is accordingly examined in a wide variety of manifestations. Positive relationships of all three characteristics can be found for the emotional manipulation of others (Nagler et al., 2014). Narcissism and psychopathy moderated the relationship between emotional control and emotional manipulation, which was closer at high levels in the Triad. In an examination of the typical type of social influence tactics, it was found that characteristics of the Dark Triad were positively associated with almost all measured influence tactics – and this across different targets, such as family, strangers, and sex (Jonason & Webster, 2012). Triad trait bearers, on the other hand, vary the chosen tactic depending on the outcome target. The authors conclude that they have a whole repertoire of tactics they can use depending on the situation, which makes them unpredictable and therefore successful. Machiavellians tend to resort to complex, long-term deception; psychopaths to impulsive deception (Roeser et al., 2016).

Negotiations represent a specific and in professional life very relevant situation of influencing the "opponent." The first studies by Christie and Geis (1970) already explored Machiavellianism in this respect and recognized the specific advantages associated with it (see Section 3.1.2). Gunnthorsdottir et al. (2002) showed that people with low Machiavellianism values are more likely to choose a reciprocal strategy, that is, they are more likely to share profits, while high scorers choose the dominant strategy, abusing trust and claiming all profits for themselves. Ten Brinke et al. (2015) found that psychopaths have advantages in competitive distribution negotiations and disadvantages when it comes to making profits integrative.

For the Triad as a whole, the results were examined in negotiation situations conducted directly (face-to-face) or via computer. For a combined Dark Triad value, Crossley et al. (2016) found that higher values contribute to success in face-to-face negotiations but worse results in those conducted via computer. Persons who scored high on psychopathy and Machiavellianism achieved higher gains than "pure psychopaths" (i.e., those who had simultaneously low Machiavellianism scores). Machiavellians scored higher in face-to-face situations but tend to score lower in computer-mediated situations.

All Triad characteristics are positively related to extraoccupational bullying in terms of direct and indirect, physical, and verbal behavior; psychopathy is strongest in each case (Baughman et al., 2012), but only with traditional, nononline-based bullying (van Geel et al., 2017). In one online experiment, psychopathy was the best predictor of trolling on Facebook, and this to a greater extent for the profile of a popular than for that of a less popular Facebook member, whereas this was true for Machiavellianism only for that of the unpopular (Lopes & Yu, 2017).

In self-reports, all Triad components are associated with various forms of explicit misconduct, from antiauthoritarian behavior, bullying, and consumption of soft and hard drugs to light and serious forms of criminality. Clearly, the strongest in each case is psychopathy. The exceptions are the missing links between Machiavellianism and narcissism and the use of hard drugs (Azizli et al., 2016). According to results of multiple regression, psychopathy was the only significant predictor here as well. The Triad characteristics also show references to more serious criminal acts; after controlling for substance use and borderline disorders, only psychopathy provided an independent explanation (Chabrol et al., 2017).

Psychopathy is associated with wearing tattoos or piercings as well as generally "cultural deviance markers," for example, clothing style. Furthermore, it is associated with various forms of criminal misconduct. Nathanson et al. (2006) investigated whether these "visual" and other conditions, such as membership in a certain peer group (together the "sociological model") or personality explain the criminal acts. After including psychopathy, the authors found this was the only significant predictor, which also applied to various categories of crime. Only in the case of drug use did the framework conditions have an additional influence, although psychopathy remained the strongest influence.

In two samples, the Dark Triad characteristics were also associated with a higher propensity for sexual harassment, and in multiple regressions, they all had a significant explanatory contribution. For Machiavellianism, there was also an interaction effect with sex in one of the two studies, according to which the tendency toward sexual harassment was highest in men with high Machiavellianism values (Zeigler-Hill et al., 2016). Carton and Egan (2017) examined violence in relationships and found psychopathy to be a strong predictor of psychological as well as physical or sexual abuse. However, low Agreeableness was the strongest determinant, and psychopathy could not explain any incremental variance. Yet, in another study, psychopathy and vulnerable narcissism were the only positive, grandiose narcissism the only negative predictor of proactive as well as reactive violence in partnerships, despite the inclusion of the complete HEXACO model – i.e., considering an Agreeableness factor (Knight et al., 2018).

A relatively new, but no less illegal, and even interpersonal particularly reprehensible form of sexual violence or crime is so-called "revenge porn" – the sharing of pornographic material of a person (often the ex-partner) to a broad public without that person's knowledge or consent. All Triad characteristics were associated with a higher probability of sharing revenge porn, sadism interestingly not (Pina et al., 2017). Again, after regression analysis, psychopathy was the only predictor of this propensity, Machiavellianism with the acceptance of such behavior, and narcissism for the pleasure of it.

Muris et al. (2017) meta-analytically summarized various areas of psychosocial consequences of the Triad: those discussed above, such as socioemotional deficits, morality, or aspects related to sexual behavior, but also those that include severely antisocial, genuinely criminal behavior. They show that, in general, all Triad characteristics are associated with negative psychosocial consequences. Psychopathy usually shows the clearly highest values, for example, for aggression-related delinquency (r=.39) and sexual behavior-related aspects (r=.32). Joint regression analyses that exclude the shared variance (see Section 3.3.2) therefore also resulted in the finding of "psychopathy runs the show" (Muris et al., 2017, p. 194). It is the only relevant predictor for almost all areas considered; for narcissism, only interpersonal problems remained; for Machiavellianism these and antisocial tactics. The authors conclude that psychopathy is the main driver for "harmful" behavior.

But psychopathy itself may still be one level too high in the search for a driver of counterproductive behavior. As discussed in Section 3.1.3 on psychopathy and in the above comments on "lifestyle," psychopathy is associated with a high level of impulsiveness, which can also be interpreted as a lack of self-control. Low self-control was suggested in the crime theory of Gottfredson and Hirschi (1990) as a cause of deviant behavior and was also used as a theoretical basis in integrity research to explain counterproductive behavior at the workplace (on counterproductive behavior, see Sections 2.2.1 and 4.1).

Wright et al. (2017) linked the two concepts and found that the Dark Triad is associated with generally higher levels of delinquency, especially violent delinquency, and that there is also an interaction with self-control: With a low degree of self-control, the Triad is more closely related to delinquency.

In the findings described here, and in the numerous other findings on differential effects of narcissism, Machiavellianism, and psychopathy made over the last 20 years, of which only a selection could be reported in this chapter, we find confirmation for the view that it is in principle worthwhile to consider the Triad characteristics separately as well, which Paulhus and Williams (2002, p. 562) concluded after their studies on the possible separation of the Dark Triad characteristics: "... distinctive enough to warrant separate measurement."

Nevertheless, one can also see from the highlighted explanatory contribution of psychopathy to the Triad (especially regarding antisocial behavior) that it is the central influencing factor. Therefore, the question has often been raised as to whether psychopathy can in principle causally explain all of the relationships found for the Dark Triad. That is why I deal with this question in more detail in the following section.

3.3 Structural and Measurement-Methodological Separation of the Dark Triad

Even before the term Dark Triad was created, the question of the overlap of the individual characteristics was discussed. It was determined that there were indeed great similarities between the construct of Machiavellianism and the most problematic components of narcissism (McHoskey, 1995), on the one hand, and narcissism and the interpersonal factor of psychopathy (Hart & Hare, 1998), on the other hand. For Machiavellianism and psychopathy, McHoskey et al. (1998) even argued that they are the *same* personality construct, and that the Mach IV (to measure Machiavellianism; see Section 3.1.2) is a measure of psychopathy in nonclinical populations. Several recent papers also support this view (e.g., Miller et al., 2017). This discussion is based on studies that have located the common measures for Dark Triad constructs in joint analyses on the same factors or show similar relationships to external criteria (Furnham, Richards et al., 2013). Thanks to the enormously increased interest in and the many recent studies on the Dark Triad (as a unit), many datasets are now available to clarify these questions on a broad empirical basis, as well as methodologically high-quality work that explicitly deals with the Dark Triad itself.

This section provides an overview of the research on the internal structure and typical measurement approaches to the Dark Triad, since both areas are not only the subject of theoretical discussion but are particularly relevant for practical, professional use. To justify a deployment in organizational HR work, one should not only demonstrate that it is worthwhile to consider the Dark Triad in this context (see Chapter 4), but one should also clarify in advance which aspects can be distinguished from one another and how these can be measured, in other words, which components of the Triad can and should be rewardingly recorded in the occupational context in the first place.

To this end, I first discuss the extent of the connections between the characteristics and which specific aspects of the Dark Triad account for them. Then, I present different views on the factorial structure of the Dark Triad and clarify whether it is more appropriate to consider one factor, two factors, or the separate measurement of all three Triad characteristics (as well as which of their subfacets). In connection with the different views on the internal relations of the Triad, another much-discussed issue is highlighted: the indicated statistical methodology in studying the relationships of Triad characteristics to external variables. Here, I discuss bivariate, regression-analytical, and structural equation modeling techniques and their respective advantages and disadvantages (Furnham, Richards et al., 2013; Watts et al., 2017). Finally, I present the theoretical explanation that has contributed to the controversial structural and analytical issues – the *construct creep* of Dark Triad research (Furnham, Richards et al., 2013). From the combination of all described findings, I propose the multidimensional view of Dark Triad features as a possible way of countering the construct creep.

Thus, I derive which structural conception and which analytical methodology appears to be the most sensible for recording and using the Dark Triad according to the current state of research, whereby supplying empirically secured recommendations for job-related application purposes.

3.3.1 Structural Concept of the Dark Triad

Shared Variance and Core Content of the Triad

One can relatively consistently determine the internal relationships of the Dark Triad through various meta-analyses and across different measures. The first relevant meta-analysis by O'Boyle et al. (2012) yielded corrected correlations from r=.30 for narcissism and Machiavellianism, r=.51 for narcissism and psychopathy, and r=.59 for psychopathy and Machiavellianism. Vize, Lynam et al. (2018) showed relationships from r=.35 for narcissism and Machiavellianism, r=.38 for narcissism and psychopathy, and r=.52 for

Machiavellianism and psychopathy. The meta-analysis by Muris et al. (2017), which included only combined studies of all Triad characteristics, arrived at average effect sizes of $r=.34$ for narcissism and Machiavellianism, $r=.38$ for narcissism and psychopathy, and $r=.58$ for psychopathy and Machiavellianism. Vernon et al. (2008), using genetic correlations of psychopathy, revealed with narcissism ($r=.48$) and Machiavellianism ($r=.66$) that these correlations have a common genetic basis. Taken together, there are strong bivariate relationships between psychopathy and Machiavellianism in particular, as well as consistently weaker (with values around $r=.30$ still substantial) relationships of narcissism and Machiavellianism.

As a possible common core of content responsible for the overlaps, low Agreeableness, Honesty-Humility, modesty, and empathy as well as pronounced antagonism or interpersonal manipulation/exploitation were suggested (see Furnham, Richards et al., 2013). All Triad characteristics share a core of low Agreeableness, Honesty-Humility, and Integrity, which was also demonstrated in a German-speaking sample (Schwarzinger, 2009) and lie in the same quadrant of the Interpersonal Circumplex (Furnham, Richards et al., 2013; see Section 3.2.3). Muris et al. (2017) meta-analytically found negative associations with Agreeableness for all three Triad characteristics: $r=-.21$ with narcissism, $r=-.43$ with Machiavellianism, and $r=-.46$ with psychopathy. With Agreeableness, Vernon et al. (2008) demonstrated genetic correlations from $r=-.42$ to $r=-.78$, which speak for this factor being a construct underlying the Triad (Miller et al., 2017). Jones and Figueredo (2013) used structural equation modeling methods to demonstrate the first psychopathy factor Interpersonal according to Hare (2003; see Section 3.1.3) as a further substantive interpretation of the core of the Triad.

Book et al. (2015) compared several models, including one that included the Big Five (it was able to explain 46% variance in the Triad), low empathy (37% variance explained), primary psychopathy consisting of manipulation and low empathy (45% variance explained), the entire HEXACO model (57% variance explained), and Honesty-Humility and low empathy (63% variance explained). Thus, a substantial part of, but not the entire, variance in the Dark Triad can be explained by either narrow content-related factors or the broad personality models. One criticism of the title of the publication "... claiming the core of the Dark Triad" and the corresponding use of terms in the text was that the statistically explained variance by a (by definition complete) overall model of personality (Big Five or HEXACO, see Section 2.1.2) cannot be regarded as a narrow core of another concept (here the Dark Triad), but rather as a broad explanatory model of all its many facets.

Hodson et al. (2018) took a somewhat different approach and meta-analytically compared the empirically extracted dark core of the Triad components (dark g-factor; see below) and the H-factor (Honesty-Humility; see Section 2.1.2). They found an almost perfectly negative correlation from which they concluded that the core of the Triad is completely identical to low Honesty-Humility. Hodson et al. (2018) further assumed, based on their findings, that all variance of the Dark Triad can be explained against the background of basal dimensions of "normal personality," thus endorsing the critical voice of Muris et al. (2017), who considered the concept of the Dark Triad as possibly redundant, since it is unable to explain much more than is already possible with traditional personality models.

This assumption is correct, as the data presented and discussed below show, but probably goes too far in its interpretation, since, on the one hand, Book et al. (2015), even using complete personality models, cannot explain the entire variance in the Triad and, on the other hand, Hodson et al. (2018) find low Honesty-Humility is only identical with the empirical core but not with the variance of the complete constructs. However, precisely the Triad constructs as a specific constellation (compound traits, see Section 2.2.2) and the consideration of all their facets (see the comments on subfacets of the Dark Triad in Section 3.3.3) represent potential additions in the application of personality factors to personnel psychology.

To summarize the overlaps between narcissism, Machiavellianism, and psychopathy and the proposed descriptions of their content, we can say that there is much variance among Triad characteristics to explain, and depending on which concept we use – a psychopathy factor, a factor of a personality model, or even one in its entirety – we discover considerable proportions of common variance among the different explanatory models and the Dark Triad. Yet, none of them can explain their entire variance. The proposals presented in this section should therefore also be understood only as cores in the narrower sense. For this purpose, we should consider interpersonal manipulation, emotional coldness, low Agreeableness, and low Honesty-Humility.

The following presents various views on how to interpret the empirical structure of the Dark Triad in all its aspects and how to regard the interrelationships and delimitability of the characteristics per se.

The Dark Triad, the Dark Dyad, or the Dark g-Factor?

The large number of common variance components of the Triad characteristics led to a single factor being extracted several times (see Furnham, Richards et al., 2013; Glenn & Sellbom, 2015). Early on, a factor was described that clarifies 61% variance and on which the NPI (see Section 3.1.1), the Mach IV (see Section 3.1.2), and the Levenson Self-Report Psychopathy Scale loaded with $r=.66$ or higher (McHoskey et al., 1998). To the best of my knowledge, the article by McHoskey and colleagues is thus the first explicitly joint investigation of all three Dark Triad characteristics, appearing a few years before the seminal work of Paulhus and colleagues. A common underlying factor was also found (exploratively) for the short procedure Dirty Dozen (see Section 5.2.2) (Jonason et al., 2009). However, in another confirmatory study, the single-factor model showed poor, whereas hierarchical and three-factor models showed significantly better model fits (Jonason & Webster, 2010).

Bertl et al. (2017) concluded that the assumption of a single superordinate factor leads to better model fits than considering the three Triad characteristics separately. However, they compared a model with single items as variables and an overlying three-factor structure with a dark-core model, in which, instead of single items, the subscales of the inventories are operationalized as manifest variables. Thus, although the models are not directly comparable in terms of their structure and parameters, they nevertheless clearly indicate the existence of a common dark core. Bertl et al. (2017) further showed that primarily the psychopathy factors Affective Deficits/Emotional Coldness and Interpersonal Manipulation explain the empirically extracted core, thus confirming the view of Jones and Figueredo (2013) that these aspects appropriately describe the content.

Good model fit was finally achieved by the parallel consideration of a superordinate factor and the individual scales of the common short inventories. A comparison of a total of five models revealed the best-fit dimensions for such a bifactor model (McLarnon & Tarraf, 2017). It should be noted that, for all the models investigated there, the authors used different methods of structural modeling or calculation, some of which are method-immanent optimized to explain as much variance as possible. While classical, "normal" confirmatory factor analyses (CFA) exclusively model a relationship to a latent factor for each item (no crossloadings, no further latent bifactor), this restriction is softened in newer structural modeling methods. Exploratory structural equation models (ESEM) allow loadings on other factors that should only be "toward zero." Bifactor models additionally assume the existence of a global factor that explains the shared variance on all items, the specific factors only the variance not covered by it. An exploratory bifactor structural equation model (B-ESEM) finally integrates both approaches (McLarnon & Tarraf, 2017).

Especially in personality research, it is well known and obvious for the Triad characteristics described as overlapping that individual item variance can be explained not only by the latent target construct but also by the other factors and common variance components. It is therefore not surprising that the classical, rather restrictive one- and three-factor CFA models are "inferior" to the new approaches, and that the B-ESEM shows the best fit-measures, as McLarnon and Tarraf show (2017). The authors also state that there was a deliberate deviation from another classic guideline – that of choosing the most parsimonious model – to explain as much variance as possible. On the other hand, they can show that there is a common variance component that exists independently of or parallel to the three characteristics, thus supporting "... both the unificationist and separatist perspectives on the underlying structure of the Dark Triad, which were previously proposed as contrasting paradigms" (McLarnon & Tarraf, 2017, p. 72).

Section 3.3.2 presents a critical examination of what is to be understood by factors modeled in this way. Unlike McLarnon and Tarraf (2017) another approach explaining the Triad structure includes the standard procedures and their subscales in the analysis, i.e., more individual, and specifically delimitable facets.

On this basis, Watts et al. (2017) found a better fit for a three-factor model with a higher order factor than that found without the assumption of such a factor; however, there was no ideal fit for both models. They then set up a series of multiple ESEMs, capturing each construct with multiple inventories and their subscales (including, for example, those on vulnerable narcissism). The model loaded all scales on one factor and produced very good fit measures; they then modeled how many factors fit "underneath," that is, how many factors lie between one factor and the number of subscales of the inventories. A four-factor model (with hardly any better indices than the three-factor model), which differs from the Dark Triad in content, proved to be the best. Its factors were named Emotional Stability, Grandiosity, Instrumentality (Machiavellianism), and Sensation-Seeking. One reason for the appearance of Emotional Stability might be the inclusion of the vulnerable narcissism scales and the broader conceptions of the psychopathy scales under consideration compared to standard and short procedures. This study shows that, using a purely empirical approach and proposals for structure optimized for fit measures, the results greatly depend on which characteristics are included, how broadly, and with which measures.

Moshagen et al. (2018) searched for and found a dark g-factor – the Dark Factor of Personality D. To this end, they included the following constructs in addition to Dark Triad short procedures: Egoism, Moral Disengagement, Psychological Entitlement, Sadism, Self-Interest, and Spitefulness. Thus, such contents are widely represented focusing on one's own advantage without consideration of or even with pleasure in the disadvantages for others. The D-factor found could accordingly be described in terms of content as the "... tendency to maximize one's individual utility at the cost of others, accompanied by beliefs that serve as justifications" (Moshagen et al., 2018, p. 656). The scales included in the

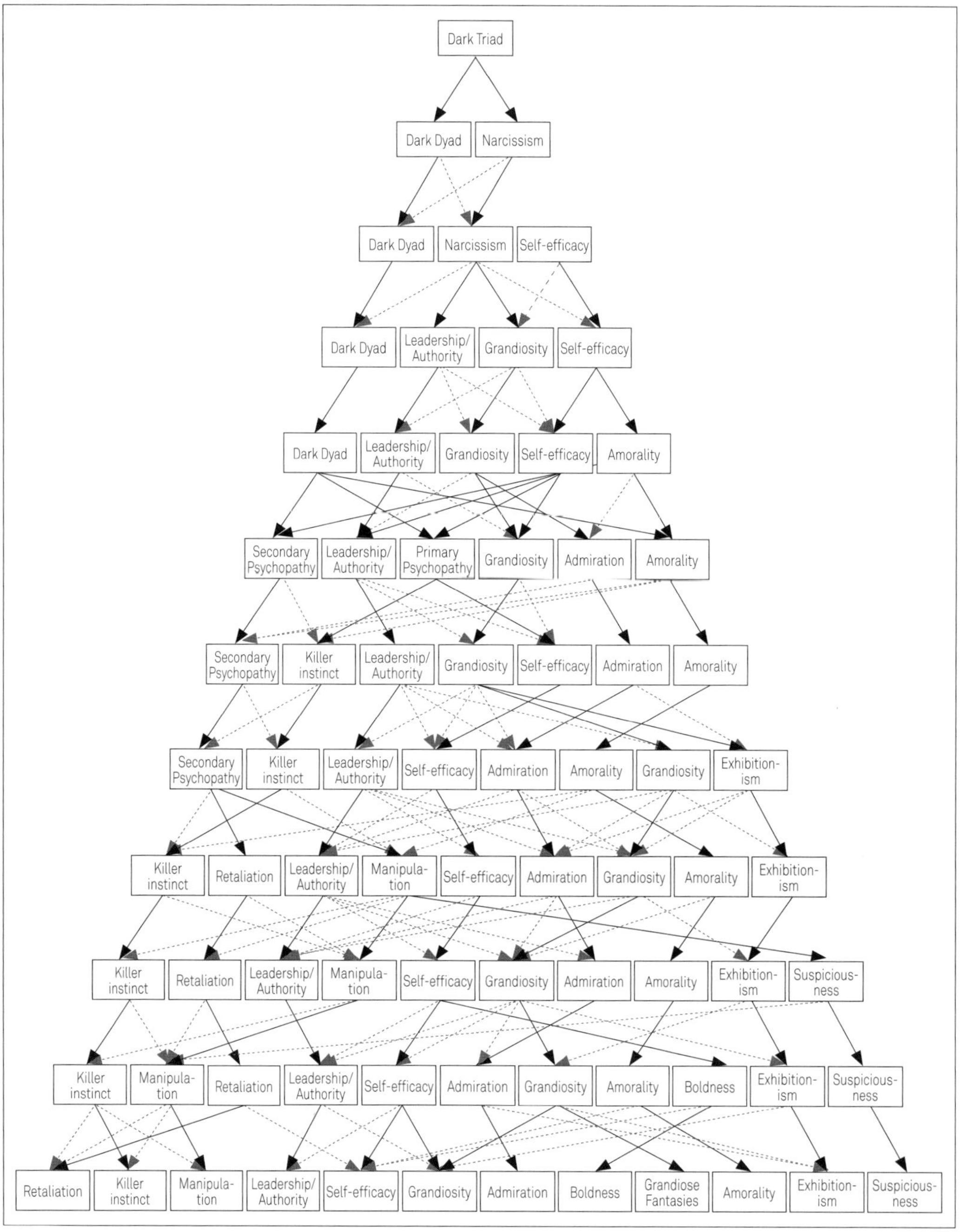

Figure 2: Hierarchical structure of the Dark Triad. Reprinted with permission from "Dark Triad traits and their structure: An empirical approach," by R. Rogoza & J. Cieciuch, 2020, *Current Psychology, 39*, p. 1294. © The Author(s) 2018.

analysis of this study resulted from an extensive literature search on dark properties in relevant journals dating back to 1999. Since, in addition to other, rather marginal, dark factors, probably the best-known dark factors (those of the HDS; see Table 2) were not included in the analysis, it cannot be clarified whether a different D-factor would have been found with them (and ideally also the Triad standard procedure with subscales).

The research by Volmer et al. (2019) and Rogoza and Cieciuch (2020) follows a more balanced and specific approach to the Triad. Volmer et al. showed that the variance under the standard procedures SRP, NPI, and Mach IV as well as SD 3 (Short Dark Triad; Jones & Paulhus, 2014) and the Dirty Dozen can be better explained by adding a bifactor D than with a three-factor model (which, however, also has good fit measures). Thus, they provide an extension of, and confirm the results of, the work by McLarnon and Tarraf (2017), who examined only the short procedures without subscales.

Rogoza and Cieciuch (2020) include the SD 3 and a standard scale for each of the three constructs. At the scale level, on which most of the approaches discussed above also work, they find evidence for the Dark Dyad solution of narcissism and psychopathy/Machiavellianism. In addition, the individual items are first condensed at the item level to explore 12 delimitable scales, and from there they compared a total of 13 structural equation models with each other based on their fit measures that, starting from one factor (Dark Triad), each have one facet more. (For the exact, somewhat more complex approach than that presented here, see Rogoza and Cieciuch, 2020.) According to their results, 12 facets form the best structural description of the classic Dark Triad items (for work-related items, 11 subscales were found; see Schwarzinger & Schuler, 2016, 2019; and Section 6.1.2). Figure 2 shows the result.

Thus, regarding the number of factors subsumed under the Triad, we can state that, using new structural modeling techniques and depending on which methods are considered and whether they are examined at the item or scale level, there is solid evidence for the advantageousness of structural interpretations that deviate from a three-factor view. However, there are some restrictions, namely, that (1), methodologically, either every conceivable variance has to be modeled, (2) completely different construct structures are created by adding marginal aspects of content (such as vulnerable narcissism), or (3) the weight of a content area in the factor solution is overestimated because of a relatively large influence of that area. But if equal proportions are used and the standard procedures are applied, there is some evidence for the delimitability of and meaningful model fits for three Triad factors, and, parallel to that, a dark bifactor can be modeled that explains additional variance. This is worth further research to theoretically understand the nature of dark properties and regarding its validity for predicting external correlates (parallel to and instead of the individual characteristics). For practical applications, the classical Dark Triad or Dark Dyad solution, but above all, a differentiated consideration of many individual facets, seems to be useful. I, therefore, discuss this finding again at the end of this chapter, also regarding its implications for occupational application (see Section 3.3.3).

Psychopathy or Dark Triad?

For practical application and for further research, Glenn and Sellbom (2015) argue that it is worth considering, especially for the prediction of external variables, that the combination of measures of related constructs and the calculation of artificial factors does not make sense theoretically, or that this and its advantageousness must first be proven (otherwise one could add any other constructs). In their opinion, it is better to measure the central factor (psychopathy) in isolation. Probably the most frequently voiced criticisms of the theoretical concept of the Dark Triad – that Machiavellianism and psychopathy cannot be conceptually distinguished or that the psychopathy construct itself is so broad as to include the other two – is raised by McHoskey et al. (1998) and currently for example by Miller et al. (2017) and Glenn and Sellbom (2015).

Using almost identical model fits for a two-factor model (with Machiavellianism and psychopathy as one factor) and a three-factor model, in combination with almost identical patterns of the two characteristics regarding external correlates, Miller et al. (2017) concluded that there is no difference between Machiavellianism and psychopathy. Glenn and Sellbom (2015) tested the incremental validity of the Dark Triad traits on psychopathy and found mostly nonsignificant – and only weak – explanatory contributions for external variables complementary to psychopathy and no interaction of the "Dark Triad residue" (= Triad without psychopathy) with psychopathy, which led the authors to conclude that there is no additional benefit in the combined measurement. They also established a confirmatory model to explain the Triad by psychopathy. This model has a matrix that is not positively definite, making it impossible to interpret or estimate, since psychopathy explains "over 100%" (!) of the variance. They conclude that no latent Dark Triad construct can be interpreted, since psychopathy explains everything (Glenn & Sellbom, 2015). It should be noted that they used a sample of prisoners, and that the study was conducted with the PPI (see Section 3.1.3), which covers a very broad range of psychopathy (according to Furnham, Richards et al., 2013, it also covers areas of Machiavellianism and narcissism). This is further evidence that the contradictory results on the structure of the Triad are strongly dependent on which scales are considered as "input variables."

Another explanation for the lack of differentiation of the other Triad characteristics from psychopathy points in this direction as well: It lies in the methodology of measurement or the preceding stages of theoretical concept definition and scale development, and states that the most commonly used measures are simply based on shared aspects, for example, items on "interpersonal manipulation" in NPI, Mach IV, PPI, and SRP (Glenn & Sellbom, 2015; Muris et al., 2017). Another explanation is that there are no differences because Mach IV does not measure some typical Machiavellian characteristics, i.e., it is deficient. (I further discuss the question of the content representation of the construct characteristics in the common scales in Section 5.2.2).

Miller et al. (2017) collected expert ratings on typical Triad profiles based on the subfacets of the FFM. Not only did their results deviate strongly from the empirically found typical Machiavellianism values in FFM, but they were also closer to the "psychopathic personality profile." However, psychopathy and the "Machiavellianism expert profile" only moderately correlated, and there were deviations from expectations in terms of impulsiveness or sensation-seeking. Even among experts, there is thus a certain disagreement as to which are the unique points of the Dark Triad characteristics.

From the contradictory findings of the studies presented on the factorial structure of the Dark Triad, there does not seem to be one correct solution. On the contrary, between one and three factors, depending on the procedures examined and the type of modeling, allow for a good representation of the data; in some cases, additional model improvements are possible by adding a fourth factor or by modeling a higher-order factor. Psychopathy and Machiavellianism do indeed appear to be very similar, for which the following section provides further evidence – but also for the usefulness of considering them separately. Psychopathy is the most multifaceted construct of the Triad and covers many aspects of the other two characteristics. Nevertheless, they also seem to have exclusive parts, something I discuss in more detail at the end of this chapter. But first, I would like to address the most frequently chosen methodological approaches to the Dark Triad.

3.3.2 Methodological Approaches to the Assessment of the Dark Triad

Watts et al. (2017) see three methodological problems in Dark Triad research:

- The uncritical assumption about the Dark Triad structure, discussed in the previous section, which only in recent years has been examined explicitly and at a higher methodological level.
- The assumption that the Triad features are delimitable, unidimensional constructs (discussed in more detail below).
- Equating the constructs with the procedures. The problem with the standard procedures is that they are seen as the "gold standard" but usually do not cover the whole construct or only a certain conceptualization. In the case of Dirty Dozen, it seems even more serious that the results of a procedure often criticized for narrowed content and demonstrably not very valid for the full constructs (see Section 5.2.2) are nevertheless used for statements on the complete constructs.

Miller et al. (2017) see a further problem in the fact that the Dark Triad characteristics are usually not considered in parallel or comparatively: The deviating bivariate relationships to external criteria are not checked for statistically significant differences, and indeed, in some cases, not even Triad intercorrelations are reported that would make this possible in retrospect.

Partialing Out

The exact opposite is achieved by the most prominent analytical approach of Triad research (besides bivariate correlations), namely, partialing out shared variance via multiple regressions (Miller et al., 2017). This involves adjusting the correlation between two variables for the influence of third variables. Paulhus and Williams (2002) proposed to capture the characteristics simultaneously and to calculate multiple regressions of explanatory external variables on them, thus revealing independent explanatory contributions, which is why a large part of the studies was oriented toward this (Furnham, Richards et al., 2013). The methodological question or criticism regarding this approach is what remains of a construct once a considerable amount of variance has been removed – in the case of a joint analysis with psychopathy, for example, 80% of that of Machiavellianism (Miller et al., 2017), according to Vize, Collison et al. (2018), at least not the original construct. This can lead to lower, higher, or even opposite relationships to external criteria because of possible suppression effects, especially in the case of highly correlated and multidimensional variables such as the Dark Triad (Sleep et al., 2017). This initially very theoretical question is of high practical relevance when deciding which Triad component to use for which application. It is decisive to know whether the findings for a particular factor or scale are to be assigned to the one or the other Triad characteristics and whether mutual influences also explain the effects. As the following sections show, unfortunately, these questions were not always addressed clearly enough, which also led to misinterpretations of the Dark Triad's causal relationships.

Primarily because of the relationships with external criteria derived from partialing out the approach has also given rise to a great deal of criticism. Sleep et al. (2017) therefore explicitly examined which effects generally result from "partialization" by investigating for various questions whether significant differences exist between raw and partialized values. For psychopathy, this resulted in relatively comparable values, for example, for the relationships with the Big Five. Only 34% of the relationships examined were different at the facet level. For Machiavellianism, on the other hand, about half of all relationships were significantly different, especially more positive appeared to Neuroticism and stronger negative ones to Extraversion for the partial components. For narcissism, even 83% of the relationships to the FFM differed between raw and partial components. In the maladaptive trait model, 25 out of 27 relationships were retained for psychopathy after partialing. However, for Machiavellianism, 83% and for narcissism fully 100% differed. Also, regarding external outcome variables, only one relationship was different for psychopathy, whereas for narcissism and Machiavellianism each was different. Contrary to the raw value, narcissism, for example, was not correlated to any of the outcome variables after partialing. Across all the relationships examined, for Machiavellianism, 71% showed differences and for narcissism 92%, including attenuated or even inverse correlations.

Precisely because narcissism suffers the greatest effects by separating the others does it seem to have the greatest autonomy. In psychopathy and Machiavellianism, 60% of the variance could be explained by the other two, but only 37% of narcissism. Sleep et al. (2017) also show that there is very little variance in the residuals in the sense of the FFM or the maladaptive personality model: in the "Machiavellianism residual," only 5% to 6%, about 12% in that of psychopathy, and 22% in that of narcissism. Herein also lies an explanation for the partly observable reversal in external relations. Narcissism has the largest independent share, and this part counteracts the effects associated with the shared variance part. The profile of the "narcissism residue," for example, is almost completely adaptive and characterized by low levels of Neuroticism and high levels of Extraversion; a description that does not initially sound detrimental to the occupational context and that, in joint analyses of all three characteristics with success criteria and with the "bad" brothers being partialed out, could give the impression that narcissism is conducive to occupational variables – which, in isolation and in all its facets, on the other hand, tends not to apply (see Chapter 4).

Sleep et al. (2017) therefore concluded that (partialized) Machiavellianism and narcissism values must be reported as such in any case since raw variables or simple correlations deviate considerably from them. The study by Jones and Paulhus (2011), for example, is therefore criticized, which reported no relationship between Machiavellianism and impulsiveness with the partial variable, whereas the raw variable did show one.

Structural Equation Modeling

Another methodological approach is to model the relationships of the Triad among themselves and to external criteria using structural equation models (SEMs), which also makes it possible to consider shared variance. Besides the issues of partialing discussed above, it should be noted that, according to Furnham, Richards et al. (2014), the methodology often overestimates shared variance (and its significance in terms of content), in the sense that existing weak relationships between aspects of a model lead to the assumption of higher factors that do not exist.

Vize, Collison et al. (2018) deal with the interpretation of residualized variables. In SEMs that model relationships to external criteria the overlap of predictors is partially "corrected." In bifactor models, for example, the shared variance is located on the bifactor, and the relationships of the "actual constructs" to external variables are thus examined based on the factors that have been partialized. This causes the problem described above in the same form as for regressions – it is unclear what the relationship of the original construct is to the dependent variable (Vize, Collison et al., 2018).

Using meta-analytical SEMs (MASEM), Vize and colleagues investigated effects before and after partialing using profile comparisons of raw and residual factors. After partialing, interpretation problems arose across all measures of the Dark Triad. Thus, once the maladaptive aspects of narcissism are partialed out, the remaining rest is adaptive and shows, for example, relationships to altruism, which is clearly contrary to the theoretical conception of narcissism. Regarding Machiavellianism, better evidence was found for some theoretical expectations with partialized, for others with raw values. For psychopathy, there are rather small effects, albeit, in any case, substantial changes in characteristics through partialization (Vize, Collison et al., 2018). A further problem lies in the question of what the residuals represent in terms of content, since there is no guarantee as to what proportion of common variance is excluded. For antagonism, for example, which is discussed as the core of the Triad in terms of content, considerable connections still exist for the residuals.

The aim of the detailed explanations at this point – and those by Vize, Collison et al. (2018) – is not to "demonize" the techniques presented, but rather to call for a more detailed examination of their purpose and proof of their usefulness:

- The raw value of a variable is better suited for many questions, such as the pure relationship to external criteria or the clarification of the nomological network of an entire construct.
- Residuals, on the other hand, are used, among other things, to investigate the common variance explanation of target variables and the contributions of the respective constructs.
- To examine the external correlates of a theoretical subaspect, measures with delimitable subscales are more appropriate than techniques of partialing, since they allow a clearer examination of the specific substantive aspects of a construct on which the relationships to external criteria are based (Vize, Collison et al., 2018).

Composite Scores

The other commonly used analytical procedure is to calculate a so-called composite score – the total value of the characteristics combined by *z*-standardization, e.g., Jonason et al.

(2009). The approach was also adopted by other authors, although the method has been criticized methodically, because the Triad composite explains less variance than the individual variables and it does not make sense to consider constructs consisting of, say, opposing aspects (e.g., impulse control) together as one factor/one variable (Furnham, Richards et al., 2014).

Watts et al. (2017) therefore, apart from the treatment of the Triad as "monolithic units," criticize primarily the practice of using composite scores. Here, the characteristics would be assumed in advance to be unidimensional (which does not apply to them) and, after being combined, would clearly level out existing differences. Thus, potential means of clarifying variance are lost. For this purpose, the meta-analysis of Mershon and Gorsuch (1988) on general personality inventories is referred to, which explains almost twice as much variance in external criteria using measures at the facet level than at the level of global factors. Watts et al. (2017) found clear evidence to confirm the advantage of not looking at the characteristics globally but at the facet level (which may even result in a different, more clearly definable factorial structure of the Triad).

The analytical approaches presented should therefore be viewed critically and their advantages and disadvantages assessed against the background of their intended use. The different methods of explaining variance provide a clear view of the individual contributions of a feature – but what is often not clear, it should be noted, is what exactly has been explained content-wise. If the relationships to external criteria are reversed, it must be questioned whether thc intended theoretical construct is still being measured. Composite scores are associated with even greater conceptual and empirical limitations, which is why, except for investigating very broad outcome variables, their use should be avoided. Above all, however, it is necessary to clearly state all techniques and the nature of the resulting target variables and always report simple, bivariate correlations.

Construct Creep

According to knowledgeable authors, the large common variance shares resulting from the measurement of Dark Triad characteristics (and thus also the latent factors that can be calculated from them and some problems with combined or partialized variables) can be traced back to one cause: the construct creep of Triad research (Furnham, Richards et al., 2013; Paulhus, 2014).

The research on the individual characteristics has expanded enormously over the long period of observation, subsuming more and more of the entire dark personality. The process has generated much redundant and confusing content, and it was discovered too late that phenomena in one's own field of research are actually attributable to other variables (both causal and primary) (Paulhus, 2014). This goes back to the Triad traits having initially been studied in different fields: Machiavellianism stems from the tradition of social-psychological research, narcissism from psychological-psychiatric, later clinical research, and psychopathy mainly from the forensic clinical context (see Section 3.1). The fact that not only related aspects but also aspects clearly belonging to other characteristics were included in each of the isolated research areas led to a confusion of content. As a result, the constructs discussed today as the Dark Triad show theoretical overlaps, and their common dimensions include aspects of each other's characteristics. Some recent studies, especially those with the short measures, and their frequently used quantitative methods discussed above further led to the assumption that the Dark Triad characteristics are a singular concept or empirically indistinguishable in the normal population. This construct creep unfortunately continues unabated (Furnham, Richards et al., 2013). Hodson et al. (2018) therefore describe the Dark Triad as a "creepy" construct, which well illustrates the problems surrounding the question of a construct creep.

These theoretical considerations may help us to explain why it is often difficult to separate the characteristics, especially Machiavellianism and psychopathy, in the empirical studies of the Triad constructs, currently operationalized primarily through the standard and short procedures:

- On a global level, on the one hand, the characteristics are identical in many central areas (substantive cores of the Triad).
- The traits also have partially similar patterns in the broad personality models and even share some common genetic foundations.
- On the other hand, extending at the edges to include related but less central aspects of the constructs in the construct definitions results in procedures that have greater overlap in content.
- If we evaluate these methods on a global factor level, which is the case in almost all studies on the Dark Triad (O'Boyle et al., 2012), this eventually produces a statistical database that allows the assumption that the Triad properties are identical or at least very similar.
- The summary of composite scores based on this assumption leads to a further leveling of differences.
- Using various methods of partialization, residuals are generated which have little independent or unclear explanatory contribution.

These approaches dominate Dark Triad research and disregard the fact that each of the Triad characteristics consists of several facets (see Section 3.3.3). For a clearer view of the actual explanatory contributions of the individual aspects, and to counter the construct creep, it is therefore paramount to split the Dark Triad constructs into subdimensions – in other words, to record them multidimensionally.

Multidimensionality

It is undisputed that the Dark Triad characteristics are all multidimensionally conceptualized (e.g., Muris et al., 2017; Watts et al., 2017); they are compound traits formed on a theoretical basis from various delimitable individual aspects, and the Triad standard procedures (such as the NPI) have specific subscales that have also been confirmed by factor analysis (see Section 3.1). Looking at the characteristics at the level of their facets best reveals the existing redundancies of the constructs and counters construct creep (Smith et al., 2018). It is therefore necessary to clarify which are the facets and which are distinguishable from each other, so that we can then also investigate which are of what importance – to theoretically clarify the structure, but also to consider their effects on external variables.

Marcus et al. (2018) performed a specific graphical analysis (LASSO) of the Triad network at the subscale level of the NPI and SRP procedures (unfortunately, it did not include the subfacets of Mach IV, Machiavellianism was recorded only as a global factor). They modeled all components of the model as nodes and their connections as paths, which are represented in different thicknesses depending on their strength; they arranged central aspects of the investigated features graphically in the middle. Especially the psychopathy factors Interpersonal Manipulation and Callousness were in different analyses each most strongly connected to all others and graphically in the center. Weakly connected and decentralized was, for example, the factor Grandiosity from the narcissism construct.

According to the results of Watts et al. (2017), the common consideration of the Dark Triad structure at the factor level is not meaningful, since the subscales often produce strongly deviating, sometimes even opposite results, and the common use of global factors levels out these findings. Jonason et al. (2011) confirmed the advantages of parallel consideration of several measurement levels, showing that the best model fits of the Triad are obtained when predicting external variables if the predictor and criterion are on the same level (see Section 2.2.2 on "bandwidth-fidelity"). Higher-order criteria, such as sociosexuality, would tend to be better predicted by an underlying dark factor, whereas mid-level variables, such as "strategies to keep a partner," are better explained by models that consider three factors separately. This means that both global factors and the specific, narrow aspects of the Dark Triad – its subfacets – need to be captured.

3.3.3 The Subfacets of the Dark Triad

Psychopathy is a very broad disorder, in Hare's model (2003) broken down into four factors and 20 subfacets. To be categorized as clinically conspicuous, a large proportion of these aspects must be highly pronounced, including actual criminal behavior, which is located on the fourth factor Antisocial. This factor and the associated behaviors are also measured in subclinical forms and procedures (see Section 3.1.3). No other Triad characteristic has criminal contents in theoretical conception or as scales/items in the corresponding measurement procedures. There are consistently much weaker links, often no links at all, between narcissism and Machiavellianism and criminal activities or serious social misconduct (especially when controlling for psychopathy, see Section 3.2.5). Also, typical extreme aspects of sexual behavior associated with (clinical) psychopathy (e.g., promiscuity, exploitative marital relationships, use of pressure or coercion) are rather weakly linked to the other Triad characteristics in comparison. The clearest demarcation of psychopathy from the other Triad traits is thus openly antisocial to severely criminal behavior and the specific sexual behavior of the psychopath.

The key aspects of narcissism are grandiosity, arrogance, and the exploitation of third parties (see Section 3.1.1). These have often been used in descriptions of psychopathy as well, e.g., "pathological egocentricity" by Cleckley (1941/1976) or "grandiose sense of self-worth" by Hare (Glenn & Sellbom, 2015). They are represented in the subscales Glibness/Superficial Charm, Grandiose Sense of Self-Worth, and Conning/Manipulative, which are located on the first factor according to Hare. This factor also exists in the SRP, so the scale also measures excessive self-esteem (Küfner et al., 2014). It was therefore found that narcissism, especially measured with the NPI (see Lynam, 2011), overlaps highly with the first psychopathy factor Interpersonal; this factor is mainly responsible for the relationship between narcissism and psychopathy. The older, two-factor solution according to Hare, in which the first factor also includes the affective aspects and cold-hearted exploitation of others, found higher correlations of narcissm to this than to the chronically unstable and antisocial lifestyle of the psychopath (Hart & Hare, 1998). McHoskey et al. (1998) found a partial correlation of narcissism to the first factor, but not to the second. Glenn and Sellbom (2015) see the concept of grandiose narcissism of the NPI fully represented in psychopathy models but note that the NPI measures narcissism more broadly. The narcissism construct also includes a heightened sense of entitlement and a factor that deals with leadership and a sense of authority (see Section 3.1.1). Aspects of leadership are not explicitly included in psychopathy scales.

Machiavellianism has no connection to typically narcissistic aspects, neither in theoretical conceptions (see Christie, 1970a) nor empirically. McHoskey (1995) found (partial) zero correlations to the NPI factors Superiority and Leadership and negative ones to Self-Sufficiency, the latter reflecting the Machiavellian's more realistic view of themselves as opposed to the narcissist's exaggerated self-esteem, while there are clear connections with maladaptive aspects of narcissism such as exploitation. Not only can these be considered the main relationship between narcissism and Machiavellianism, interpersonal manipulation and exploitation are also assumed to be a core of the Triad as a whole (see Section 3.3.1; Jones & Figueredo, 2013). There are therefore also closer connections to the psychopathy factor that captures these – in the older Hare model Primary Psychopathy – than to Secondary Psychopathy (McHoskey et al., 1998), which can be traced back to the classic Machiavellian aspects contained in the Coning-Manipulating scale.

Another factor, and perhaps the closest thing in common with Machiavellianism, is the second factor – Affective according to the current Hare model – which stands for affective foundations such as emotional coldness, emotional harshness, and ruthlessness or unscrupulousness. Compared to Machiavellianism and psychopathy, narcissism is only weakly associated with low empathy (Jonason & Kroll, 2015), and there is no scale for this in the NPI, nor did a corresponding factor ever appear in narcissism factor solutions (see Section 3.1.1). For Machiavellianism, a relative lack of feelings in interpersonal relationships was theoretically assumed (Cloetta, 1972), and there is a body of evidence that sees emotional coldness or "cool syndrome" as a core characteristic of Machiavellianism (see Sections 3.1.2 and 3.2.2).

As already mentioned, Machiavellianism and psychopathy are largely very similar and difficult to distinguish from each other. From a theoretical perspective, however, some differences were emphasized. One, even postulated as a central element of Machiavellianism, is the cynical attitude toward third parties (subscale Views, see Section 3.1.2), which has also been confirmed empirically (Jones & Paulhus, 2009). However, there are no explicit references to this in the literature on psychopathy (Glenn & Sellbom, 2015), and there are also no such scales or items in current psychopathy inventories. Accordingly, a connection to cynicism was shown for the Dark Triad residue (without psychopathy), which is why this factor can be seen as the characteristic of Machiavellianism that differentiates it from psychopathy (Glenn & Sellbom, 2015).

Further theoretical assumptions for Machiavellianism indicate a rather long-term oriented, rational-strategic approach to goal attainment, in contrast to psychopathy, a construct for which impulsiveness and low behavioral control are definitory and scale aspects have been empirically proven in many cases (see Sections 3.1 and 3.2). These are a central component of the third psychopathy factor according to Hare – Lifestyle – or the term Secondary Psychopathy previously used for this. By utilizing various correlates from the typical life and behavioral styles of the Triad members (see Section 3.2.5), it was possible to show a different pattern in this respect. Accordingly, neither impulsive behavior nor lack of planning is a characteristic aspect of Machiavellianism (or narcissism).

In summary, the unifying components of narcissism and psychopathy are grandiosity and arrogance of the first factor Interpersonal according to Hare; the aspect of this factor shared by all Triad characteristics is "manipulation." According to Hare, Machiavellianism and psychopathy are empirically united by the Affective factor. The differentiating feature of psychopathy from the other two is factors three and four of the psychopathy model: the typical lifestyle characterized by impulsiveness, irresponsibility, and the lack of realistic goals; and actually criminal behavior. These aspects not only distinguish them from the others, but they also make psychopathy the most destructive feature of dark personalities (Mathieu & Babiak, 2016a). Machiavellianism is the only one not characterized by self-exaltation but by a pragmatic, realistic attitude. Moreover, cynicism is the unique point that differentiates Machiavellianism. Aspects typically associated with narcissism, such as leadership and an overly demanding attitude, are not part of Machiavellianism and are not part of the psychopathic construct or corresponding scales.

Thus, there exist both theoretically well-founded and subscale-backed specific aspects of the Triad characteristics that differ. Analyses of the Triad characteristics at the global level, frequently used short procedures that do not allow the identification of subscales, and statistical measures that model latent factors or composite scores limit the constructs so much as to prevent potential explanatory contributions. Analytically speaking, attention should also be paid to how the measurement level fits the explanatory variables. Higher-order constructs can be better explained by latent factors, narrower aspects more accurately predicted, or a maximum of variance explanation can be achieved by using a finely attuned measurement at the facet level. For this reason, and because of the many differential relationships to external criteria exhibited, it is not only important to consider the Triad features separately (or, in addition to composite scores or regressions, also in isolation), but also to consider the individual facets of the multidimensional Triad constructs (Watts et al., 2017). This is also important for applied questions of personnel psychology, as these sometimes show considerable variations in their explanatory contribution, such as narcissism facets for counterproductive behavior or stress/work satisfaction (Schyns, 2015). The following chapter discusses further relationships of the characteristics to variables relevant for aptitude diagnostics.

4 Findings on the Dark Triad Relevant to Aptitude Diagnostics

Psychologists have considered the effects of the dark side of personality in professional life since the 1920s (see Sackett et al., 2017, and Section 2.2). Since about the turn of the last millennium, however, the topic has rightly enjoyed new and increased attention, as witnessed by the numerous findings on dark-side traits and work-related issues (see Section 2.3). In the current research, the dark side has mostly been operationalized using features based on the official DSM disorders and in some studies by linear combinations of facets of the FFM, but mostly with the Hogan Development Survey (HDS; see Section 2.3.3). In practice, this method has been used almost exclusively to date. Some of the results obtained with this method were nevertheless published under the names of the Dark Triad characteristics, such as the curvilinear relationship between narcissism and leadership effectiveness (see Grijalva et al., 2015), which is based on data from the Bold scale of the HDS.

The Dark Triad itself has yet to be sufficiently researched in the workplace, even though, along with the other dark-side traits, it recently entered the mainstream of organizational research (Harms & Spain, 2015). Particularly in comparison with the many discussions in the media, few explicitly job-related research articles appeared in the first 10 years of dealing with the Dark Triad, marking a high numerical divergence between scientific papers and general-media publications (Cohen, 2016). Smith and Lilienfeld (2013) pointed this out in their review on psychopathy at work and illustrated the gap shown in Figure 3.

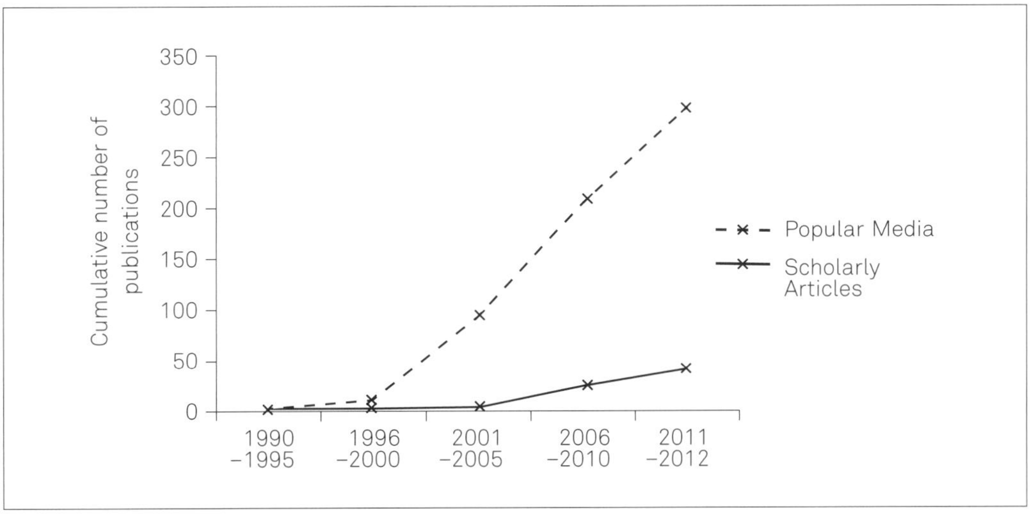

Figure 3: Articles on psychopathy at work in general media vs. scientific journals. Reprinted with permission from "Psychopathy in the workplace: The knowns and unknowns" by S. F. Smith & S. O. Lilienfeld, 2013, *Aggression and Violent Behavior*, *18*, p. 204. © Elsevier.

The actual, reliable state of research on the Dark Triad of personality at work is far less abundant and unambiguous than popular scientific and public reception would have us to believe. However, to justify their use in aptitude diagnostics, common criteria of occupational performance in representative samples and contexts must be capable of being predicted using the Dark Triad characteristics (see Chapter 5). In the following sections, I present those study results that demonstrate such relationships and the utility of the Dark Triad. But before that I discuss the specific suitability of different research studies for this purpose.

Some of the papers presented are not suitable for clearly demonstrating the aptitude-diagnostic benefit of the Dark Triad and thus for justifying its use, as they are mostly theoretical-conceptual, as Campbell et al. (2011) state in their review on narcissism in organizations. They often conclude several obvious relationships about the presumed effects of the Dark Triad on work behavior or performance. Several empirical studies of Triad research are also unsuitable for justifying an application for operative aptitude-diagnostic purposes because of the samples used or the context in which they were conducted. One can use the meta-analysis by Vize, Lynam et al. (2018) as an indicator of the subjects commonly used in Triad research: Of the 159 datasets examined, 86% were collected among college students or with the commercial service MTurk from Amazon, the remainder being from the areas of school, general population, and business (the share of the latter area is likely to be significantly below 10%). Also, not all studies on the Dark Triad and occupational issues were conducted in a representative context and were based on samples in which sufficient professional experience was available. However, the main limitation associated with some of the published workplace-related findings lies in the procedures or measurement approaches employed in some cases, some of which on closer examination do not allow for a demonstrably valid measurement of the characteristics. (I discuss these measurement approaches and other methods of recording Dark Triad characteristics in detail in Section 5.1.) Smith and Lilienfeld (2013) therefore note that it is premature to rely on the anecdotes often shared in public (and to act accordingly in practice) before robust studies in the occupational context with valid measures are available.

In the meantime, there has been a noticeable increase in the number of relevant publications. LeBreton et al. (2018) presented the first comprehensive, specific review on the subject of the Dark Triad and work behavior. After the rapid increase in findings on the Triad, they see it as a good idea to pause for a moment to clarify which findings are truly relevant to the organizational context.

In the following sections, I heed this call, focusing on works that allow the assessment of an explicit use for aptitude diagnostics. My focus lies primarily on those studies that examine whether the common criteria of occupational performance or occupational success or failure can be predicted, as described in Section 2.2. For reasons of space and relevance, I cannot acknowledge all research work conducted on the effects of the Dark Triad on the job or on professional aspects, especially not the many conceptual and older works from the long research traditions of the features. Instead, I limit myself to current empirical work, ideally combined for the Triad characteristics and carried out in working populations or within companies (which, according to the sample designs of Triad research described, unfortunately, cannot always be adhered to). In addition to the generally applied criteria of job performance, I report on the relationships of the Dark Triad to various constructs and concepts relevant to aptitude diagnostics in the field of personnel selection and professional counseling. In addition, I address additional personnel-psychological questions and tasks the Dark Triad could contribute to solving.

With this, I want to make a statement as to if the Dark Triad of personality is a concept whose use is fundamentally useful in aptitude diagnostics and promises to be beneficial to them. Chapter 5 takes up whether and how its application is possible. Chapter 6 presents an exemplary procedure for this purpose.

4.1 Predicting Counterproductive Behavior in the Workplace

Probably the most studied and best-documented work-related relationship of the Dark Triad is that with "counterproductive work behavior" (CWB; Spain et al., 2014; see Section 2.2.1 for a definition). In a meta-analytical study, O'Boyle et al. (2012) showed a positive correlation of all Triad characteristics with CWB, though surprisingly it was weakest for psychopathy and strongest for narcissism with corrected $r = .43$. Grijalva and Newman (2015) found only a meta-analytically corrected correlation for this relationship of $r = .23$. Of the two moderators tested, each of whom was only weak, in the first-mentioned meta-analysis culture (collectivist vs. individualist) proved to be the stronger one for narcissism compared with the degree of authority of the employee role. Grijalva and Newman (2015) confirmed the finding that the connection between narcissism and CWB is weaker in collectivist cultures. Machiavellianism showed a robust relationship with CWB, even when considering moderators, whereas the strength of the narcissism–CWB relationship is most likely because of moderation effects (O'Boyle et al., 2012). Psychopathy explained only about 1% of the variance in CWB and was unexpectedly weak, with a corrected $r = .07$ correlated with it. Authority moderated the effect in the sense that the relationship of psychopathy to CWB was somewhat weaker in authority roles. The Triad explained 28% of the variance in CWB; all three characteristics were significant predictors in a regression model. Narcissism dominated this with a relative weight of 67%, and psychopathy had an inverse relationship to the bivariate one – according to which psychopathy, considering the other two Triad characteristics, would be associated with lower CWB values as a result.

O'Boyle et al. (2012) provided three reasons for this surprising finding: Statistically, a suppressor effect could be effective, arising from the low psychopathy–CWB relationship with a simultaneous high correlation of the Triad characteristics among themselves. Methodologically, a sampling effect may exist, since the psychopathy samples were composed mainly of persons in authority roles (primarily police officers) who were moderators of the relationship of psychopathy to CWB. Finally, theoretically, the statistically remaining "residue" of psychopathy may have led to less CWB if the negative aspects of psychopathy shared with narcissism and Machiavellianism are partialized (see Section 3.3.2).

The last explanation is described by the authors of the study themselves as unlikely, and according to the explanations in Section 3.2, the "rest" of psychopathy hardly seems to be unproblematic. On the contrary, the fourth factor Antisocial (and the third factor Lifestyle) are closely related to rule-breaking, criminal behavior. A sampling effect is therefore much more probable, which also allows the fundamentally very low bivariate correlation and thus the suppressor effect. O'Boyle et al. (2012) themselves explained: Police officers would simply not show the typical behavior recorded with the CWB scales (e.g., committing theft), but might show others that are not recorded (e.g., provoking suspects to treat them harshly). In my opinion, the CWB-psychopathy relationship found in the meta-analysis underestimates the existing level because of the sample selection. Of the 146 studies on achievement/CWB, 60 are from police populations, 9 from the military, 17 from the educational sector (mostly teachers), and only 11 each were in the areas of sales/marketing and management, the rest in mixed populations. As evidence for the presumed underestimation, we refer to Scherer et al. (2013), who use subclinical psychopathy to explain considerable variance in CWB and even incremental over the FFM (see Section 2.1.2).

One possible reason for the partly weak relationship of the Dark Triad to CWB in O'Boyle et al. (2012) lies in their failure to consider other mediators and moderators of this relationship. Cohen (2016) therefore proposes a conceptual model that explains the relationship between the Dark Triad and CWB, according to which the Triad operates through the level of organizational politics and necessary accountability perceived. The first describes organizations in which there is scope for exerting an influence that is conducive to self-interest; the second describes the perceived need to justify one's own behavior. Thus, a higher level of organizational policy and lower pressure to justify oneself benefit carriers of high levels of Dark Triad, while increasing the level of CWB. In this model, the relationships are moderated by an individual's political skill, the level of transparency that exists in the organization, the existing regulations against CWBs, and the organizational culture.

In the meantime, various subareas of the model have been reviewed, and I present the results briefly below. Baloch et al. (2017) found that, despite the inclusion of the mediator organizational politics, there was a direct relationship between the Triad and CWB. However, the organizational policy had a moderating effect: the Triad had a stronger influence on CWB in organizations with more room for their own influence. Palmer et al. (2017) investigated whether perceived organizational support, as an expression of how much the organization values its employees and cares about their well-being, has a moderating effect on the relationship between Dark Triad and CWB. Lower organizational support strengthened the relationship of narcissism to production-related deviance (e.g., deliberately slow working), even under the control of the other two Triad components. They found a similar relationship for psychopathy as well as a positive relationship with further subaspects of CWB. Machiavellianism had a negative relationship with CWB while controlling for the other characteristics, which the authors explain by the fact that only the shared variance of the Triad characteristics leads to CWB and not the Machiavellianism-specific parts.

DeShong et al. (2015) used structural models and comparative path analysis to show that the Big Five can explain more variance in CWB than the Dark Triad. In a reduced model, Agreeableness and Conscientiousness were the only predictors necessary to explain counterproductive behaviors targeted toward both an organization and an individual. From this they concluded that the common core of Disagreeableness could be the reason for the positive relationship of the Triad to CWB. Low Agreeableness is primarily associated with CWBs directed against individuals (CWB-I), whereas those that are aimed at the organization (CWB-O) are associated with low Conscientiousness (Berry, Ones, & Sackett, 2007). Accordingly, a closer connection with CWB-I was postulated for the Triad (Cohen, 2016). DeShong et al. found a connection with both forms of CWB, in each case for psychopathy the strongest, whereas narcissism was somewhat more strongly associated with CWB-I, and the other two Triad characteristics were more strongly related with CWB-O, but essentially at similar levels.

A frequently studied form of CWB-I is workplace bullying, i.e., emotional and physical mistreatment of employees or colleagues. Boddy (2011) found that, when a psychopath leads employees, they report more harassment in the workplace and feel more often unfairly treated; the interest in the employee of psychopathic managers is rated lower. Tokarev et al. (2017) showed that the relationship of narcissism and psychopathy of the manager to depression among their employees can be fully explained through the mediation of workplace bullying. When analyzed together, however, only psychopathy remained as an influencing factor, causing the authors to conclude that the shared dark core of characteristics probably leads to harassment in the workplace (and via this to depression among subordinates).

Schütte et al. (2018) found a connection of CWB-I with the psychopathy factor Self-Centered Impulsivity, measured with the Psychopathic Personality Inventory (PPI; see Section 3.1.3); the factor Fearless Dominance only showed such a connection if the own possibility of interpersonal influence (an aspect of political skill) is assessed as low. CWB-O was also associated with Self-Centered Impulsivity, and Fearless Dominance was in turn moderated: At low educational levels, high levels of this factor lead to greater CWB-O (Blickle & Schütte, 2017).

Castille et al. (2017) showed that, when there is a lack of organizational resources, i.e., when they are in a competitive environment, Machiavellians undermine or weaken their colleagues, and if there are no restrictions, they refrain from doing so. The same situational framework conditions apply to the CWB-O aspect of production-related deviance.

In Penney and Spector (2002), the connection between narcissism and CWB is moderated by job constraints and anger. More severe work limitations, such as poor work equipment and higher narcissism levels, lead to increased CWB. Angrier narcissists behave more counterproductively. Similarly, Michel and Bowling (2013) showed a moderating effect of aggression: Narcissism leads to greater CWB among those who are more aggressive.

Blickle et al. (2006) found on average narcissism to be more pronounced in a sample of imprisoned managers than in noncriminal managers. Similarly, Ragatz et al. (2012) examined white-collar crime and psychopathy, comparing this type of imprisoned criminal with those who have not committed economic crimes. There was a tendency, albeit insignificantly, toward higher values on the factors of the psychopathy scale PPI but higher values on the subscale social potency.

Ray (2007) examined attitudes to white-collar crime among students. The overall value and the first factor of psychopathy – but not the second factor, which here captures the impulsive way of life – were associated with positive attitudes and intentions to commit this type of crime. Ray and Jones (2011) studied the finding in detail regarding the (hypothetical) crime of illegal toxic waste dumping. Again, the factor Fearless Dominance was associated with positive attitudes toward it, the scales Machiavellian egocentricity and Carefree nonplanfulness even with the willingness to commit this offense.

Less destructive to the environment, but associated with considerable damage for companies, is the inequitable behavior of cutting corners at work, which entails working as little as possible or purposefully with as little effort as possible to achieve a result. Jonason and O'Connor (2017) found that all Triad characteristics are related to this behavior and provided incremental validity to the Big Five in predicting this style of working. A study by

Roczniewska and Bakker (2016) examined the connections between the Triad characteristics and a similar skill, job crafting, which is understood as how people shape or (to their mind) change the way they do their work. On zero-order, narcissism and Machiavellianism were associated with the proactive "reduction of work demands" (= changes that make work easier), Machiavellianism and psychopathy negatively with "seeking structural resources" (e.g., the acquisition of additional skills), and narcissism positively with "seeking social resources" (e.g., the help of colleagues).

In case studies, Babiak (1995, 1996) characterized the typical profile of a "corporate psychopath" as having high values on the first, interpersonally effective factor and low values on the second factor that captures the lifestyle (Babiak, 2007, p. 415). High scorers were described by superiors as charming and effective and accordingly as "high potentials." They negatively impacted colleagues, through manipulation and fraud or bullying. They also tended to delegate their work to subordinates and had above-average expense accounts. Other case studies provided very similar descriptions, according to which psychopaths were seen as the "stars" in the organization by those hierarchically above them but at the same time showed misbehavior "downwards" by harassment and intimidation. Highly psychopathic individuals showed ineffective management, characterized by "very poor levels of personnel management, directionless leadership, miss-management of resources and outright fraud" (Boddy et al., 2015, p. 530).

A fundamental attitude or behavioral disposition, termed "integrity," plays a role in the omission of obviously negative or even criminal behavior at the workplace and in the (successful) execution of the actual work task (see Section 2.2). Box 3 presents the relationships of the Dark Triad to this characteristic, which is important for operative personnel selection and is accordingly more frequently used in practice.

Box 3: Relationships of the Dark Triad With Integrity

- For Machiavellianism and narcissism, Schlenker (2008) found substantial negative associations with integrity in two studies.
- Narcissism is negatively associated with overt- as well as personality-based integrity tests (Mumford et al., 2001) and supervisor assessments of integrity (Blair et al., 2008).
- Psychopathy was negatively related to both types of integrity test results, scales such as *manipulation or lack of guilt were* strongly correlated, while the psychopathy facet Affective Deficit/Emotional Coldness was uncorrelated (Connelly et al., 2006).
- A negative relationship to integrity could be demonstrated for all Dark Triad characteristics in a German-speaking sample (Schwarzinger et al., 2010).

As these explanations show, all Triad characteristics stand in a relationship to counterproductive behavior in the workplace which can be meta-analytically generalized. Initial evidence can also be found for negative and destructive (abusive) forms of leadership; more is presented in the following section. The connection with acts directed toward an individual seems to be generally somewhat higher than with deviance directed toward the organization. An explanation for this may be found in the low level of Agreeableness that characterizes the Triad characteristics. The exact interdependencies are influenced by several moderators such as authority and perceived influence, anger, educational level, organizational culture, or lack of resources/competitiveness. As to contrary dispositions – behaving correctly – there are obvious signs of negative relations with the Dark Triad. People with high values of narcissism, Machiavellianism, or psychopathy are not prone to integrity, which leads to the preliminary conclusion that persons with high Triad values are potentially damaging to the organization (or one of its members), and that, whether as employees or managers, they represent a correspondingly increased risk.

4.2 Predicting Job Performance and Success

The behavior and success of a person in the workplace concerning the Dark Triad are often examined in terms of their role as a leader. Particularly regarding narcissism, of central research interest is "leadership" or the leader. This is, indeed "one of the longest running issues" in the relevant research (Campbell et al., 2011, p. 272); I discuss it in greater detail in this section than the other Triad characteristics because more data are available.

4.2.1 Leadership Effectiveness and Abusive Supervision

Judge et al. (2009) established a comprehensive conceptual model for explaining leadership success, the leader trait emergence effectiveness heuristic. Starting from a genetically determined development of basic traits (including narcissism and Machiavellianism), this model includes mediators that help to turn a person into a leader; then, depending on moderators, objective and subjective leadership success is achieved. I first present findings on narcissism based on selected parts of this model and then turn to the relationships of the other two Triad components to leadership.

Regarding the act of "taking the leadership role" (leader emergence), Brunell et al. (2008) showed that narcissistic persons are more likely to emerge as group leaders in group discussions – both in their own assessment and in the assessment of others. After they completed teamwork (in which narcissism was linked neither to one's own performance nor to the group's success), the effect continued to occur in their self-assessments, though the group no longer saw the narcissistic person as a leader. In a group discussion among managers, narcissistic persons also crystallized as leaders, whereby the criterion was externally assessed by experts. Nevicka et al. (2011) provided a similar finding for team simulations. Narcissists tended to become leaders regardless of their actual performance (narcissism was not associated with performance here either). Teams with narcissistic leaders communicated less, and their members made fewer individual decisions. In contrast, narcissists performed better in the context of "high rewards interdependence," i.e., depending on whether gains were made at team level (high interdependence) or an individual level – whether cooperation or self-interest was rewarded. Under this condition, teams led by narcissists communicated more and gave more help to each other. Since these relationships did not apply to teams with leaders who had low narcissism values, one can assume that a particular context is needed in which the narcissists can "shine" to motivate them to perform well. This confirms the findings of Wallace and Baumeister (2002), who determined that narcissists only show higher performance if they have the opportunity to present themselves in a positive light.

De Hoogh et al. (2015) found that narcissism is negatively associated with perceived "leader effectiveness," which is, however, moderated by sex, in a form that is not very flattering to men: Female narcissists were rated worse, and for narcissistic men there was no effect. Women were generally rated worse by their male superiors but not by their female superiors. Narcissism by male subordinates was negatively associated with the effectiveness of the female manager but not the male manager. This effect did not exist among women.

In the meta-analysis of Grijalva et al. (2015), narcissism was associated with leader emergence but not with the performance/effectiveness as a leader. This relationship also weakened with the longer acquaintance of the person being assessed. In addition, the relationship was fully moderated by Extraversion in the analysis. Thus, there is no linear relationship between narcissism and leadership performance, although an inverted U-shaped relationship could be shown in all six samples examined, but significant in only two of the samples. The curvilinear relationships were not explained by Extraversion. This means that low levels of narcissism are associated with rather weak leadership performance, medium levels of the trait are associated with the best estimates of leadership effectiveness, and negative influences on leadership effectiveness occur from about one standard deviation above the mean of narcissism (Grijalva et al., 2015).

In one study with self- and other-assessed leadership performance (peer assessments), Judge et al. (2006) found narcissism to be positively associated, in another study to be negatively associated with the third-party assessment of leadership performance (by superiors) and at the same time positively associated with self-assessments in this regard. In addition, narcissism was negatively associated with externally assessed contextual performance; in all substudies, the self-assessments were significantly more positive than the external assessments. In Blair et al. (2008), narcissism is also negatively associated with the interpersonal performance of managers, namely, "participation," "confrontation effectiveness," "team building", and "sensitivity." Interestingly, these relationships existed only in the assessment of superiors, but not in that of subordinates.

Owens et al. (2015) found a moderator in the factor Honesty-Humility of the HEXACO model (see Section 2.1.2). With simultaneously high values on this factor and narcissism, positive assessments of leadership effectiveness and the performance of subordinates regarding subjective and objective measures emerged. Ong et al. (2016) showed that perceived leadership performance decreases over time. On the one hand, among subjects who did not know each other before, narcissistic persons were attributed leadership qualities at the time of group formation, but not at the other times studied. On the other hand, among persons who already knew each other, narcissistic persons were not attributed increased leadership qualities at the first point in time and even decreased in the further course of the study.

Ellen et al. (2019) assumed that narcissistic managers create stress in employees, and that they are better able to deal with narcissistic leadership if they have their own abilities to "manage resources." Among people who do not have this ability, narcissistic managers have led to greater "emotional exhaustion," "depressed mood," "job tension," and less organizational citizenship behavior (OCB; see Section 2.2.1) and poorer self-assessments of job performance. Among those with higher corresponding abilities, the level of the manager's narcissism level had no negative effects.

Hurst et al. (2017) found a similar adaptive aspect to psychopathy in employees whose manager shows "abusive supervision," i.e., destructive or abusive leadership behavior. Such a leadership style includes strategically exploitative as well as directly offensive behavior, such as bullying, toward the subordinate. Employees with high scores on the first psychopathy factor Interpersonal possessed advantages or the appropriate protective mechanism and showed positive affect and work commitment even under the influence of abusive leadership. However, the moderation effect results primarily because the less psychopathic employees suffer greatly from abusive leadership behavior, whereas the psychopathic employees are relatively independent of the type of their leader.

Leadership by a Machiavellian leads to greater "emotional exhaustion" of employees according to Gkorezis et al. (2015). This effect is mediated both directly and partly by "organizational cynicism" and is operationalized by the employees' assessments in this regard. Higher Machiavellianism values of the manager are related to a style considered abusive by the subordinates and is fully mediated by the authoritarian leadership style of the Machiavellian (Kiazad et al., 2010).

Andrea and Conway (1982) studied various aspects of leadership performance and showed that Machiavellianism is generally related to task orientation rather than person orientation. The curvilinearity of the relationship explains the weak effects of each criterion. For several variables, they found the closest relationships around the mean value for Machiavellianism, with values falling above it from about one standard deviation onward. This effect existed for such variables as "concern for people" and "integration." For criteria such as "productivity" and "representation of the interests of those led" (to third parties), however, leadership performance rose again at very high Machiavellianism values.

Babiak et al. (2010, p. 174) assumed difficulties in measuring psychopathy in the workplace as the reason why there are only a handful of "small-sample studies, anecdotes, and speculation" on the subject. They contrast this with an empirical study of over 200 working adults, mostly managers up to C-level executives, who were assessed using the Psychopathy Checklist (PCL; see Section 3.1.3). In percentage terms, these managers reached the cut-off value for psychopathy on the PCL more frequently than the general population (although on average they achieved lower values). Accordingly, although psychopathy was not linked to hierarchical status, some very high levels of psychopathy ("real psychopaths") were found in senior management positions. Increased psychopathy values were associated with poor ratings as "team players" and with management style and performance appraisal, but positively with ratings on "communication," "strategy", and "innovation."

For Sanecka (2013), higher psychopathy values in managers are associated with lower organizational commitment and less job satisfaction among their subordinates. Furthermore, the employees express very low satisfaction with the manager. Mathieu et al. (2014) showed a connection between high psychopathy values of the manager and higher stress and lower job satisfaction in employees; also, in structural equation models, higher psychopathy values were the strongest predictor of lower job satisfaction. In Mathieu and Babiak (2016b), higher psychopathy values of the manager are related to abusive leadership behavior as well as lower job satisfaction and more frequent intent to terminate their employment on the part of employees. In structural equation models, on the other hand, psychopathy was only indirectly related to intent to terminate and (lower) job satisfaction. In one model tested, psychopathy influenced employee job satisfaction via abusive leadership behavior.

Wisse and Sleebos (2016) examined the extent of abusive leadership behavior associated with the Triad characteristics. Elevated values in Machiavellianism and psychopathy among managers were associated with such "leadership style" in the assessment of individual employees. At the team level, they found no effect for narcissism and psychopathy, for Machiavellianism only if the leader had a high "position power."

In joint studies of all Triad characteristics, the narcissism value of the executive in regression analyses was a positive predictor of higher salary and more employee promotions, the Machiavellianism value a negative predictor of their career satisfaction (Volmer et al., 2016). Indicators of employee well-being, such as emotional exhaustion and job satisfaction, were negatively influenced by the Machiavellianism or psychopathy of the leaders.

4.2.2 Criteria of Individual Performance

Meta-analytically, a weak negative correlation was found with global job performance for all Triad components, which is not significant for narcissism (r= –.03, corrected). Machiavellianism is negatively related to job performance (r= –.07, corrected), which is a significant but small effect, the direction of which is not consistent in all samples. Psychopathy has, comparatively speaking, the strongest negative correlation to job performance (r= –.10, corrected) (O'Boyle et al., 2012). In a meta-analytical regression model, the entire Dark Triad achieved a virtually irrelevant effect of 1% explanation of variance in job performance, where only psychopathy was a significant predictor. O'Boyle et al. (2012) state that the Dark Triad explains little to no variance in job performance, and that it has limited value in predicting occupational performance compared to more elaborate procedures such as intelligence tests, which have high predictive validity.

According to the nearly nonexistent direct and linear relationship of the Triad and performance evaluations, some authors proposed considering various specific criteria, moderators, and curvilinear relationships. Most of the them examined situational factors of influence, which are discussed in more detail below. A presumably more promising approach is to look at variables that lie within the person. As an explanation for the success that is partly attributed to some bearers of dark traits, Templer (2018) consider the variable political skill as a moderator. Dark personalities with high values in this variable achieve better managerial assessments of their task- and contextual performance. (Unfortunately, the study operationalizes dark characteristics by low values on the H-factor of the HEXACO model, which cannot be considered a dark-side trait in the true sense of the word.)

Schuler (2014a) regards integrity as a possible influencing factor interacting with Dark Triad characteristics in the workplace; O'Boyle et al. (2012) and Muris et al. (2017) prefer the person's intelligence. During the development of the occupational procedure TOP (Schwarzinger & Schuler, 2016, 2019), the authors tested the correlations of these variables and found no confirmation of the assumption regarding the effect of intelligence. On the other hand, they did show that integrity moderates the relationship between Machiavellianism and occupational performance: If they also possess high integrity, Machiavellian individuals receive better performance estimates; with low integrity, they receive worse estimates (a detailed presentation of the study can be found in Chapter 6).

Zhang and Goffin (2018) found no validity for the interaction of the Dark Triad with intelligence in predicting "counterproductive behavior." However, the criterion was only operationalized by "smart" lies to colleagues to gain personal advantage and measured by a situational judgment test (SJT) among students, so the question needs further research.

For Smith et al. (2016), the overall relationship between the Dark Triad and performance is still too muddied, especially since only a few studies address positive aspects such as OCB, and the criterion performance has too rarely been differentiated into its components task and contextual performance. Thus, despite the important meta-analysis by O'Boyle et al. (2012), the relationship to occupational performance remains not yet fully clarified, as also no distinction was made between task and contextual performance (see Section 2.2.1). The low or nonexistent relationships of the Triad with the criterion could, for example, result from the performance measures used (see the comments on the sample selection of the study in Section 4.1).

For O'Boyle et al. (2012), the relationship of psychopathy and Machiavellianism to performance is not moderated by the authority of the role the person plays or the level of collectivism of the organization. For narcissism, performance is weaker in collectivist culture and in positions of high authority. Wallace and Baumeister (2002) found the "perceived self-enhancement opportunity" offered by the performance situation to moderate the relationship between narcissism and individual success. In a simulation among students, they investigated four different performance criteria and means of self-enhancement. Narcissists performed better when the situation was challenging, when they were under pressure, or when they were being evaluated by others. In general, the situational conditions had little effect on people with low levels of narcissism. Wallace and Baumeister (p. 831) clearly summarize their findings: "Narcissists performed relatively poorly when feedback would be known only to themselves, but they outperformed everyone else when the feedback was anticipated to be made public." Thus, narcissists are primarily concerned with presenting themselves – not with the result as such. In a large sample of managers, Guedes (2017) showed that narcissism is associated with higher evaluations of one's own performance and consequently with its overestimation, as there was no connection to objective performance criteria.

In the years after its introduction, the Machiavellianism construct was researched concerning its influence on job performance, especially in the sales and advertising sector, regarding the ability to convince others, which it connotes, since precisely "marketing" is criticized for enticing people (against their will) to engage in unnecessary consumption (see Sparks, 1994). Some of these studies found correlations to individual measures of success (Turner & Martinez, 1977), whereas others did not (Hunt & Chonko, 1984), which led to an expectation derived from the theoretical considerations on the Machiavellianism construct to be repeatedly examined: the moderating effect of "latitude for improvisation."

As it turns out, the performance of Machiavellians among advertisers was lower in situations of low latitude for improvisation, but in situations of high latitude for improvisation there was no difference to people with low Machiavellianism values (Sparks, 1994). A broad analysis of the entire sales staff of a timeshare company by Crotts et al. (2005) revealed that there is no correlation with better sales performance – on the contrary, it was worse for high scorers than for the "low Machs" group, the explanation being the high "organizational structure" of the temporary employment agency.

Machiavellianism and the structured or regulated nature of the working environment interact in Shultz (1993) such that, in poorly structured situations, i.e., where more decision-making power is available and fewer rules must be adhered to, the criteria "sales performance" and "customer loyalty" were positively associated with increased Machiavellianism values. In highly structured organizations, on the other hand, Machiavellians performed less well than people with low Machiavellianism values. However, Shultz's study compared two different occupational fields and did not compare different "improvisation possibilities" within one occupation (Sparks, 1994).

Where identification with one's job is low (low job involvement), there is no relationship between Machiavellianism and performance criteria, whereas there is a substantially positive relationship where job involvement is high; there was no isolated relationship between involvement and Machiavellianism or performance (Gable & Dangello, 1994). Machiavellians were at an advantage when the supervisor exercised little control, while under high control there were no differences (Gable et al., 1992).

Recent work found that higher sales in commerce and industry are associated with higher levels of Machiavellianism (Ricks & Sterrett, 2002), but, interestingly, these individuals have poorer self-assessments and receive poorer managerial assessments of job performance. Ricks and Fraedrich described this unusual finding in *The Paradox of Machiavellianism* (1999). The performance ratings of people who sell more (which was especially true for Machiavellians) were even worse than those of people who sell less. So, Machiavellians seem to have problems "selling" their better sales performance. This could be because of their disposition not to push themselves into the foreground and "present" themselves, or it could be because of their relationship with superiors.

Smith and Webster (2017) examined possible factors influencing the connections between Machiavellianism and the assessments of superiors. Using a complex model, they found only an indirect effect of the interaction of Machiavellianism and "social undermining" on higher performance ratings (via political skill) but otherwise no relationship between Machiavellianism and managerial assessments. Also, only under the condition that Machiavellians feel "undermined" do they show more "political tactics" and thus achieve good performance ratings. Kuyumcu and Dahling (2014) also showed that Machiavellians obtain better assessments from their superiors only in the condition that they compete with their colleagues for resources – their "career orientation" leads to performance gains in the competitive situation of low resources. Dahling et al. (2009) found no direct effect on task-related performance, but they did find an interaction effect of Machiavellianism and "seniority levels": Moderated by longer tenure, there was a positive relationship to performance.

Titze et al. (2017) examined the influence of psychopathy on sales performance and found a curvilinear relationship in which the best sales performance was associated with values of about one-third of a standard deviation below the mean on the PPI factor Fearless Dominance, while higher values were associated with lower sales performance. As a moderating effect, Blickle and Schütte (2017) showed that people with a high level of education show a positive relationship of this factor to task-related work performance, while people with a low level of education show a negative one.

Ten Brinke et al. (2018) coded typical nonverbal behaviors and visual characteristics for the Triad traits in semistructured interviews of hedgefund managers and found that psychopathic individuals had lower financial gains; narcissists took higher risks (but balanced their gains and losses). Machiavellianism is not associated with any financial performance indicator, according to their findings.

Smith et al. (2016) distinguished superior assessments of task-related and contextual performance and related both criteria to the Dark Triad and the facilitator "promotion focus." Machiavellianism had no relationship with task performance, narcissism had a negative relationship with task performance, and psychopathy had a negative relationship with contextual performance. With higher "promotion orientation," both narcissistic and psychopathic employees received lower scores on both criteria. A likely explanation for the negative performance ratings is that the negative traits of the characteristics become particularly visible (and negatively conspicuous) when high scorers are motivated to achieve goals and therefore show their true colors (more openly).

In DeShong et al. (2017), OCB showed no relationship to any of the Triad constructs, though detailed observations reveal findings that differ from these. For example, narcissism is positively associated with self-assessed OCB but not with others (Judge et al., 2006); psychopathy is negatively associated with "supportive behavior," an OCB-like variable (Smith et al., 2016); Machiavellianism is negatively correlated with both individual and organizational OCB, and the trait explains significantly more variance in the latter (Becker & O'Hair, 2007). Zettler and Solga (2013) also found negative correlations to several delimitable aspects of OCB, also revealing curvilinear relationships for Machiavellianism and OCB.

4.2.3 Career Success

Spurk et al. (2016) examined the connection between the Dark Triad and the objective measures of success – salary, hierarchical position, and leadership responsibility – in professionals at the stage of the career at 25–34 years of age. (This was considered a critical age since it is where problems with organizational or professional socialization would arise.) In their analysis, they controlled for a whole range of variables such as sex, age, organization size, job tenure, work hours, and education and found a positive relationship of narcissism to salary, whereas psychopathy was negatively associated with career satisfaction as well as salary and leadership position (the latter only if the control variables were included). Machiavellianism was positively associated with holding a management position and, after controls, also positively associated with career satisfaction. Like the relationships to performance O'Boyle et al. (2012) showed meta-analytically, the effects of the Triad on career success were also small and explained only 1.5–2% of variance beyond control variables. In addition, joint analyses sometimes revealed inverse relationships or relationships that became significant only after including controls or other Triad characteristics. Like job performance per se, the Triad characteristics do not appear to be particularly strong and good predictors of professional success – in contrast to the views often expressed in the press and public discussion.

In Jonason et al. (2016), narcissism is associated with a higher self-reported salary and better socioeconomic status. As to salary and leadership position, there were positive relations of narcissism – and even some additional explanation beyond the Big Five – and negative ones of psychopathy for salary (Paleczek et al., 2018). Jonason et al. (2018) examined factors influencing income and revealed that all Triad characteristics were associated with higher salaries. Men reported higher incomes than women and higher narcissism, neuroticism mediated the gender effect. According to the authors' interpretation, women may report lower salaries because they are on average more neurotic, whereas men report higher salaries because they are more narcissistic.

Hirschi and Jaensch (2015) found only a weak relationship of narcissism to salary: In joint analyses with occupational self-efficacy, self-efficacy mediated the relationship such that there was only an indirect relationship of narcissism to higher salary via greater perceived occupational self-efficacy. Satisfaction with one's career was also only weakly connected, and the direct effect disappeared after the authors included the variables self-efficacy and career engagement.

Early work on Machiavellianism discovered relationships to measures of success such as academic achievement among "masculine" women (Ames & Kidd, 1979) and regarding higher "social mobility" (Touhey, 1973); as regards the latter criterion, highly intelligent and highly Machiavellian men were superior to other groups. Turner and Martinez (1977) showed a moderating influence of education on professional success: Machiavellianism was positively associated among highly educated people with "occupational prestige" and income; among poorly educated people, it was negatively associated with income.

Ullrich et al. (2008) demonstrated that psychopathy does not correlate with life success. The factor Interpersonal was not associated with achieved status and financial wealth, whereas the factors Lifestyle, Affective, and Antisocial were negatively associated with criteria of life success. Howe et al. (2014) examined employees in the New York financial sector who showed higher values on the factor Interpersonal than the general population. Values on this factor were associated with higher annual salaries and higher hierarchical positions (albeit not linearly, only in group comparisons). There was no correlation between the total value or the other two factors and the corresponding criteria.

Eisenbarth et al. (2018) emphasize the need to take a multidimensional view of psychopathy as well as to distinguish professional success measures according to objective, material criteria and subjective satisfaction. In their study, the overall value of the PPI was not associated with any measure of success, Fearless Dominance was positively correlated with material and subjective measures, Self-Centered Impulsivity was negatively correlated with satisfaction, and Emotional Coldness was uncorrelated with all subareas. After controlling for the Big Five, work experience, and sex, they found that Fearless Dominance was not significantly associated with material success, whereas Self-Centered Impulsivity was associated with higher career satisfaction.

Muris et al. (2017) concluded that there is little evidence that increased Dark Triad values had positive effects on performance and success criteria. Apart from the objective measures of success Spurk et al. (2016) found, there are few positive work-related effects – or at least they were clearly overshadowed by the overall negative effects of narcissism, Machiavellianism, and psychopathy. Thus, over the past 10 years, nothing seems to have changed decisively from the descriptions given by O'Boyle et al. (2012, pp. 557 and 570): "Overall, the link between the DT [Dark Triad] and work behavior is tentative, with a substantial number of positive, negative, and null findings" and "... the DT as currently operationalized is better apt to explain dark behavior, rather than positive behaviors such as task performance and citizenship behavior."

Nevertheless, some new and more detailed insights into the effects of the Dark Triad at the workplace were gained since that meta-analysis; I present some selected ones in the following box.

Conclusion
Relationships of the Dark Triad to Job Performance and Success

As a conclusion to the relationships described above between the Dark Triad and professional performance and success, although there are indications of some positive effects on individual, specific criteria, overall negative effects on one's own performance and success can be expected in general.

There are no or weakly negative relationships to task and contextual performance measures; the relationships are partly dependent on moderators such as one's own independence or the possibility of self-representation, or differ depending on the partial aspect of a characteristic. The same applies to the relationships with professional success measures.

The Triad characteristics, on the other hand, are associated with negative leadership performance or behavior and corresponding effects on the well-being and performance of employees. Increased manifestations of the Dark Triad also lead to potentially large individual and financial damage in the workplace because of the associated increased probability of counterproductive behavior.

Several studies have demonstrated the usefulness of the Dark Triad for diagnosing aptitude. Together, they form the basis for assessing the effects of elevated forms of narcissism, Machiavellianism, and psychopathy on an organization and its members. We can thus use the effects presented to justify the use of Triad characteristics in practice, for example, for the selection of employees. In the next section, I discuss which other relationships relevant in the professional context have frequently been researched for the Dark Triad and could represent possible areas of application.

4.3 Further Fields of Application in Personnel Psychology

Personnel psychology deals with all aspects of the behavior and experience of people at work, often also decidedly from the perspective of the organization (Schuler, 2014b). Besides personnel selection, there are numerous applied fields of personnel psychology, such as performance assessment, personnel development, or teamwork. Little is known to date about the impact or use of the Dark Triad in these areas of intervention and interaction that deal with already employed people (Smith et al., 2018). This book also focuses on measuring the characteristics themselves for the purpose of personnel selection. For reasons of space and because of the less extensive state of research, I cannot go into similar depth on the different personnel-psychological applications of the Dark Triad – which nevertheless all require a valid assessment of the characteristics in advance.

In this section, I accordingly report findings for those fields of application that, based on an individual measurement, can provide contributions to personal advice to the person in choosing a job or career path – such as typical professional interests or the field of entrepreneurship. In addition, I present the relationships of the Dark Triad to constructs that have an interacting effect with them at the workplace, such as professional motivation or political skill, and to subjective criteria of professional success, such as well-being and job satisfaction, which can be of interest in operative personnel work. First, however, I give an overview of the research on the impact of the Dark Triad at the top levels of organizations – the founders, the CEOs, and the political leaders.

4.3.1 The CEO and President Personality, and Entrepreneurship

In the research history of the Dark Triad, narcissism has often been studied primarily in terms of the personality of CEOs and US presidents. In most cases, these studies did not use personality tests filled out by these persons to determine their characteristics, but rather various forms of external assessment or content analytical procedures. (In Section 5.1 I discuss the quality of some of these approaches.)

In a study often cited in the relevant publications on the Dark Triad and job performance (which, as far as the measurement of predictors and criteria is concerned, is hardly suitable for clarifying this relationship), Deluga (1997) examined the narcissism value of US presidents (retrospectively and externally assessed) in connection with various "presidential" performance and success measures. Narcissism was associated with positively connoted achievements such as "good decisions" or "greatness." Machiavellianism among former US presidents is also associated with better performance ratings of "perceived greatness" (Deluga, 2001). Watts et al. (2013) had US presidents assessed by experts based on the FFM prototype for narcissistic personality disorder (NPD; see Section 5.2.1 on the so-called "FFM PD Counts"), also regarding grandiose and vulnerable narcissism, linking the values to various performance and success values subjectively assessed by historians and objective data such as the length of the presidency or the number of "scandals." The facet of grandiose narcissism (but not vulnerable narcissism or NPD) was positively related to the survey values on "public persuasiveness," "agenda-setting," "crisis management," and "winning public elections," but also to the negative criteria of "impeachment proceedings," "putting political success before effectiveness," and "unethical behavior." The assessments of NPD and vulnerable narcissism were also linked to such negative, but not to positive criteria of success. Watts et al. concluded that only the grandiose aspects of narcissism lead to (some) success with actual performance values (mostly ethical aspects), but that mostly negative relationships exist.

Resick et al. (2009) examined the CEOs of US professional baseball clubs using the bibliographic account technique. The analysis of personality based on books or, in this case, mainly (sports) magazines, which evaluated a collection of statements and descriptions and combined them to form a "biographical sketch" about various constructs also included direct quotations from the CEOs. The results were incorporated into a model with different management styles and measures of success. Narcissism had a negative relationship to contingent reward leadership (an aspect of transactional leadership) and no relationship to transformational leadership – although the relationship was significant on zero-order. However, it was precisely this style of leadership that was responsible in their structural model and analysis for the relationship to objective success variables – narcissism correspondingly not.

Peterson et al. (2012) received self-assessments of narcissism by CEOs, a rare find in this context. Narcissism was negatively associated with "servant leadership," i.e., putting oneself at the service of the organization, and corporate success, and was accompanied by lower organizational commitment.

O'Reilly et al. (2014) examined the salaries or structures of the "salary packages" of CEOs whose narcissism value was assessed by employees. Narcissistic CEOs received higher salaries, especially those who have been with the company for a longer time. However, O'Reilly et al. (2018) also found that companies led by narcissistic CEOs have more and more protracted lawsuits (regardless of the overall conditions such as industry, size, or age of the organization). In simulations, narcissists accepted less advice and information about possible risks, and in risk situations, they tended to opt for potentially more problematic decisions (launching new products, settling lawsuits), presumably because they questioned the competence of the advisors (compared to their own).

An example of such a risky decision situation would be the takeover process of another company. Aktas et al. (2016) estimated the narcissism value of CEOs by analyzing their speeches and counting the ratio of first-person singular pronouns to first-person plural pronouns. Companies striving to acquire other companies have higher CEO narcissism values; the discrepancy between their own value and that of the "opposing" CEO also tended to play a role. If companies with higher narcissism values among their CEOs were the target of the purchase, they were able to achieve higher profits in the negotiation; in the case of an acquisition, this relationship was very weak. The duration of the acquisition process was significantly shorter among narcissistic CEOs.

Chatterjee and Hambrick (2007) developed the measurement technique described above in their often-quoted study on CEO narcissism and company performance; however, at least the partial measure "first-person singular" has since proved to be invalid (see Section 5.1.2 on the problem of so-called "proxies"). Their narcissism inventory was constructed from various objective data, in addition to the above-mentioned indicator, others being the prominence of the CEO photo in corporate publications and the salary differential to the other members of the board. Using the overall measure, the authors found, among other things, that narcissistic CEOs buy more and larger companies, and their companies achieve more extreme annual results (both very good and very bad).

In her review article, Braun (2017) compiled further findings on narcissistic CEOs and the success rates or development data of the companies they manage, which I summarize here shortly. CEO narcissism led to the increasing internationalization of the company, but not to an increase in risky business abroad. Narcissistic CEOs tended to make aggressive investment decisions in new technologies, especially those in the public eye. Corporate social responsibility measures were initiated by narcissistic CEOs purely for external or self-promotion reasons. Even publicly visible financial aspects, such as dividends, were positively associated with CEO narcissism. However, because of short-term effects such as discounts, the increases did not lead to a sustainable increase in company value. Concerning tax avoidance, positive relationships were found between CEO narcissism and "uncertain tax benefits" and negative relationships to financially effective, better tax rates. An objective CEO narcissism measure was related to allegations of fraud.

Finally, Zhu and Cheng (2015) make a direct aptitude-diagnostic connection: Narcissistic CEOs tend to hire managing directors with similarly high narcissistic tendencies.

A professional activity thought to be ideally suited to the ideas of high-level Dark Triad bearers is start-ups, which is why the Triad characteristics have been considered more often in this context. The general intention to become entrepreneurially active and the "perceived desirability" to do so (but not the "perceived feasibility") were positively associated with narcissism and psychopathy, primarily the interpersonal factor; narcissism was also associated with the expressed inclination and steps already taken to start such a business. Machiavellianism, however, had no relationship to any of the variables (Kramer et al., 2011). Akhtar et al. (2013) found bivariate associations between psychopathy and different measures of the tendency to found a company and the results of such efforts, but not after the inclusion of control variables. Only primary psychopathy remained negatively associated with social entrepreneurship.

Hmieleski and Lerner (2016) confirmed the correlation between higher entrepreneurial intention and narcissism, and after regression analysis, it was the only predictor. They showed that only narcissism (and only in one of two samples) is associated with productive motives (i.e., generating common benefits) for starting a business. Psychopathy was negatively associated with productive motives in both samples, and all Dark Triad characteristics were also associated with unproductive motives (i.e., expecting individual benefits). Therefore, business schools, sponsors, and state funding agencies thus have the duty to identify founders who act from the wrong motives or who are endowed with a risky personality. Smith et al. (2018) assumed that there is a great practical benefit in giving prospective entrepreneurs the opportunity for "self-assessment" in their education and in dealing with the possible effects of dark and bright personality traits.

4.3.2 Vocational Interests and Career Orientation

Jonason, Wee et al. (2014) investigated the connection between the Dark Triad and professional orientations or interests according to the RIASEC model of Holland (1997). Psychopathy was the only component that positively predicted interest in realistic activities; narcissism positively predicted interest in artistic activities, Machiavellianism was associated with less interest in such activities, and the same applies to social interests. For enterprising interests, there was a positive relationship with psychopathy and narcissism and a negative one with Machiavellianism. After regression analyses, narcissism was the only independent and positive predictor for this area. The relationships found in the analyses were partly moderated by sex. In a second study, Machiavellianism was negatively associated with careers related to caring for others, and psychopathy was positively associated with practical activities. For cultural professions, in a regression analysis psychopathy was a negative predictor, narcissism a positive predictor.

Regarding a broader constellation of professional interests, Schneider et al. (2017) found that the Triad characteristics have incremental validity to the Big Five regarding five of nine interest dimensions. In return, the Big Five explain significantly less additional variance beyond the Triad, which means that the latter can potentially add diagnostic value. In relative weights analyses, the Dark Triad characteristics usually showed the strongest independent shares of variance explained: narcissism 54% in Assertive (exercising control over others), 48% in Enterprising, and 42% for Conventional; psychopathy in the latter two 28% and 48% for Socialized.

Using the same model but with the standard procedures and with different names for the factors, Kowalski et al. (2017) also showed almost consistent relationships for narcissism and all its subscales to the Artistic factor; psychopathy and Machiavellianism, on the other hand, were negatively connected with Social Interests in all individual facets.

Machiavellianism had no connection with the Business factor, while narcissism and psychopathy had a positive one.

This constellation of interests is also reflected in the choice of study fields. Students of economics/business have the highest Machiavellianism values compared to those of psychology, law, or political science as well as almost consistently higher values in narcissism (Vedel & Thomsen, 2017). Law students scored higher in dark qualities than psychology students but not higher than political scientists. The strongest effect sizes, and thus the clearest differences, were found for Machiavellianism and the subjects of economics and psychology. These relationships were also present when the sexes were considered separately. (A difference between the subjects could have been explained by the high proportions of women and men in psychology and economics, respectively, in accordance with the known gender effect existing for the Triad. However, women studying economics scored even higher in Machiavellianism than male students of psychology.) There was no significant effect of psychopathy between subjects, although business students had the highest psychopathy scores and psychology students had the lowest. Regarding applicability in aptitude diagnostics, Vedel and Thomsen (2017) argue that self-selection occurs in the choice of study field because of one's own dark characteristics. The choice of a career in law and economics by Machiavellian scholars is a classic finding (Fehr et al., 1992; Jones & Paulhus, 2009).

4.3.3 Occupational Motivation, Political Skills, and Well-Being at Work

Section 3.2 reports findings on the typical motives and goals of persons with high values in the Dark Triad. They are interested in power, success, and money. Whether in competition with others, in relationships, or through criminal behavior, they try to achieve their own goals and satisfy their own needs at the expense of others and sometimes without regard for their own health. Many behavior patterns associated with Dark Triad characteristics outside of professional life are likely to emerge at work as well. In Section 4.1, I discuss the most serious consequences of counterproductive behavior. In the following, I present further effects that have been researched for Dark Triad characteristics in the workplace or that can be used as criteria of subjective professional success, such as job satisfaction.

Achievement motivation or the general striving for performance is usually assumed to be positively correlated with narcissism (e.g., DuBrin, 2012; Gerstenberg et al., 2014). Soyer et al. (1999), on the other hand, were able to show that narcissism is not generally correlated with striving for performance or "sales performance indicators" (but with a positive attitude toward ethically questionable sales tactics). Contrary to expectations drawn from concept definition and the research literature (Fehr et al., 1992), only weak evidence was found for a positive relationship of performance motivation with Machiavellianism. The relationship of psychopathy to performance motivation differs between its two central factors and the nature of the performance goals: Secondary psychopathy is negatively associated with commitment to achieving goals and with cooperation, whereas primary psychopathy is positively associated with "hypercompetition," a highly competitive form of motivation (Ross & Rausch, 2001).

Jonason et al. (2012) examined how people with high scores on Dark Triad traits strive to advance professionally by using numerous tactics categorized as either soft or hard. Machiavellianism and psychopathy were associated with hard tactics such as threat, Machiavellianism and narcissism with soft tactics such as flattery. Machiavellianism was associated with the use of most different tactics.

A special form of asserting one's own interests lies in using political skills to influence others at work and to behave in a way that contributes to the achievement of personal or organizational goals (Ferris et al., 2005). This type of influence, understood as a specific construct, has been considered a moderator variable in Triad research on several occasions (see Sections 4.1 and 4.2). In Kessler et al. (2010), political skills are negatively associated with Machiavellianism, which can be attributed to the Power subscale (the other two subscales of the Machiavellianism Inventory were uncorrelated to this). In a model by Smith and Webster (2017), Machiavellianism interacts with "social undermining" in the sense that Machiavellians who felt they had been "undermined" responded with higher political skills or behaviors; but there was no bivariate correlation between the two variables. As noted above, Schütte et al. (2018) demonstrated an aspect of political skills as a moderator to explain the relationship between psychopathy and CWB: CWB occurs more often in the presence of (self-estimated) diminished personal influence. Templer (2018) sees political skills as a means of explaining the relationship between dark traits and job performance, but, as described in Section 4.2.2, he does not examine them with "real" dark-side traits, but rather with the "H-factor" of the HEXACO general personality model.

Narcissism is associated with greater enjoyment of work and work commitment (Andreassen et al., 2012): Managers showed higher levels of narcissism than managed employees in the study. Mathieu (2013) refers to individual studies that establish a negative relationship between narcissism and job satisfaction, all of which do not originate from the organizational context: Negative relationships were found with more clinical measures, but not with the NPI (see Section 3.1.1). In an original study, Mathieu shows a negative relationship of narcissism to job satisfaction beyond the variance elucidation by the Big Five, which is explained by narcissistic employees believing that they deserve a better job.

Other typical narcissistic patterns can describe the narcissist's own experience at work: Maynard et al. (2015) showed that narcissists feel overqualified, regardless of actual (over) qualification. Narcissists are more likely to respond to negative feedback on their performance with anger (at others) than people with low narcissism scores. In the case of success or high achievement, narcissists tend toward personal attribution (almost exclusively to their own "superior" skills). In the case of failure, on the other hand, they attribute it to the situation, for example, to task difficulty (Stucke, 2003).

Narcissism is sometimes associated with higher job satisfaction and greater commitment (Michel & Bowling, 2013). Zettler et al. (2011) used the Affective Commitment scale of the questionnaire by Felfe et al. (2010) to show that higher values in Machiavellianism are associated with low commitment to others, but that there is a positive relationship with "self-related commitment," i.e., with one's own career.

Machiavellianism is usually seen in a negative relationship with one's own well-being and especially with job satisfaction, (see Section 4.2.1 and Jones & Paulhus, 2009). Machiavellians claim to feel little valued and suffer from stagnating careers (Corzine et al., 1999). In a meta-analytical study, Bruk-Lee et al. (2009) found a weakly negative relationship of job satisfaction to narcissism and a substantially negative one for Machiavellianism.

Jonason, Wee et al. (2015) associated higher values of all Triad characteristics with lower satisfaction; the respective employees also think more often about termination. They also found some typical circumstances for satisfaction in which the Dark Triad characteristics differ: There is an interaction of Machiavellianism with the perceived "competitiveness" in the workplace such that, if the latter was highly rated, a negative prediction of satisfaction and a positive prediction of thoughts of termination were possible. Regarding the "autonomy" of the workplace, however, it was the other way round: A higher degree of expression was accompanied by higher satisfaction and fewer thoughts of dismissal. With narcissism, it was the perceived "prestige" of the workplace that led to the same effects. So, only through interaction with variables of the workplace was the Dark Triad related to job satisfaction (Jonason, Wee et al., 2015).

In addition to the harmful effects on third parties and the organization, which can be reduced by the negative selection of carriers of high levels of the Dark Triad characteristics, further questions and applications can thus be found in which the use of the Dark Triad in aptitude diagnostics for personnel psychological purposes appears profitable (see Box 4).

Box 4: Further Fields of Application of the Dark Triad Besides Classic Personnel Psychological Interventions

In addition to the use of the Dark Triad for personnel selection and other common functional applications, such as personnel development or coaching, the following useful applications also exist:

- *Vocational interests:* Interest constellations are rarely used for selection purposes, but rather for advisory purposes (Schuler, 2014a). To support self-selection, the Dark Triad could be used diagnostically in the context of student counseling or interest tests, for example, if the actual content of a desired occupation does not show any potential for satisfying the motives associated with a dark personality structure.
- *Entrepreneurship:* Even though founders usually do not take part in classical aptitude diagnostics in the sense of a selection or placement decision, the use of the Dark Triad is conceivable in start-up-related orientation and consulting, for example, in the context of start-up seminars and as a diagnostic instrument in the selection for financial support programs or loans.
- *Selection of top personnel:* The two groups under consideration, CEOs and heads of government or politicians in general, are (unfortunately) rarely explicitly diagnosed regarding their suitability but are nevertheless selected by smaller (supervisory boards) or larger groups of people (voters). The findings described above give an impression of the effects of the characteristics whose consideration in such (selection) decisions offers potential benefits for organizations or the governed.
- *Motivation structure:* Persons with elevated values on the components of the Dark Triad have specific motives and perceptions at work. The Triad characteristics are not necessarily associated with actual task-related motivation. The interest of these persons is related more to the satisfaction of their own needs. They also do not generally have better political skills, but rather an adaptive way of achieving their own goals. However, these and other influencing factors and framework conditions seem to be moderators for whether and which aspects of the Triad characteristics lead to positive or negative effects at the workplace.
- *Well-being in the workplace:* Job satisfaction and the commitment of people with high levels of narcissism, Machiavellianism, and psychopathy are rather low. Some of the typical aspects of narcissism and Machiavellianism, such as perceived overqualification or cynical worldview, can be cited as reasons for such experiences.

Knowledge of the mechanisms of action of the Dark Triad is thus relevant for many other fields of personnel psychology applications beyond just personnel selection. The characteristics must therefore be further researched in the future in connection with measures of operative work with employed personnel, such as in personnel development. However, the clearest benefit of the Dark Triad of personality for aptitude diagnostics seems to lie in the further research and prognosis of counterproductive behavior at the workplace, especially destructive leadership. Ideally, both should be done together with and in contrast to integrity, the characteristic that has developed into today's scientific term because of efforts in practice to predict counterproductive behavior. If the Dark Triad is to be used for the purposes described in this chapter, it must follow the path taken by integrity – but in reverse: from theory into practice and thus into a target field that has various specific requirements and is highly regulated. I discuss these in the following chapter and examine on this basis whether and how the Dark Triad of personality can be used for operative vocational-aptitude diagnostics.

5 Requirements for a Diagnostic Procedure for Assessing the Dark Triad in Organizational Practice

Research on the Dark Triad in the workplace no longer addresses only general job-related issues, for example, whether a narcissist is more likely to emerge as a team leader. Rather, it explicitly talks about personnel selection based on dark characteristics (e.g., Jonason, Wee et al., 2014; Reichin et al., 2019; Schyns, 2015). The increasing scientific consideration of the Dark Triad in this regard marks the beginning of its use for aptitude-diagnostic purposes in practice; the present chapter serves to inform about the possibilities and limitations of such applications.

According to O'Boyle et al. (2012), only a few studies have used Dark Triad characteristics as a basis for personnel selection decisions, and these were limited to clinical psychopathy scales such as those of the *Minnesota Multiphasic Personality Inventory* (MMPI; see Section 2.3.3). Even today, with an explosion of studies on the Dark Triad and work-related behavior and criteria and its wide discussion in media, there are only a few actual uses of the traits in operative organizational or professional contexts, apart from its role in scientific research. To the best of my knowledge, there is no published study in which the Dark Triad as a whole and in its common form was used for actual personnel selection decisions. In contrast, there is a broad use of the only procedure for DSM-based dark-side traits in the professional context to date, the *Hogan Development Survey* (HDS; see Section 2.3.3). Thus, because of the lower extent of occupation-related research (in the field) compared to other dark-side traits (e.g., the 11 scales of the HDS), our knowledge about the use of the established procedures for the Dark Triad in organizational practice remains scarce.

To assess the potential uses of narcissism, Machiavellianism, and subclinical psychopathy in the diagnosis of occupational aptitude, we must first clarify to what extent the existing measurement approaches are suitable for use in practice, in addition to proving the validity of the constructs themselves (see Chapter 4). For this reason, this chapter presents the assessment methods proposed in Triad research and evaluates their practical applicability based on relevant guidelines for personnel selection. Following this compilation, I derive concrete requirements for the applied organizational use, especially employee selection and general aptitude diagnostics, of the Dark Triad.

For dark-side measures, the same professional guidelines that apply to other aptitude-diagnostic procedures play a fundamental role in evaluating their role in organizational practice. Internationally, these are the *Standards for Educational and Psychological Testing* (AERA/APA/NCME, 2014), the current development *ISO 10667* (ISO, 2020), or the more field relevant *SIOP Principles for Test Use* (Society for Industrial and Organizational Psychology (SIOP), 2018) and the *Guidelines for Occupationally Mandated Psychological Evaluations* (APA, 2018). The latter two form the main basis for the discussion.

Background of the Issue

Several countries widely consider actual clinical assessments of dark traits illegal in personnel selection, and even some broad dimensional personality traits, such as Neuroticism, were recently considered to potentially be problematic as clinical and normal range personality are integrated (Melson-Silimon et al., 2019). Some of the traditional self-report inventories have been criticized for their psychometric properties or lack of validation, whereas others, such as the Self-Report Psychopathy Scale (SRP; Hare, 1985), include items on sexual and criminal behavior, which seems problematic in organizational settings concerning testtakers' perception and acceptance.

As I show here briefly, some of the very basic existing requirements for the applied organizational use of psychological constructs and measures for personnel decisions are questioned for some of the scientifically used instruments for the dark side of personality. Several issues must first be considered before applying dark traits, especially transferring novel measurement approaches to practical personnel psychology and the use of any form of dark-side assessment for personnel selection. In particular, this includes those that go beyond the repeatedly discussed legality of dark personality consideration in the selection regarding laws such as the Americans with Disabilities Act (ADA, 1990) and respective EEOC guidance (2000), which applies only to the USA. This limits the necessary discussion focusing on this matter.

To raise awareness of the open questions that need to be addressed, and to provide recommendations on what is possible and what should be avoided when measuring the dark side at the workplace, the present chapter briefly points out the issues commonly raised to date and complements these by adding the viewpoint of professional standards related to personnel decisions, the goal being to contrast the different proposed types of measurement methods of the Dark Triad with both.

In the responses to the focal article by Melson-Silimon et al. (2019), several authors begin making general recommendations on how to best design and apply dark-side traits in personnel practice, especially regarding dark-side personality tests and concerning legality (e.g., Christiansen et al., 2019; van Someren et al., 2019). This chapter builds upon these works to (1) expand the notions made there concerning dark-side measurement to all assessment strategies, especially the more recently proposed types, and (2) go beyond them by explicitly discussing the proposed dark-side measures regarding the professional standards for application in organizational settings, especially personnel selection. To this end, I present some main principles of the basic and most important requirements defined in the professional guidelines of psychological associations and the legal regulations relevant to psychological diagnostics in occupational practice. It is crucial to contrast them with the available and recently proposed dark-side assessment strategies.

The chapter thus strives to go beyond the ongoing theoretical debate of whether it is generally legal to assess dark personality in the workplace, as the research dealing with this issue, briefly presented above and discussed for the concrete dark-side measurement strategies in detail below, shows that, according to the current legislation and court law, it is perfectly legal when applied in a proper and defensible way. I thus prefer to shed light on how measuring dark personality in the workplace in fact can be done and when it is better avoided.

The SIOP Principles as a Reference for Evaluating Dark-Side Assessments

The *SIOP Principles for Test Use* (SIOP, 2018) aim to "specify established scientific findings and generally accepted professional practice in the field of personnel selection psychology" (p. 1). For this purpose, they contain various chapters on, for example, the validation process, operational considerations, and recommendations for application in practice. The most important aspects of the Principles for the assessment of dark personality are probably job-relatedness, the criteria and predictors considered, validation and transportability of evidence, and acceptance. Regarding the first aspect, it notes (SIOP, 2018, p. 4):

> The essential principle in the evaluation of any selection procedure is that evidence be accumulated to support an inference of job-relatedness. The job-relatedness of a selection procedure has been demonstrated when evidence supports the accuracy of inferences made from scores on, or evaluations derived from, those procedures regarding some important aspect of work behavior.

Therefore, one should always analyze work carried out before planning and applying a selection procedure, to first derive the requirements of the job. This seems especially important for dark personality. To protect oneself against potential legal action, to ensure the best possible criterion validity, and to enhance the acceptance of candidates, it is crucial to establish a causal connection between a specific dark trait (i.e., its behavioral outcomes) and criteria of success or failure in a specific job or workplace. Criteria in the sense of the Principles accordingly "need not be all-inclusive, but there should be a clear rationale linking the criteria to the proposed uses of the selection procedure. Criteria can be measures of overall or task-specific work performance, work behaviors, or work outcomes" (SIOP, 2018, p. 11).

Referring to the different strategies through which validity can be proven for a selection procedure and transportability of validity evidence, the Principles (SIOP, 2018, p. 19) note:

> [E]ven when different strategies are employed for gathering validation evidence, the inference to be supported is that scores on a selection procedure can be used to predict subsequent work behavior or outcomes. (p. 5) and depending on the context and purpose of a selection procedure, sufficient accumulated validity evidence may be available to justify the appropriateness of applying a selection system in a new setting without conducting a local validation research study.

This means that establishing construct-related or internal validity of, say, a novel assessment approach for capturing a dark trait would only serve as a psychometric prerequisite to a potential validation strategy – not a sufficient validation as such.

It is important to note that selection procedures according to the Principles generally can include not only traditional procedures like job interviews and psychological tests, but a wide variety of other means of assessments including "machine learning methods (e.g., harvesting information about candidates from social media sites, resumes, or other sources of text or information), gamification, and computer-based simulations of varying levels of technological sophistication" (SIOP, 2018, p. 3). Additionally, it is important to highlight the notions the Principles expound concerning such strategies (SIOP, 2018, p. 13):

> Scores produced by algorithms [...] that are used to make selection decisions should also be recognized as predictors. In cases where scores from such algorithms are used as part of the selection process, the conceptual and methodological basis for that use should be sufficiently documented to establish a clear rationale for linking the resulting scores to the criterion constructs of interest.

In addition, of course, one must show the relationships of a specific dark trait to important work-relevant criteria. It is generally considered possible to transport evidence of validity from external studies to the target application. Of special importance in this respect is meta-analytic generalization, while of course ensuring "the conditions for the application of meta-analytic results are met; and the application of meta-analytic conclusions is appropriate for the work and settings studied" (SIOP, 2018, p. 20).

For dark personality, when not conducting one's own job analysis and validation study, it seems to be at least necessary to make sure there is sufficient scientific evidence that the trait under consideration itself relates to relevant work-related outcomes, that the studies, including meta-analytic ones, were carried out in representative samples, and that the measures intended to apply in the selection setting can be regarded as valid indicators of the constructs assessed in the original studies or meta-analyses.

I use the principles described above throughout this chapter to assess the applicability of the diverse assessment procedures suggested for the Dark Triad. But first I discuss the most common form, namely, personality-based tests, and one of their general limitations for applied use: the faking of results.

5.1 Overview of the Different Measurement Approaches and Their Special Features

The most widespread means to measure personality (at the workplace) and especially for selection purposes are *self-evaluation procedures* (Smith et al., 2018). For this purpose, they have demonstrated unrivaled economic applicability with simultaneous predictive validity, notwithstanding all the inherent shortcomings and criticisms associated with self-assessments (see Section 2.2). I therefore focus my considerations in this chapter on this type of procedure.

I first discuss the most frequent point of criticism – the possibility of manipulating self-assessments – in more detail because of its significance. This is followed by a discussion of potential alternative measurement approaches using the overviews by Smith et al. (2018) and Spain et al. (2014), deducing which types of procedures currently appear to be fundamentally suitable for job-related diagnostics of the Dark Triad of personality. At the same time, I give general recommendations for action and application which are also valid for other measurement approaches not presented here or which may be developed in the future.

5.1.1 Faking Test Results

A presumably serious problem for the meaningful applicability of a test is that of *faking* – the deliberate manipulation of test results. Although test persons are quite capable of doing this, and some applicants are willing to do so, the effects on the validity of test results for personnel selection are probably smaller than often assumed (see Sackett, 2011; Sackett et al., 2017). Despite individual papers arguing to the contrary (e.g., Hogan et al., 2007), it is undisputed that there will always be "fakers" – Griffith et al. (2007) estimate their number to lie between 22% and 49% of all applicants. Contrary to this alarming percentage, however, the impact can still be considered rather small. For example, Smith and Ellingson (2002) failed to find any influence on construct validity, and Ones and Viswesvaran (1998) found neither increased nor decreased criterion-related validity. Ziegler and Bühner (2009), on the other hand, concluded that there are indeed effects on both validity indicators, especially at the facet level. The reason for the rather low effects in selection situations is probably that *all* persons tend to try to simulate "better" characteristics; this was also confirmed meta-analytically (Birkeland et al., 2006; Viswesvaran & Ones, 1999). The real problem arises when not all simulate or not all simulate to the same extent. This shifts the ranking of the applicants, which can cause major problems with "top-down selection" (Ziegler et al., 2011). For integrity tests, for example, the extent of falsification in various faking studies has been indicated at between half a standard deviation and one standard deviation (Sackett, 2011). Marcus (2000) assumed that this type of procedure is no more or less faked than other personality tests, and that the effects occur more strongly in faking studies than in actual selection situations. Correspondingly, for example, they discovered only minor deviations from practical and research situations (Sackett, 2011).

Faking is a complex phenomenon, which makes it necessary to operationalize and further research it (Bühner, 2011). An overview of the diverse issues discussed here as well as reliable findings on and theoretical explanations for faking can be found, among others, in a special issue of the journal *Human Performance* from 2011 (Volume 24, Issue 4).

Numerous papers theoretically address possible problems for the Dark Triad caused by faking, as fraud is the essence of the traits in terms of content, typical behavior, and motivational structure (e.g., Spain et al., 2014). It is often assumed that persons with, for example, high psychopathy scores falsify procedures for measuring the Dark Triad, thus casting doubt on their fundamental effectiveness and applicability. A look at the findings on the psychopathy construct, however, shows it is more likely that psychopaths can and will cheat in principle and not just on Dark Triad procedures, affecting *all* personnel selection methods and test contents. Moreover, the question is not whether faking is easier for them, but whether it is actually practiced (and whether it influences the validity of the selection decision). As is typical for some parts of Dark Triad research, many anecdotes and speculations but hardly any reliable findings exist on this highly relevant question, and the results obtained under laboratory conditions described below are also inconsistent among the characteristics and across the methods used.

Psychopaths, for example, can fake personality tests (here to capture the Big Five) if they are instructed accordingly (Fisher et al., 2018). Unfortunately, choosing the type of scale does not solve the (supposed) problem: Psychopaths practice faking inventories to capture the Big Five in both Likert-scaled and forced-choice procedures (see Section 5.1.3), even when warnings are given. These two approaches mitigated the extent of faking but could not completely solve the problem.

Regarding the question of whether they also fake better or more successfully than others, MacNeil (2008) provided only weak confirmation that psychopathy and Machiavellianism are associated with higher success in *faking-good* (i.e., being able to present oneself in a more positive light than others without being recognized as a "faker" in a corresponding procedure). For this purpose, several partial studies were carried out in the research setting, and various procedures or methods were compared that operationalize "successful faking." I mention some of the core findings of the extensive study here and strongly recommend the full read of the original publication.

Regarding psychopathy, in a partial study among inmates (MacNeil, 2008), it was not the overall value but only the individual factors that were associated with success in faking-good on personality inventories; there was no connection to *faking-bad* (i.e., successfully simulating worse values). In a further substudy among students, psychopathy could only predict success in faking-good regarding one of three methods of assessment; Machiavellianism in two, narcissism in none. Again, none of the characteristics in this sample were associated with higher success in faking-bad. In a third substudy, in which the veracity of the person and the believability of their statements was assessed based on videos with self-presentation as a measure of successful faking, psychopathy and narcissism were positively associated with believability but not with veracity. Machiavellianism was even associated with *less* success in faking-good, operationalized by less perceived believability and less veracity.

In a more comprehensive study on the nature of faking, the Triad characteristics were, among others, examined as possible influencing factors in regression analyses (Bensch et al., 2019). None of the Triad characteristics made a significant contribution to explaining faking-bad (although sex and an aspect of social desirability did). For faking-good, besides social desirability, Machiavellianism provided positive explanatory contributions, narcissism even negative ones; psychopathy had no influence in either study. According to the results described above, narcissism seems to be virtually unrelated to faking, and psychopathy only in individual studies and in the form of individual subfacets. Only for Machiavellianism is there evidence in several studies and based on theoretical expectations of more successful faking-good.

One finding to be considered in the discussion about the expected effects in personnel-selection practice is that Machiavellianism and psychopathy are even negatively associated with (self-assessed) socially desirable response behavior – out of little fear of consequences (Kowalski et al., 2018). Whether persons with high Triad scores fake more and more successfully than others in an actual selection situation has yet to be investigated.

In summary, the problem of faking tests exists and is not completely solvable, but it is probably smaller than commonly assumed and in practice less significant than feared. Nevertheless, the phenomenon needs to be better and further researched, explicitly also for Triad characteristics, in real personnel-selection contexts. Laboratory studies with appropriately instructed subjects have little explanatory value in practice, since instructed faking differs from actual faking in both extent and quality (Sackett, 2011). Deviations between research and selection situations were found for procedures used for personnel selection, such as integrity tests. Therefore, context-specific norms should be provided for a test which reflect the general effect of socially desirable response behavior and thus make it possible to largely control this in practice. Scales for measuring social desirability, on the other hand, have often proven to be of little use in practice because they are themselves prone to faking (Sackett, 2011). Moreover, they provide only indications of a possible distortion; one cannot calculate the exact extent or even correct for faking. It is recommended to use tests only for preselection and with a low cut-off value to prevent displacement of suitable (or, in the case of dark characteristics, unproblematic) applicants and enable a check in later selection stages, for example, in interviews (Sackett, 2011). This also applies to the Dark Triad.

Moreover, faking must also be considered in the context of the entire selection process. Schuler (2014a) observes that criticism of test procedures is often voiced by people who are more gullible toward other diagnostic approaches, for example, by uncritically believing answers in interviews that flatter the company. Paulhus et al. (2013) simulated *recruitment interviews* and found that more narcissistic students were more likely to be evaluated as potential hires and were considered more intelligent. One reason for this assessment was their generally higher word volumes, expressed in explicit self-praise in the form of positive statements about themselves rather than in an exaggerated presentation of their abilities. The degree of self-portrayal by narcissists was higher when the counterpart was perceived as an expert, operationalized by the interviewer having previously described them as experts or laymen. All Triad characteristics are also related to the use of deceptive impression management tactics in interviews (Roulin & Bourdage, 2017). People with high scores use different tactics that are appropriate to the recruiting organization, depending on the situation.

Conclusion
Faking

Faking is a complex phenomenon that requires further research and cannot be easily prevented, though its impact on practical selection decisions is less than is often assumed. Faking can affect Triad procedures, other test procedures in Likert- and forced-choice format as well as other modes, such as interviews. Contrary to popular belief, higher dark Triad values do not automatically lead to more and more successful faking. The findings on this are unclear and inconsistent for the characteristics, the effects depend on the respective goal and situation. At present, no studies speak against the possibility of using Triad methods and thus obtaining relatively unadulterated values. To dispense with fundamentally valid tests because of possible faking, only to be dazzled in the interview, does not appear to be a sensible option for personnel selection anyway.

5.1.2 External Assessments and Information Technology-Based Measurements

Various *external assessments* have been suggested in Dark Triad research. In the case of external personnel selection, these are difficult to obtain (in an unadulterated form) and could even be associated with a possible fear of consequences, especially from Triad high scorers (Schyns, 2015). In addition, third parties rarely have insight into relevant internal processes, which makes accurate measurements difficult, especially of the dark side, because outwardly visible expressions could be characterized by representational tendencies, especially with these characteristics. Until recently, it was unclear which dark characteristics are suitable and how well suited they are for peer assessment (Spain et al., 2014). Malesza and Kaczmarek (2018) provided valuable insights with their study on the agreement between peer assessments and Dark Triad test values. The correlations for third-party assessments of narcissism, Machiavellianism, and psychopathy by close acquaintances and the standard procedures NPI, Mach IV, and SRP (see Section 3.1) lie between $r=.33$ and $r=.49$.

Lämmle et al. (2021), using the same three measures, analyzed the agreement of observers of peers, parents, and students answering the inventories and found narcissism to be relatively well observable as well as consistent between different other-raters; both parties rely on the same informational cues. Regarding the other two Dark Triad traits, self-other agreement was rather small, and, more importantly, the other-raters under-estimated the traits in their expression and derived their rating by using different information, which the authors interpret as the ability to "hide" these traits or display them differently according to the situation or target person.

In conclusion, the moderate convergent construct-related validity values shown are insufficient for operative occupational purposes. But more importantly, predictive validity studies for this approach are still lacking, and in practice employers will likely find it difficult to obtain unbiased assessments of the Triad values of a potential employee from their close acquaintances.

For that reason, various methods of external assessment based on freely available biographical data or indicators have repeatedly been proposed, mostly for narcissism. Such *proxies* can be coded and calculated, e.g., based on annual reports or speeches by CEOs (Chatterjee & Hambrick, 2007; see Section 4.3.1), biographies (e.g., of US presidents, see Deluga, 1997, 2001), or Twitter communications of professional teams of the American basketball league NBA (Grijalva et al., 2020). These approaches, sometimes described as "unobtrusive," appear to be suitable methods for research purposes, especially for otherwise hard-to-reach groups of people such as NBA stars, CEOs, and (deceased) US presidents. In contrast, the operational use for personnel selection is fraught with problems. On the one hand, proxies are, by definition, only auxiliary variables incapable of measuring the entire actual construct. For example, the Twitter proxy for narcissism from Grijalva et al. (2020) is only related at $r=.31$ with the NPI, though the variable is used as "narcissism." In the case of auxiliary constructs (and all other forms of procedures such as peer-ratings), regardless of insufficient construct-related validity, it is probably better to determine the predictive validity of this proxy or procedure itself before using it for personnel selection, and not to take an inadmissible detour via the available findings for the characteristic narcissism. From a viewpoint of the Principles standards regarding validation and transportability, making use of the available findings for the characteristic, e.g., the meta-analytically derived general validity estimates found for narcissism by standard measures such as the NPI, seems not to justify the use of an indicator that merely approximates the respective variable as operationalized by the given inventory. Put succinctly: If the NPI has a relation of $r = .50$ with CWB and is thus able to predict 25% of the variance in CWB, it may therefore be considered useful for employee selection. When a proxy relates to $r = .50$ to the NPI (thus sharing 25% of the variance with it), that doesn't mean the proxy shares exactly the 25% of the variance with the NPI that predicts CWB. So, the proxy might approximate narcissism but no work-relevant aspect of it at all.

Furthermore, the data material usually required for the approaches presented (annual reports, speeches, etc.) is not available for applicants – though it could nevertheless be generated in the application situation, for example, using voluntary and specially prepared texts such as a letter of motivation. The use of this type of data without consent, such as that of public Twitter accounts, and the question of whether the procedures, in this case, can really be considered "unobtrusive" is discussed below.

First and foremost, the approaches presented have not yet been researched in a way that could justify their use for the purposes of operative personnel diagnostics. They must meet the same criteria as common measurement approaches or provide the usual proof of psychometric quality and validity for the criteria of interest. Carey et al. (2015), for example, show that the often used (and deemed a valid proxy for narcissism) increased use of first-person singular pronouns is not construct-valid for detecting narcissism. Across several research groups, measures, survey contexts, and languages, narcissism is related to this measure in a way that approaches zero. Yet, this indicator is widely used in the study of work-related topics of narcissism, although as Van Scotter (2020) showed in their review of dozens of studies on the archival approach, it has extreme limitations regarding reliability and criterion validity.

According to the current state of knowledge from the perspective of the Principles, proxies and third-party assessments of the Dark Triad can, therefore, in light of their use and proven validity in the past, not be recommended for practical personnel selection.

Implicit procedures that are better tested and have proven their validity and lower falsifiability (independent of the Dark Triad) are conditional reasoning tests (CRT) and implicit association tests (IAT). Across different target groups and instructions (such as to act like an applicant), these approaches produce stable results and less faking – although this effect seems to be fully effective only if the measurement intent has been disguised (LeBreton et al., 2007; Smith et al., 2018). These types of procedures themselves have not yet been tested in the selection context in a way that would allow reliable findings to emerge concerning their predictive validity and effectiveness against faking (Schuler, 2014a). Many authors regard them as valuable measures of dark characteristics, although no published IATs or CRTs are yet available for dark-side traits. One promising exception is an IAT for antagonistic narcissism recently introduced by Heinze et al. (2020). The validation findings for an IAT for the Dark Tetrad (narcissism, Machiavellianism, psychopathy, sadism) turned out so poorly that even the test author advises against its use (Mörzinger, 2012). An implicit measure of psychopathy in the workplace, the Logical Inference Exercise, measures "aberrant self-promotion" in the form of a CRT and thus core features of subclinical psychopathy (Gustafson, 2000). But there are no published findings for this measure, which makes its use for operative purposes appear too early (Smith & Lilienfeld, 2013) – with no change in sight.

Benz (2018) developed a *CRT to detect the Dark Triad in the occupational context* (CRT-DT) in the form of a screening procedure for the dark core. In accordance with the intention of the test development, the procedure was not designed and validated regarding measurement of the three Triad characteristics, but only regarding detection of the underlying core (operationalized via scales of the SRP and the H-factor). It has some (psychometric) limitations, corresponding to the high complexity involved in drawing conclusions about (dark) personality from reasoning; however, its further development and validation for job-related criteria are potentially promising, and this type of procedure is a very interesting approach.

This also applies to a "digital work simulation" to assess Machiavellianism and compliant behavior (Dubbelt et al., 2015). With its extensive "cover story" and five tasks, each with five alternative answers, the procedure represents a less economical, but demonstrably valid option. Not only was it less prone to faking than self-assessments, but it was also able to predict CWB incrementally to the MPS (a Machiavellianism self-assessment scale;

Dahling et al., 2009). Such a digitally based SJT – or this type of procedure in general – therefore also appears to be a feasible approach. However, there is also a small limitation here, regarding less the predictive validity provided for the recorded target criterion than the construct-related one: In this study, the results of the procedure are weakly related to the Machiavellianism scale used (r=.22 to .31). So perhaps in this case one should rather speak of a digital work simulation that predicts counterproductive behavior (while at the same time correlating with Machiavellianism) than of a "work simulation to assess Machiavellianism."

Generally speaking, the last three types of procedures presented here do not usually measure a personality trait in the strict sense. SJTs or work simulations belong to the simulation-oriented procedures according to the *trimodal concept of personnel assessment* (Schuler, 2008), which, depending on the instruction, record typical or maximum behavior in a described situation that is critical to occupational success and are thus intended to predict occupational performance. With a suitable design, however, SJTs can also be used to validly record narrow personality traits (Mussel et al., 2018).

According to Smith et al. (2018), technological advances and cost-cutting have also greatly facilitated the use of elaborate (neuro-)biological procedures, which have a rich tradition, particularly in psychopathy research. Compared to other methods, they are still not very economical, and to date validation studies for the target criteria are also unavailable. The road to using functional magnetic resonance imaging *(fMRI)* in personnel selection fortunately remains quite long.

There have also been suggestions to use *information technology (IT)-based methods* to infer Triad characteristics from communication behavior on social media. Analyses of Facebook profiles enabled predictions of narcissism values relatively accurately, whereas Machiavellianism and psychopathy could not be predicted at all (Vander Molen et al., 2018). Sumner et al. (2012) compared approaches using machine-learning methods (a form of *artificial intelligence*) to capture the Dark Triad through communication behavior on Twitter. For psychopathy, the best method could correctly assign 2 out of 125 persons of the top percentile of the distribution (without false positives); a modeled increase in the rate of correct assignments led to strong increases in the false-positive rate. The approach is therefore not suitable for purposes of personnel selection because of its lack of accuracy. Furthermore, the use of such technologies is subject to regulation to determine the circumstances under which a personality prognosis based solely on user profiles of social media is ethically acceptable at all (Sumner et al., 2012). Many people mistakenly regard such platforms as private and disclose much more information about themselves than they would like to. The use of this data without consent or regulations to protect against misuse should therefore be viewed critically. Data protection and the ethical justifiability of personality diagnostics based on information shared on the internet are fundamental questions that do not apply specifically to Dark Triad characteristics. Nevertheless, I discuss them below in my discussion of the other ethical and legal issues associated with measurement (see Section 5.2).

From a legal point of view, in the event of an intrusion into the private sphere of applicants, the organization must have a convincing interest in such information and evidence of its suitability and diagnostic relevance, ideally determined by a job-analysis in the sense of the Principles. Another relevant matter in the operational considerations of the Principles concerning dark personality assessment seems to be acceptability:

> Some organizations find certain types of selection procedure questions unacceptable. [...] personality inventory items may be viewed as an invasion of privacy, even if they can be shown to be related conceptually and empirically to the criterion measures or the requirements of the job. Cultures also differ in the acceptability of different kinds of selection procedures, so candidates' willingness to complete the assessment should be taken into consideration. (SIOP, 2018, p. 26).

To ensure this, it is recommended to have a valid selection procedure that can also provide people with feedback on their results, expressed by notions like "Generally, the greater the similarity between the selection procedure and the work performed, the greater the acceptability to candidates, management, and other stakeholders" and "Communications regarding the selection procedure, the constructs measured, and the role of incumbents and managers in developing the procedure may improve understanding and acceptance of a selection procedure" (SIOP, 2018, p. 28).

Conclusion
Novel Assessment Strategies Applicability in Practice

Several interesting measurement approaches to the Dark Triad have been proposed and need to be explored and studied further. None of them is currently documented and validated in a form that would make it appropriate to use them for employee selection purposes in practice according to professional standards of the field, e.g., the SIOP principles. For third-party assessments, proxies, and similar approaches to measuring dark properties, it was stated that they are "in their infancy and only time will tell whether or not they will prove effective for research and practice" (Harms & Spain, 2015, 18). Not much has changed in this respect: Nearly all proposed assessment methods have only been studied in research settings, fail to meet some psychometric quality criteria for applied use in high-stakes settings, and, above all, have not been validated and tested for such purposes. Some have great potential though to be developed further and validated and thus are promising new approaches to dark side assessment in the future.

5.1.3 Self-Assessment Procedures with Forced-Choice vs. Likert-Type Formats

The only type of procedure in research on the Dark Triad that basically corresponds to the criteria used in vocational-aptitude diagnostics – or that can be evaluated for such purposes based on the available data – is currently self-assessment. The answers are usually recorded on *Likert scales*, which require a free self-assessment of an item (in response to a stimulus). In addition, procedures with several alternative answers or stimuli *(forced-choice)* have been developed, and both variants have been compared with each other for some time (e.g., Bartlett et al., 1960). Forced-choice items are primarily intended to remedy the frequently discussed problem of faking, which they succeed in doing, at least to a certain extent. However, this answer format often causes psychometric problems, such as limited reliability, validity, or an unclear factorial structure (Brown & Maydeu-Olivares, 2013).

Christiansen et al. (2014) regarded the further exploration of this response format as a possible solution to the problem of faking. In one study (Fisher et al., 2018), people with high psychopathy scores were less susceptible to faking than on a Likert scale, but the forced-choice items were also answered in a socially desirable way – so they do not offer complete protection either.

Paulhus and Jones (2015) presented an overview of all self-assessment measures for Dark Triad properties known to that date, 18 in total, some of which were short versions of the standard procedures. Among them are the three standard scales *NPI*, *Mach IV*, and *SRP* (see Section 3.1), which are of paramount importance and are used almost exclusively; and the short measures *Dirty Dozen* (DD) and *Short Dark Triad* (SD 3; Jones & Paulhus, 2014), which have recently become increasingly important. Other Triad inventories, like the short methods, that allow a combined measurement of properties are the *Mini-Markers of Evil* (Harms et al., 2004) and the Dark Triad *Screening Measure* (MacNeil et al., 2007). Because of their limited relevance for the state of research, I discuss neither of these two here; they have not yet been used outside of the development studies or no publications have been presented, apart from conference contributions. Thus, as already noted by Furnham, Richards et al. (2013) as well as Paulhus and Jones (2015), there is still not enough information available to allow a meaningful consideration. In Section 5.2.2, I present the quality criteria of the above-mentioned standard and short procedures.

Regarding the Dark Triad, to date and to the best of my knowledge, no narcissism scale focuses on the sphere of work-life, and there is only one work-related Machiavellianism scale (OMS; Kessler et al., 2010) that contains explicit job-related formulations in about one-third of the items. However, there are at least four occupational measures of psychopathy. The B-Scan (Mathieu & Babiak, 2016a) maps the four factors according to Hare (2003) with work-related items and as such also enables a multidimensional view, which is of high relevance in the case of psychopathy given the differential work-related effects of its subfactors (e.g., Blickle & Schütte, 2017). B-Scan shows good psychometric quality and construct-related validity and is currently undergoing further validation, though additional criteria-based studies are necessary before it can be used for operative personnel decisions. Nevertheless, it already appears to be a promising measure of psychopathy at work (Mathieu & Babiak, 2016a). A more recent development is the Corporate Personality Inventory (CPI-R; Fritzon et al., 2017), which is composed of work-related items and shows sound basic psychometric properties, though it covers subfactors that differ from the ones proposed by Hare (2003). A very promising measure is the Triarchic Psychopathy Measure Adapted for Work (TriPM-Work; Sutton et al., 2020), which contains only work-related item formulations, yields the same, theoretically sound factor solution as the original TriPM, has already been shown to be a valid predictor of relevant job-related criteria such as abusive supervision and is available in both self- and other-rater forms. The Psychopathy Measure – Management Research Version (PM-MRV) seems to be a less successful procedure. Jones and Hare (2016) sharply criticized the scale developed and used by Boddy (2011, 2017), stressing that their criticism is not an academic discussion, on the contrary: If characteristics are used for actual personnel decisions, theoretically sound and developed measures must be used that rigorously adhere to standards and are ecologically valid for the context.

Special emphasis on the latter aspect was given in the development of the measure Dark Triad of Personality at Work (TOP; Schwarzinger & Schuler, 2016, 2019), which captures the main contents of the Dark Triad traits at both the subscale and factor level, was developed with work-related items, successfully validated against the standard scales, several work-relevant constructs, and criteria of interest such as job performance and CWB, among both working adults and in the organizational context. Moreover, it has been tested in high-stakes settings and for acceptance by testtakers. Extensive user information is available in the form of a test manual, informing about validation findings, ways to correctly apply the test and provide useful and acceptable feedback to testtakers, aided by detailed narrative feedback reports. TOP is described in detail in Chapter 6.

But first I would like to discuss below the specifications and requirements for the applied diagnostic use of dark properties in the workplace in more detail and refer to the legal, technical-formal aspects as well as aspects derived from the theoretical preliminary considerations on dimensionality and the viewpoint of the diagnosed person. In addition, I look at a requirement that is relevant to all areas mentioned: the relevance of the procedure, i.e., the relevance of its contents for professional life. Thus, I present the current standard and short procedures as representatives of the proposed self-evaluation procedures for the Dark Triad and their suitability for use in applied personnel-psychological purposes is discussed. On this basis, general expectations for an organizationally applicable procedure for the Dark Triad of personality are derived.

5.2 Legal and Technical Requirements for Practical Operational Use

The necessary legal prerequisite for any kind of psychological diagnostics is the legality and justifiability of its use. This is implied in various individual laws, professional standards, and ethical guidelines of psychological associations around the globe. Of primary relevance is the protection of the general personality rights, to prevent an inappropriate intrusion into an individual's private sphere. In this respect, dark personality tests do not differ fundamentally from other forms of occupational psychological diagnostics, which is why I discuss the relevant aspects below together with the other professional standards for the assessment of aptitude diagnostic tests.

5.2.1 Legal, Subclinical Measurement of Dark Personality Traits

A special case regarding the legality, however, is that many of the dark personality traits – in the case of the Triad narcissism and psychopathy – have a clinical background and are based on the corresponding personality disorders from this field (see Chapter 3). Yet, according to the prevailing opinion in personnel selection, medical "health diagnoses," including mental health, are not permitted – if they are made without announcement and consent; they are permitted in the context of an occupational health examination. In the United States, for example, they are prohibited under the *Americans with Disabilities Act* (ADA) and in Great Britain under the *Disability Discrimination Act* (DDA) (see e.g., Guenole, 2014; Wu & LeBreton, 2011) when used for the preselection of applicants. The reason is that a restriction in the selection process could pose a potential disadvantage that is not problematic later in the actual job (Christiansen et al., 2014). Medical health diagnoses are permitted, however, in connection with a binding job offer, but in principle only if the presence of the recorded characteristics would restrict "essential functions" that are central to the job and would prevent the (successful) performance of the job. A pure measurement of personality disorders just for the sake of it, on the other hand, is never allowed (Guenole, 2014).

In the United States, several labor-court rulings have clarified that the Minnesota Multiphasic Personality Inventory (*MMPI*; see Section 2.3.3) may not be used for personnel selection until the entrepreneurial necessity or *occupational relevance* is first demonstrated (Guenole, 2014). Occupational or *requirement relevance* is basically given only for dark characteristics that stand in a critical relationship to common criteria of job performance or success, but not for behaviors that do not necessarily affect the fundamental tasks and duties of the respective workplace, such as self-harming behavior or compulsive hand-washing (Dilchert et al., 2014).

Therefore, apart from waivering individual questions that may prove problematic (discussed below in the context of acceptance and occupational reference), a prerequisite for the permissible use of dark personality traits is addressing only those traits that are related to basic requirements of the respective workplace. Furthermore, a subclinical measurement with the classification of results on continuously distributed, dimensional scales must be guaranteed, and no classification of persons into categories (i.e., no clinical measurement) is allowed (see Section 2.3.1).

In light of the demonstrable relationship of the Dark Triad to occupational performance criteria (see Chapter 4) – and if only a quantitative and not a qualitative differentiation is made between individuals – the use of the dark personality characteristics for personnel selection is formally legal (see Wille et al., 2013). All available standard and short procedures are based on self-assessments on dimensional scales and provide continuously distributed data. Moreover, they do not originate from clinical psychology but from the study of characteristics in the general population or have been tested for this purpose (see Section 3.1). Some of the more recently presented inventories focusing on the Dark Triad at work even show ecological and face validity. Thus, the introduction of subclinical procedures has solved the basic problem, making legal measurement of the Dark Triad possible with all current procedures. Guenole (2014, p. 86) summarizes the principle of this approach as follows: "Our rationale is that we are not screening for a disorder, we are measuring maladaptive personality traits with implications for job performance."

Recently, however, this perception has been questioned once again, the argument being that because normal and abnormal aspects of personality are now integrated along a continuum by developments in clinical psychology toward a dimensional view of disorder, even standard personality measures and subclinical dark-side procedures could come in conflict with legal regulations, as they may be considered a medical examination (Melson-Silimon et al., 2019). Several responses to this focal article regard this view as too restrictive and not backed by existing case laws and regulations, indeed the product of their misinterpretation (e.g., Winterberg et al., 2019). Reichin et al. (2019), for example, responded by reviewing the relevant criteria in the EEOC guidelines which define a medical test, concluding that, in the case of the subclinical standard measures NPI and SRP, no single point would deem them a medical exam and as such illegal for use in personnel selection.

In conclusion on this point, if we follow the argumentations in the respective works, clinical diagnoses, procedures originally developed for this purpose or those being used by respective professionals are not considered appropriate for personnel preselection.

Problematic would be, for example, the MMPI (see Melson-Silimon et al., 2019) or the personality inventory for the DSM-5 maladaptive trait model (PID-5; APA, 2013), whose results can be used to calculate even official categorical disorders. All subclinical assessments usually employed in the scientific literature enable the measurement and display of results on continuously distributed scales but not a classification into clinical categories or the respective interpretations and were not designed for that purpose and thus can be regarded as legal for personnel selection.

Calculating the Dark Characteristics Based on General Personality Factors

Studies on the diagnosability of clinical categories with the FFM (see Section 2.1.2) show that the welcome impetus formulated by Guenole must be adhered to even with clearly dimensional and non-dark personality traits. Using this approach, namely, with linear combinations of its narrow facets, one can calculate prototypical *personality disorder types* or so-called *FFM PD Counts* (e.g., Miller et al., 2005; Wille et al., 2013).

Ahmetoglu et al. (2016) successfully used such "FFM personality disorder values" for the prognosis of occupationally relevant criteria in an organizational context. De Fruyt et al. (2009) discussed the use of the "count technique" for personnel selection and to collect data in the selection context. In their study, FFM PD Counts are linked to various criteria in the selection process and the final hiring decision. Wille et al. (2013, p. 214) showed the incremental validity of the normal Big Five in predicting career success with FFM personality disorder prototypes "derived from clinical personality disorder constructs ...". They explicitly addressed the legal aspect and emphasized that "... assessment of the FFM aberrant tendencies does not break legal regulations" (p. 212), since this uses subclinical procedures developed on "healthy" populations, which show a normal distribution of scores.

This line of argument overlooks the fact that the legal validity of their use is based less on the instrument, or the raw values achieved on it, than on offsetting and interpreting its results.

Regarding certain FFM linear combinations, it is possible to define values from a definitive cut-off point as a category; for example, a *T*-value of 65 was suggested as a warning signal for a DSM disorder (De Fruyt et al., 2009). Thus, one could use even normal personality inventories in an unintended and potentially illegal way in the personnel-selection context, inferred by the approach that "individuals scoring beyond a certain cut-off above the mean are 'flagged' as being at risk for this particular aberrant personality tendency" (Wille et al., 2013, p. 213). The authors consider screening for dark characteristics to be possibly warranted, as the *Employers' Liability (Compulsory Insurance) Act 1969* requires employers to protect the health and safety of their employees, for which the deselection of high scorers is an effective means. This may be true, but it does not absolve the employer from treating potential "offenders" and indeed all applicants who never become problematic in a legally correct manner. The decisive question, therefore, is whether the various FFM PD count techniques can be considered legally permissible in the personnel-selection context.

De Fruyt et al. (2009) emphasize that the values recorded in this way are not considered "pathological" but only as potential indicators of a disorder and thus do not substitute clinical diagnoses. The various forms of FFM aberrant compound values are not real disorders, and in organizational practice, the "diagnosticians" are generally no medical personnel but recruiters, often not even psychologists, which is why the reigning professional ethic guidelines, such as that for OMPP (APA, 2018), would not apply to them. Because they are not trained clinicians, any result obtained in this way cannot be considered the diagnosis of a personality disorder. Thus, also the use of FFM PD Counts in selection should be possible, as no clinical personnel is carrying out the diagnosis and the underlying tests are not specially designed for diagnosing personality disorders (EEOC, 2000).

In fact, only the corresponding result of an assessment by an accredited and authorized professional according to the common criteria of the DSM (see Section 2.1.1), possibly supported by demonstrably valid clinical scales, can represent the official diagnosis of a personality disorder.

The use of FFM PD Counts in the selection context should be legally possible; nevertheless, it represents a gray area or a slippery slope, and even more problematic would be the use of the PID-5, whose results can be used to calculate official categorical disorders (see Section 2.3.1). Even if there is nothing legally wrong with using FFM PD Counts, the possible categorical classification and the terms employed result in great conceptual proximity to official disorders and an empirical connection with them. Even just diagnosing an indicator or the high probability of an official personality disorder in the context of personnel selection must be viewed very critically. Christiansen et al. (2014) therefore also considered ethical issues to be applied when using inventories such as the *NEO-PI* (Costa & McCrae, 1985) and advised personnel practitioners to refrain from utilizing any scales or approaches named after a clinical diagnosis. The better choice is procedures that relate exclusively to workplace behavior.

However, the use of dark qualities is clearly not prohibited by law in the context of actual personnel selection, neither those directly related to the DSM nor to the Dark Triad. That is the conclusion of several authors (e.g., Harms et al., 2019; Reichin et al., 2019) in an issue of the journal *Industrial and Organizational Psychology* (2019, Volume 12, Issue 2). That issue discusses many legal and theoretical arguments, both for and against the use, and implications of the practical application of dark qualities, which is why it is a useful source of further information for interested parties and those working in personnel-selection practice.

The indicated procedure for the job-related use of dark personality traits thus consists of a measurement on dimensional scales and a resulting normal distribution of results. Ideally, such an instrument should be developed in and for samples from the general population. The use of clinical procedures and corresponding diagnoses by licensed professionals is not permitted for personnel-selection purposes. Therefore, it is also better not to categorize results in groups that are labeled as personality disorders.

Such a classification is also irrelevant in personnel selection; what is of greater interest is the job-related effects of the constructs recorded. If it is absolutely necessary to build categories, from the aptitude-diagnostic point of view, there is more to be said for – and nothing legally opposed to – placing applicants with high Triad scores in a "risk category" for demonstrably associated effects, such as CWB (see Section 4.1) – and therefore rejecting them.

5.2.2 Technically Correct Measurement: Quality Criteria of Established Standard and Short Procedures for the Assessment of the Dark Triad

Of foremost importance are the psychometric properties of an instrument, especially its validity, as well as the criterion of job-relatedness and more specifically its *requirement relevance* (i.e., whether the characteristics measured by the procedure have a clear reference to the actual job requirements – whether they yield suitability characteristics). I discuss questions of occupational and requirement relatedness further below in a separate section (5.3.2) and illustrate them using example items. In the following, I assess the established procedures NPI, Mach IV, SRP, Dirty Dozen, and SD 3 regarding their psychometric quality and their basic suitability for aptitude-diagnostic purposes.

The Standard Procedures: NPI, Mach IV, and SRP

The *Narcissistic Personality Inventory* (NPI; see Section 3.1.1) has often been criticized regarding its psychometric characteristics but mostly regarding its unclear factorial structure (e.g., Ackerman et al., 2011; Küfner et al., 2014), primarily because deviating factor solutions have often been proposed and the vulnerable aspect of narcissism is not covered (Paulhus & Jones, 2015). The forced-choice scale used also generates additional complexity when used in combination with other Likert-scaled procedures (Jonason & Webster, 2010). The reliability of the NPI total and the seven originally proposed subscales was investigated concerning *test stability* and *internal consistency*, and only the overall value was found to be satisfactory (del Rosario & White, 2005). Ackerman et al. (2011) confirmed a three-factor solution as more reliable, although the factor Entitlement/Exploitativeness showed alpha values below .50 in three studies.

The *Mach IV* for recording Machiavellianism (see Section 3.1.2) has been criticized regarding its psychometric properties, item formulations, and validity (Küfner et al., 2014); its reliability is often given at only around .70 (Jonason & Webster, 2010). In principle, the scale is adequately reliable; even with Mach IV, the factorial structure is the main point of criticism (Jones & Paulhus, 2009). As I discussed in Section 3.3.1, the scale does not cover all theoretically postulated aspects of Machiavellianism. To date, only two of the expected factors could be confirmed in the development of the scale, and it remains mostly used as a one-dimensional scale. According to Paulhus and Jones (2015), more recent scales by Kessler et al. (2010) and Rauthmann and Will (2011), on the other hand, capture content that is too broad and thus potentially contributes further to the construct creep (see Section 3.3.2).

The most used psychopathy scales have been criticized mainly regarding their length (Jones & Paulhus, 2014). The *Psychopathic Personality Inventory (PPI;* see Section 3.1.3), for example, consists of 154 items, which means almost half an hour of processing time. Furnham, Richards et al. (2013) consider the inventory to be too comprehensive and a good example of construct creep: The development oriented toward mapping as many aspects of psychopathy as possible led to the integration of elements of Machiavellianism and narcissism. The *Self-Report Psychopathy Scale* (SRP; see Section 3.1.3) addresses the criminal "consequences" of psychopathy through items for mapping the factor Antisocial and thus (depending on the conceptual view of psychopathy; see Section 3.1.3) shows *criterion contamination.* It is now available in its fourth version as an official test including a manual (SRP 4; Paulhus et al., 2016). The manual reports good alpha coefficients and retest reliabilities for this version. The most problematic of all the Triads' standard procedures in terms of content is thus probably the one most fundamentally suitable – in terms of its documentation and procedural instructions – in aptitude diagnostics.

Despite the criticism voiced regarding the unclear factor structure and the partial lack of reliability of the standard procedures for the Dark Triad, from a psychometric point of view they can still be considered fundamentally appropriate for aptitude diagnostics. There is some evidence for the factor solutions presented in Section 3.1, and there is broad agreement on the core features of the scales and the possibility of multidimensional measurement. The results obtained with the standard procedures (still) dominate the Triad research quantitatively and represent a large part of our knowledge about the characteristics. They revealed several relationships to criteria relevant for aptitude diagnostics (see Chapter 4), and for organizational variables, they have been considered to be the presumably most valid predictors of the Dark Triad (LeBreton et al., 2018). A major point of criticism for the applied use is the time intensity of their combined use (Jones & Paulhus, 2014; Küfner et al., 2014). Primarily for reasons of *time economy,* short procedures were therefore proposed, which are discussed below.

Dark Triad Short Scales: Dirty Dozen and SD 3

Jonason and Webster (2010) developed a short procedure with 4 items per Triad factor, the so-called *Dirty Dozen* (DD). This scale has been translated into numerous languages and demonstrated its suitability for predicting many of the behavioral and outcome criteria usually associated with the Triad (see Section 3.2). The DD are often used because of the short duration of the procedure, although precisely this brevity explains the deficits of DD. For example, Jonason and Webster (2010) found low alpha reliabilities below .70 already during test development, which in their opinion is compatible with the scale length, though after the rather short timespan of 3 weeks yielded a retest reliability of on average only r_{tt}=.80. In addition, problems with the discriminant validity of the Machiavellianism scale to the SRP were already apparent during development (see Jonason & Webster, 2010). Using *item-response theory*, Webster and Jonason (2013) showed good discrimination and difficulty values but too high item intercorrelations, which indicate that the scales are too narrow. Kajonius et al. (2016) found a bimodal distribution for all three factors using the same method based on almost 4,000 participants. In the first instance, the lowest response category, which rejects the item most strongly, was chosen, indicating social desirability in response behavior (see also Section 5.1.1). The data indicate a certain reluctance to truthfully answer the Machiavellianism and psychopathy items of the DD, whereas those for narcissism tend to produce normal response patterns and value distributions, whereas the latter hardly contributed to the discrimination of individuals. The above-mentioned problematic forms of distributions can lead to considerably distorted results of multivariate procedures in small samples (Kajonius et al., 2016).

Furnham, Richards et al. (2014) report further studies that attest to the low validity (Miller et al., 2012) and predictive power (Lee et al., 2013) of DD. However, the main problem with

DD lies in the opposite or different pattern of relations of its factors compared to the standard procedures (Jonason & Tost, 2010), probably because not all aspects of the heterogeneous constructs could be covered. Watts et al. (2017) found several differences between the DD and standard procedures at the facet level of the FFM as well as the HEXACO model (see Section 2.1.2) and concluded that the DD do not cover many of the typical and relevant components of the characteristics. Miller et al. (2012) examined the psychopathy scale of DD specifically from this point of view: The psychopathy items lack relevant aspects such as manipulation, grandiosity, and low impulse control, and regarding construct validity, the correlations with (low) Conscientiousness and individual proportions of (low) Agreeableness are too low. There are moderate correlations to other psychopathy scales, especially to their antisocial aspects, but only weak correlations to the aspect of "Fearless Dominance" of the PPI, for example. The DD psychopathy scale shares only less than a quarter of the variance with the SRP. Miller et al. (2012) stated that scale shortening does not absolve the user adhering to common psychometric demands, and that the use of DD is expected to change the relationships in the study of variables associated with psychopathy, which is why it is not advisable to use DD as the sole measure of psychopathy. Maples et al. (2014) explained that DD psychopathy lacks the characteristic "disinhibition," whereas the DD narcissism scale includes "antagonism" but not the aspects of narcissism related to Extraversion. In addition, one item on the DD psychopathy scale ("I tend to be cynical") can clearly be counted theoretically and regarding content as Machiavellianism (see Section 3.1.2).

According to Jones and Paulhus (2014), DD seems to be simply too short, so no recommendation for its use can be derived from a summary of empirical findings. In addition to the limitations mentioned, they particularly emphasized the lack of *discriminant validity*, i.e., the relationship to other aspects is in some cases higher than the *convergent validity*. The convergent relationships to standard procedures are also partly low, so DD covers only a very limited proportion of the contents of the constructs.

For this reason, the development of the *Short Dark Triad* (SD 3; Jones & Paulhus, 2014) included items for many aspects that were highlighted in the theoretical study of the Dark Triad constructs. A three-step factor-analytical process (isolated exploratory analysis for each construct, joint exploratory examination of all items, and final confirmatory testing) found 27 items that exhibit good fit measures, loadings on assigned factors, and validity regarding the standard procedures. The SD 3 was subsequently certified to have better psychometric properties than the DD and good predictive quality for variables of interest (Furnham, Richards et al., 2014).

Maples et al. (2014) compared the DD and SD 3 directly. Based on a literature review, they first summarized that DD scales generally have lower convergent validity with standard procedures than the SD 3, and that Machiavellianism on the DD is highly associated with other factors, especially psychopathy. In their subsequent analyses, there were also too few discriminatory relationships, which manifest themselves in very high intercorrelations with the respective noncorresponding constructs of the other procedure and within the inventories. Thus, DD-Machiavellianism and DD-Psychopathy are more closely related to each other than the latter to SD 3-Psychopathy and almost as highly related to SD 3-Machiavellianism. The Machiavellianism scales of both inventories are more closely related to psychopathy in the other test than to the Machiavellianism scale of the other test. A study with the standard procedures found higher correlations throughout for SD 3, which covers a wider range of content (mean item intercorrelations of .33 on average compared to .67

for DD). No relationship to antisocial aspects remained for DD after the partialization of SD 3. The higher convergent validity with SD 3 was found for all other Triad scales tested (except for one scale that covers vulnerable narcissism and has no relationship to SD 3).

Maples et al. (2014) concluded that the widest possible measurement should be taken, i.e., the standard procedures (i.e., NPI, Mach IV, SRP) could be used in principle, and the SD 3 in applications with a short survey time. All studies comparing the short procedures prefer SD 3 (e.g., Furnham, Richards et al., 2014), because, from a psychometric point of view, it is better suited to capture the Dark Triad according to common standards. With the DD, big question marks remain, especially regarding its construct-related validity.

Multidimensional Measurement

In Section 3.3 on the structure of the Dark Triad, I presented various theoretical and empirically justifiable views on the type and number of factors and subscales among the Dark Triad properties as well as practical approaches to their assessment. I wanted to make it clear why only a *finely graded measurement* can clarify open construct-related questions and to fully exploit the possibilities in the prediction of various target variables – especially when individual aspects of a characteristic run opposite to criteria.

Apart from global criteria, such as professional success, multidimensional measurement is relevant in aptitude diagnostics when specific aspects of job performance or misconduct are to be predicted. However, few studies have been conducted or results reported at the *facet level of* work-related characteristics, and the mere collection or publication of results at the global factor level means results in all facet information being lost (O'Boyle et al., 2012). The occupational literature on the Dark Triad has therefore also noted the need to view its components as multidimensional constructs from different traits (e.g., Wu & LeBreton, 2011) and called for ensuring that all individual aspects of the constructs are represented (Harms & Spain, 2015).

This is possible with the standard procedures. As I showed in Section 3.1, the standard procedures presented in the previous section have a theoretically and empirically comprehensible structure consisting of subfacets and the superordinate factor (with restrictions for Mach IV, for which no respective official scoring keys exist). Narcissism and psychopathy are very heterogeneous and complex and are difficult to capture with short measures (Maples et al., 2014). For this reason, the proposed short procedures cannot provide subscales simply because they are too short. As I explained in Section 3.3, this is partly behind some of the confusion surrounding the structure of the Dark Triad, and this narrowing – only part of the definitional core content is covered – and mixing – which may level out opposing relationships of individual aspects – also decrease explanatory power. The short scales DD and SD 3 are thus associated with potential limitations of their predictive usefulness when used for aptitude-diagnostic questions.

Conclusion
General Triad Procedures and Aptitude Diagnostics in Practice

Regarding the *psychometric properties,* there is some criticism for all the methods presented in the previous section, particularly strong criticism of the Dirty Dozen. The standard measures have provided acceptable values over many decades and hundreds of peer-reviewed articles in journals and could therefore be used in principle in the diagnosis of occupational aptitude from a psychometric perspective. Their target field-related problems are more likely to result from the secondary quality criteria of economy of use and *standardization*.

The latter restriction applies to all the procedures presented and is related less to the available database than to formal reasons, as there are numerous sample characteristics for a variety of questions and over long periods (see, e.g., Section 3.1.1 on the history of research into narcissism). The procedures were developed for the research context, albeit not for the diagnosis of occupational aptitude – and no test manuals were prepared for them (except for SRP 4 and PPI-R). Therefore, apart from the mentioned manual of SRP 4 and PPI-R, (to my best knowledge) no published, explicit collections and comparisons of norm values or standardization samples are available, especially not from professionals or even from the selection context. An exception is a paper by Hunt and Chonko (1984), which reports Mach IV mean values and associated standard deviations for six samples of employed persons (the mean difference between the highest and lowest performing sample there is, interestingly, three standard deviations). The lack of manuals also means that there are no detailed procedural and application instructions, which may exclude the use of the methods in fully compliant HR processes anyway. However, it is conceivable to compile all this information in the form of manuals and to collect and publish norms of the working samples from the published studies.

For use in personnel selection, the characteristics outlined in the SIOP principles or similar professional guidelines of psychological organizations around the globe must be adhered to if the suitability diagnostic process is to conform to them. Such standards in many countries have neither legally binding effects nor do they reflect the orientation of the overwhelming majority of companies. Because of the originally distant measuring intention of the general Triad procedures, an assessment of the procedures based on this standard does not seem accurate and fair (but must be done if one wants to assess their suitability for studies or real applications in practical personnel work).

As a requirement regarding professional standards, however, even for general Dark Triad procedures, at least the adherence to common psychometric quality indicators must apply, which is largely given for the standard procedures and SD 3. For DD, it must be questioned whether such a frequently and clearly criticized scale is appropriate for the decisions to be made in personnel selection; Spain et al. (2014) take the view that it is not.

Regarding the aptitude-diagnostic usability of common Dark Triad self-evaluation procedures, it can be stated that they all have a *theoretical foundation* but not regarding their use in a professional context. The findings known in this respect were later established through their application to occupationally related issues (see Chapter 4). This deficit in the theoretical foundation (for the occupational context) leads to the fact that general Dark Triad procedures contain irrelevant, but above all not requirement-related content for use in personnel selection. This circumstance, in combination with the resulting presumably low acceptance of the items from this as well as the lack of procedural instructions and standards, argues against the use of classic Triad procedures in personnel-selection practice.

The Applicant Perspective – Socially Valid, Accepted, and Job-Related Measurement

In addition to observing legal and professional standards and adopting a methodological approach indicated by the current state of research, when using dark personality traits in practice, one has to give a further criterion particular attention: the reaction to or *acceptance of* the procedures by the applicants. Variables important for organizations, such as commitment and fluctuation, are influenced by whether the applicant accepts the recruitment process (Shotland et al., 1998). A meta-analysis confirmed that a positive perception of the hiring process is associated with a more positive image of the organization and a higher probability of accepting a job offer and recommending the company to acquaintances (Hausknecht et al., 2004). Here, *face validity* was a significant influencing factor; too invasive or inappropriate elements of the selection process can lead to less "employer attractiveness" – which is relevant, considering the legal requirements outlined above, to a potential increase in legal actions. Shotland et al. (1998) therefore recommended ensuring an apparently valid selection process by making it as occupation-related as possible.

Applicants generally accept personality tests less than, say, interviews (Anderson et al., 2010). Schwarzinger and Schuler (2016, 2019) tested the acceptance of the commonly used Dark Triad short scales DD and SD3 for potential personnel-selection purposes in comparison to the job-related measure TOP and bright personality traits used in this context, such as organizational commitment; I present the results in Section 6.3. In the following Sections 5.3.1 and 5.3.2, I discuss two aspects of professionally and ethically correct personnel selection that must be observed in principle and that should be conducive to the acceptance of applicants beforehand: the social validity of the process and the relationship of the procedures used to the occupation in question.

5.2.3 Social Validity

The question of correct treatment of applicants is not primarily about preventing legal action; rather, it is part of the desirable basic ethical attitude in dealing with applicants, which was formulated in the concept of *social validity* (Schuler & Stehle, 1983). Nevertheless, efforts to adhere to its principles contribute to a more positive experience of the application process (Köchling & Körner, 1996). Social validity goes far beyond compliance with professional quality standards, such as the appropriate psychometric characteristics of a procedure, and refers to the form and extent of *information*, *participation/control*, *transparency,* and *communication of judgments* extended to the applicant in the social contract situation (Schuler, 2014a).

For a socially valid and well-accepted use of dark personality traits in personnel selection, one therefore has to ensure that applicants are properly informed about the requirements of the job to the extent that they can establish a connection to the queried characteristics (e.g., to leadership-relevant aspects from the narcissism construct in a management position). In the present case regarding diagnostic procedures per se (the concept of social validity refers to the entire personnel-selection process), the requirement for information is equivalent to the aspect of *transparency*. One can ensure this by establishing the task or job-relatedness for the procedures used, so applicants are transparently informed about what is part of the procedure and how its parts relate to aptitude for the job in question. In the diagnostic situation, the participant must be allowed their own control, which, in case of, e.g., a personality test, ranges from completion to nonexecution. In the case of the IAT or CRT procedure types presented in Section 5.1.2 above, the participant's control is much more limited, and in the case of remote diagnoses via proxies or social media-supported "profiling," for example, it is not given at all. The loss of control that occurs when diagnoses are made without the knowledge of the person and without the person knowing the purpose is the opposite of social validity (Schuler, 2018).

The communication of the assessment should be upfront (within the necessary protection of the selection process and its procedures), and in any case the *feedback* should be considerate and supportive. Especially the feedback of results, which "should facilitate integration into the self-concept" (Schuler, 2014a, p. 371), raises difficulties with the standard and short procedures and generally for the applied diagnostics of dark personality traits. How, for example, should one give feedback to a candidate who is deemed highly "psychopathic" according to the test results, who may be completely unaware of the content and meaning of the construct or – worst case – even equate it with the characteristics of a serial killer? How then to tell them why one has used the procedure for personnel selection? This is where candidate acceptance, social validity, and the diagnostic purpose as well as the interests of the organization, such as its public image, come into conflict. This makes it even more important to establish a work-relatedness in the entire selection process, but especially for the individual procedures, so that the important face validity exists. Problematic content that is not related to the job or job requirements should be excluded, and it is generally necessary to carefully consider and plan in which way and which results are reported back to applicants.

The potential problems of *indirect procedures* have already been raised regarding the issue of transparency and are discussed again here. It was emphasized that there is an advantage to being able to calculate personality disorder indicators retrospectively (and without having to obtain a renewed and specific consent?) from available FFM test results (see De Fruyt et al., 2009; Wille et al., 2013; see Section 5.2.1). Wille et al. see this procedure uncritically: Because the "normal" personality is usually already part of a selection procedure, one can readily use the available data. Such an approach, however, would allow suitability diagnoses to be carried out without any transparency. The same applies to indirect procedures such as CRT or IAT, when the intention to measure is concealed from the testees – which seems to be a prerequisite for their "faking resistance" (LeBreton et al., 2007). If FFM PD counts are calculated ex post, as the proponents suggest, in extreme cases, this communicates a different intention to measure at the time of the survey.

Use of Social Media, Big Data, and Artificial Intelligence Approaches

In contrast, the use of the various other approaches mentioned, such as proxies or the analysis of social media sites, would be even more problematic in personnel selection if the testees did not even know about their participation in the "aptitude-diagnostic procedure."

The question of the ethical and legal limits to the use of information about applicants on the internet, as already mentioned, must be clarified independently of the applicability of the Dark Triad for personnel-selection purposes. I address this here only because procedures for recording the Dark Triad based on analyses of a person's social-media presence have also been proposed (see Section 5.1.2). Yet, the corresponding procedures are not considered aptitude-diagnostic procedures, which is why no consent requirement is prescribed for them.

Sackett et al. (2017) deal with the use of data available on the internet for personnel-selection purposes and conclude that enormous amounts of data with information about people (and their personality) are now available, and that the methodology for evaluating and using this information is steadily increasing. The personal, as it were "manual" evaluation of *Facebook profiles* by recruiters has no validity for aptitude-diagnostic criteria (Van Iddekinge et al., 2013) and cannot be recommended under any circumstances at this point from an ethical, legal, and validity point of view (Jeske & Shultz, 2016) – especially because protected categories such as sexual orientation can be recorded and this much more precisely than the actually job-related characteristics of the person. The Triad, for example, could not be validly diagnosed, as explained above (Vander Molen et al., 2018). However, statistical analyses of Facebook profiles can be used to assess a person's personality according to the FFM (Bachrach et al., 2012). Irrespective of the possible influence this may have on an enormous number of people with high effect sizes (Matz et al., 2017), which has led to great criticism of the methodology and its misuse (see the Cambridge Analytica scandal), regarding the occupational context and the present question, it seems to be possible to use psychological characteristics recorded in this way as predictors of occupational aptitude. An example would be a Facebook like-based Conscientiousness score in employee preselection.

However, it is still unclear how valid such techniques are for personnel selection, and it is not yet possible to assess modern approaches in comparison to other, more common types of procedures. Sackett et al. (2017) therefore expressly warn against the rapid and ill-considered use of novel approaches of any kind, especially without having carried out the necessary studies using established standards and procedures regarding reliability, factor-analytical foundation, and their validity. The same applies unreservedly to corresponding proposals for the Dark Triad. One problem here is that the functional logic of novel procedures and their signature functions (especially of big-data analyses and approaches to artificial intelligence) partly contradict or challenge the classical principles and statistical procedures of psychology (Liem et al., 2018), and only recently have methods been developed to combine both areas (see Cheung & Jak, 2018).

It is therefore likely to become even more uncontrollable for applicants (and HR managers) if it is no longer recruiters themselves who search the internet for an applicant, or if Facebook likes are linked to personality using the methodology of linear regression, but complex algorithms of *artificial intelligence* scan voice or image recordings of applicants, search their application documents or even the whole internet for information, and link them all together. Schuler (2018) assumes that information technology-based procedures will soon be much more valid and far exceed the possibilities of current diagnostics, based solely on automated pattern recognition. Classic and standard technical and legal requirements continue to apply in principle to novel approaches, but they must adapt to the new circumstances (McFarland & Ployhart, 2015).

Whether they can do so is debatable. Professional ethical and legal regulations, and above all the willingness to comply with them, will probably not be able to keep pace with the development and unregulated use of artificial intelligence (Schuler, 2018). For example, some companies offer personnel-selection procedures with the support of artificial intelligence without independent proof of validity (Kanning, 2018) or legislators having clearly approved the use of these procedures.

The questions concerning the ethical implications of the automated processing of data and use of information (on the internet) are thus of a fundamental nature and go far beyond the use of the Dark Triad for personnel selection – but also beyond the entire field of professional aptitude diagnostics. In comparison with the potentially far-reaching, harmful effects of modern IT methods and big data on individuals and entire societies when misused via mass media, job-related specifications for these approaches may appear to be of secondary importance. But they are of great relevance for future developments in this field: for ensuring the validity of corporate selection processes but above all for the protection of the applicants' rights.

5.2.4 Occupation-Related Measurement

To solve the problems arising from novel measurement approaches for personnel selection (not only in the case of Dark Triad diagnostics), it may be helpful to concentrate on a further criterion: the occupational and requirement relevance of a procedure or its *content-related validity*. A content-valid procedure adapted to the target context of "profession and organization" not only increases the acceptance among applicants but at the same time contributes to ensuring the central legal requirement of the professional relationship and relevance of the test procedure, as already mentioned above. Professional standards require the content of personnel-selection procedures to be related to the actual work performed. The reasoning for this lies in protecting an applicant's rights against irrelevant or excessive intrusion into their intimacy and privacy as well as unauthorized investigation of their personality. The procedures can refer to both direct performance requirements and contextual performance (Guenole, 2014).

A further reason for designing diagnostic procedures as contextualized as possible is the resulting increase in reliability and predictive validity for work-related success criteria (Lievens et al., 2008). The *frame-of-reference effect* responsible for this leads to higher measurement accuracy and thus greater predictive power, because it reduces intrapersonal inconsistency in the response behavior of applicants, since a *cognitive scheme* is effective for all items – in the present case "at work." Therefore, to increase criterion-related validity, the content of the procedure has to conceptually overlap with the criterion (Lievens et al., 2008).

Guenole (2015) notes that item content must be designed to "work" for a wide range of people (in this case, the working population) but still capture the underlying constructs. As a solution, he proposed transferring the item contents of "maladaptive" procedures to the occupational context and in this process clarifying questions of privacy, occupational reference, and legality. Very private or hidden aspects of personality, such as self-harming behavior, avoidance of intimacy, or generally intimate areas such as sexual behavior (but also, e.g., religiousness), are potentially problematic in the professional context (Christiansen et al., 2014; Guenole, 2015), even though many dark procedures address some of these aspects. From a legal point of view, in the event of an intrusion into the private sphere of applicants, the organization must have a convincing interest in such information and evidence of its suitability and diagnostic relevance. Applicants are likely to have a greater sensitivity to item content and its possible legality precisely in the selection context (Jackson, 2014).

Both the standard and the short procedures for recording the Dark Triad (see Section 5.2.2) do not have an occupational development background or purpose and thus have virtually no work-related items concerning success-relevant work behavior, that is, no contextualization or even a requirement reference. The main prerequisite for the permitted application of dark personality in practice is therefore to assess only those traits that are related to basic requirements of the workplace.

At the same time, work-related items and job relevance are some of the main guidance Melson-Silimon et al. (2019) gave for making dark-side assessment legally defensible in case of lawsuits. The standard procedures also contain items that can be described as even irrelevant to the job or as too invasive, because, although they do not deal with illegal areas or pose illegal questions, they do deal with very private attitudes or private life. Examples of such items in the NPI concern joy in showing off one's body, in the Mach IV one's opinion whether sick people should have the freedom to choose death, and in the SRP sex with strangers, including items of the psychopathy factor Antisocial, which ask about criminal acts actually committed, for example, on drug use, gang membership, or theft. In contrast, the DD's formulations are less problematic, although items about exploiting others or lying and cheating to get ahead may also seem too invasive for the professional context.

Overly invasive questions about the private life of applicants are prohibited by law, so assessing the psychopathy items mentioned in the personnel-selection context can be seen as highly problematic to illegal (Mathieu & Babiak, 2016a), not to mention the acceptance issues of applicants. Moreover, none of the short procedures has explicitly wording related to worklife.

Using inventories designed for the workplace – with work-related item content and wording – was recommended as one of the key aspects in making dark personality assessment legally defensible in personnel selection (Christiansen et al., 2019; van Someren et al., 2019). Although the usual scales allow for subclinical measurement, individual items are thus potentially problematic in terms of acceptance or even legality; at the very least, their content does not address the relevant requirements of the occupational context.

Conclusion
Social Validity Principles for Candidate Acceptance

As a conclusion on the subject of accepted use of Dark Triad characteristics from the applicant's perspective, it can be stated that the requirements of the concept of social validity should be observed. In particular, no information may be collected without the knowledge of the applicants; instead, it should be requested in as transparent a form as possible, and a high level of acceptance should be ensured by task- and requirement-related contents.

In light of the specifications presented in this chapter and the available information on the usual methods used for measuring the Dark Triad, none of the presented methods fully meet the requirements of an aptitude-diagnostic application in an organizational context. However, because of the increasing interest in researching the effects of dark personality traits such as narcissism, Machiavellianism, and psychopathy in professional life and the opportunities offered by the applied use of these traits specifically for aptitude diagnostics, precisely such a procedure is of major interest. What is needed is a psychometrically suitable, job-related procedure for the Dark Triad of personality which measures the characteristics jointly, multidimensionally, and meets the legal requirements of the context and the special demands made by the target group (the applicants). In the following chapter, I provide a short description of the development and validation of a test procedure that is intended to fulfil just these goals – the *Dark Triad of Personality at Work* (TOP; Schwarzinger & Schuler, 2016, 2019) – as well as initial findings on its application in personnel practice.

6 Work-Related Measurement of the Dark Triad – The Example of TOP

As the explanations in Chapter 4 have shown, the consideration of the Dark Triad in personnel work promises a potentially great benefit, as it depicts additional areas of personality relevant to professional success which are not covered by common constructs. At the same time, the evaluation of the currently available procedures in Chapter 5 made it clear that these do not allow the high professional standards required of psychodiagnostic test procedures in personnel practice to be fully maintained.

To close this gap, the Dark Triad of Personality at Work (TOP) personality test was developed between 2010 and 2015 at the Department of Psychology at the University of Hohenheim, Germany, under the guidance of Professor Heinz Schuler and published at the end of 2016 in German (Schwarzinger & Schuler, 2016). The UK and US adaptation was validated in 2019 and published, and based on this, ten further language versions are being planned between 2020 and 2023 (see reference list). This chapter describes the construction and validation of the method and reviews the requirements that have been derived regarding the necessary psychometric quality and the application-related needs of Triad measurement in practice. Using the example of current test development, I show which challenges and necessities exist for the use of the Dark Triad in vocational-aptitude diagnostics and give general recommendations for the use of narcissism, Machiavellianism, and subclinical psychopathy in human-resources work, especially in job-aptitude diagnostics.

6.1 Design of the TOP

As a personality test, the TOP was conceived as a self-description procedure and developed using classical test theory. Accordingly, I present the common parameters of item and scale development, their factorial validity, and the main and secondary quality criteria of psychological tests (see Amelang & Zielinski, 2002). For reasons of space, this presentation is provided in the form of a brief overview of the construction of the method and its most relevant parameters; I also briefly discuss secondary quality criteria such as economy of use, acceptance, or availability of norms. For further and more detailed information, please refer to the test manual (Schwarzinger & Schuler, 2016, 2019).

6.1.1 The Requirements, Objectives, and Database of Test Development and Item Construction

At the time of test design, no other method was available to measure the Dark Triad characteristics in the workplace, taking into account all derived requirements, so a complete redesign was necessary to overcome the shortcomings of existing methods. This led to the following objective of the test development: the construction of an objective, reliable, and valid personality test for the combined measurement of the Dark Triad characteristics narcissism, Machiavellianism, and subclinical psychopathy which meets the requirements for applied professional aptitude diagnostics and is accepted by the target population.

The development of the TOP was based on the stages of test development according to Bühner (2011) and initially included a careful demand analysis, planning, and literature search. Subsequently, a first test design was created, which was then optimized over several stages of item and scale analysis. Lastly, the final test version was determined by factor analysis and was then validated and standardized.

The theoretical foundation of the features to be tested included both basic and current theoretical work concerning the constructs of interest, common test procedures, and empirical work on their effects in the target field "occupation and organization." Because of the rapidly growing level of knowledge about the Dark Triad in the workplace, anyone interested in using the Dark Triad in the context of their personnel work is recommended to research the current and specifically relevant state of research.

The target group "employed persons" made it necessary to carry out all studies on persons with professional experience or working people to ensure the representativeness of the results for the later target population. The samples used originate from various industries and contexts and various hierarchical levels (from trainees to managers). Among the total of 12 individual studies, some were conducted within an organization and some were conducted independently of the employer. The overall sample consists of $N = 1{,}584$ subjects who took part in the TOP development studies between autumn 2010 and autumn 2015, 58% of whom were women; the mean age of all participants was 31 years ($SD = 11.5$). The UK/US adaptation was carried out in 2018 and 2019 with $N = 2{,}001$ employed adults; the demographics, scale statistics, and reliability data on this version are presented below.

The determination of the target group and the planned purpose of personnel selection also necessitated the formulation of items in a job-related manner to comply with the need for closest possible job and requirement reference and face validity, and to achieve the highest possible acceptance among the test persons (see Section 5.3.2). By increasing the content-related validity that can be achieved in this way, the developers also aimed at achieving a potential increase in the criterion-related validity (see Shaffer & Postlethwaite, 2012).

Scale Type and Item Construction

As is most frequently practiced for personality tests, a Likert-type rating scale was chosen as the response format for the TOP. In the present case, a 7-level (i.e., rather broad) scale was chosen (according to Bühner, 5 levels are the most common form), since more scale points allow for better differentiation of the test persons and potentially increase the reliability and validity (Bühner, 2011). The individual scale points were verbally anchored, which according to Krosnick (1999) also leads to improved reliability and validity; they were labeled as follows: *strongly disagree, disagree, slightly disagree, neutral, slightly agree, agree, strongly agree.*

All items of the TOP are coded in ascending order in the direction of construction, i.e., positively formulated in the direction of a high characteristic value. This decision was made after careful consideration of the possible advantages and disadvantages, which I will briefly discuss here. Many common inventories contain polarity changes, which serve primarily to avoid acquisition, i.e., the tendency to consent. If one considers the empirical findings on this topic, however, negatively poled items create more problems than they solve: Factor analyses of scales with alternating polarity often result in two factors (one of which usually contains the negative items). Factors of this kind have been interpreted in various studies as methodological factors (see Podsakoff et al., 2003) or as a content dimension that captures a particular response style (Steyer & Eid, 2001). Lastly, in the TOP items, alternating apparently positive aspects, such as self-assessment as an outstanding leader, and negative ones, such as one's own willingness to lie, makes mere "blind" agreement unlikely. Bühner (2011) also concluded that they are dispensable, not the least because they can simply be "overlooked," resulting in an answer contrary to the actual intention and correspondingly incorrect interpretations.

Two different methods were used to obtain and select the items, the aim being to compensate for the respective "shortcomings" of the other: First, for item formulation, the rational questionnaire construction or deductive method, which selects items according to content aspects, i.e., where an existing theoretical basis is the basis for item construction. Finally, the principle of inductive questionnaire construction was pursued using statistical analysis procedures of item reduction (e.g., factor analyses), in which the dimensions found are used for theory formation or, in the present case, for control (Bühner, 2011).

Central contents of the constructs of narcissism, Machiavellianism, and psychopathy from the item pool of existing inventories were included in the scale development by formulating their occupation-specific equivalents. The procedures used in this regard were the German NPI-R (Schütz et al., 2004), the Machiavellianism scale of Cloetta's Questionnaire for recording Machiavellianism and Conservatism (MK; 1972), and the Kiel Psychopathy Inventory (Köhler et al., in preparation). For translating the contents into the professional context, the goal was to transfer the content, such as a certain behavior or characteristic, but of course not to copy the original items. To give an example:

- Item from the MK: "Almost all people are only concerned with personal gain in what they do."
- Item transferred to the professional context: "At our company, everyone only looks out for themselves."

Further items were constructed utilizing an expert survey based on definitions of constructs (and their subscales) or diagnostic characteristics according to DSM (see Section 2.1.1). The $N=7$ participants were, on the one hand, scientists with a focus on aptitude diagnostics and, on the other hand, personnel practitioners with many years of experience in personnel selection, with frequent direct contact with applicants and customers in high-level to top hierarchical positions in fields such as industry and management consultancy.

All items formulated in this way were assigned to the subscales and factors of the Triad constructs derived from the theory (see Section 3.3.3). Since this did not allow for an equal representation of all subscales, the authors of the TOP "filled up" scales that consisted of only a few items (again deductively based on the definitions of the expert survey). Special attention was paid to introducing aspects that had been missing until then. Finally, all items were reviewed according to the common rules for item formulation (e.g., no double negations) and improved where necessary. The result was a total of 433 work-related Dark Triad items which formed the basis for the following quantitative and statistically oriented test development.

6.1.2 Item Analyses and Dimensionality Testing: The Structure of the TOP

To evaluate the item raw value distributions in the present case, span, skewness, and kurtosis were initially tested on a first sample (N=105). Any items that appeared to be problematic concerning at least one of the criteria mentioned were removed, and the remaining items were grouped into the theoretically intended scales and examined for difficulty, discriminatory power, and homogeneity. A total of 170 items remained after this procedure for further test development.

To verify the factorial structure underlying the TOP items, the authors collected additional data and calculated exploratory and confirmatory factor analyses (structural equation models). After a first exploration of possible dimensions of the item material, we examined the obtained factor solution again exploratively on an independent dataset and slightly revised it, finally verifying the resulting version of the TOP by confirmatory analysis (such a multistage procedure was also used by Jones & Paulhus, 2014, in the construction of their SD 3).

Because of the described overlaps in the content of the examined Triad components, the first set of factor analyses was not calculated based on all items, but separately for the three constructs. The alternative would have potentially led to a strong reduction of the dimensions and thus of the displayed contents already in the first stage. The goal of a multidimensional measurement of the Dark Triad derived in Chapter 5, on the other hand, requires an as multilayered as possible representation of the facets of narcissism, Machiavellianism, and psychopathy.

Principal axis factor analysis (PAF) and maximum likelihood factor analysis (ML) are suitable for finding latent dimensions in item material (see Bühner, 2011). The first step foresees a separate analysis of the items of the constructs narcissism, Machiavellianism, and psychopathy by PAF. ML was also used in the joint factorial testing of all Triad items, since the results of this step were later verified by confirmation, for which ML provides a good basis (Bühner, 2011). In each case, Promax (for oblique, i.e., correlated factors) was chosen as the rotation technique, as this is the method of choice for the factors present here, which are assumed to be correlated; it is suitable for achieving a so-called "simple solution" (Bühner, 2011).

For reasons of space, I do not show the results of the first analyses separated by constructs here. The goal of reducing the number of 170 items while retaining the full content of the characteristics as far as possible was achieved, since theoretically meaningful interpretable scales could be delimited despite the significantly reduced number of items. In the next step, the 120 remaining items were examined together, and thus the factorial structure of the entire Dark Triad and the mapping of its scales by the items of the TOP were checked on a dataset of N=334. The aim was to find as many aspects of the items subsumed under the Triad constructs as possible in the factorial solution, which is why, for example, no extraction techniques were carried out with a "constraint" on three factors. One should check whether the scales found in separate analyses can be further delimited when the TOP items are analyzed together.

I briefly present the results here. The initial eigenvalue curve points to 28 factors. The Scree-Test speaks only for 5 factors. The parallel analysis according to Horn points to 15 factors, the MAP test (minimum average partial test) in the original version to 12 factors, in the revised version to 18. 15 factors can be interpreted clearly (eigenvalues: 24.9; 10.5; 3.9; 3.6; 3.4; 2.6; 2.5; 2.3; 2.1; 2.1; 1.9; 1.7; 1.6; 1.5; 1.5). At least three items load on these with at least .35 which do not have cross-loadings with other factors, which would make their interpretation difficult. A total of 73 items could be extracted, representing 15 occupation-related components of the Dark Triad characteristics.

Based on this research version, further studies were subsequently conducted to obtain additional samples independent of the first dataset. Thereupon, the final factorial structure and item composition were determined.

The new data obtained were divided according to the proposal of Fabrigar et al. (1999) to determine the final version of the procedure through independent exploratory and confirmatory factor analyses. For this purpose, the factor structure of the TOP research version was replicated and slightly revised in a partial dataset ($N=391$); it was then examined whether the scales found in the TOP are based on the three Dark Triad constructs. The structural model for the TOP procedure derived based on these exploratory analyses was then checked for its fit on a second, independent dataset ($N=263$).

For the replication of the factorial structure, a total of five individual samples from different occupational contexts, age groups, and hierarchical levels were combined to achieve the most representative representation of the target population possible, and ML and PAF were calculated with the criterion eigenvalue >1. Both methods produced quasi-identical factor solutions. The initial eigenvalue curve indicates 15 factors each, the extracted factors 11 (eigenvalues: 17.1; 8.4; 3.1; 2.9; 2.1; 1.9; 1.8; 1.7; 1.5; 1.4; 1.4). The Scree-Test speaks for 4 factors. The parallel analysis points to 12 factors. The MAP test, in both the original and revised versions, indicates 11 factors. 11 factors can also be meaningfully interpreted in both analysis methods. The solutions also show identical scales and almost identical item assignments and sequences. The method invariance indicates a stable solution. In addition, the factors represent an extensive replication of the initial factor solution of the research version and reflect the theoretically expected subscales. Thus, both statistical and logical reasons speak for the solutions found. The decision was finally made in favor of the PAF solution with 60 items, as it has slightly lower cross-loadings than the ML.

Eleven of the 15 scales of the initial solution could be replicated and were named according to their content as follows: need for authority, extenuation, assertiveness, flexibility, claim to leadership, impulsivity, appetite for risk, skepticism, unsentimentality, sense of superiority, and belief in persuasive power. Thus, many central aspects discussed under the Triad characteristics are available as delimitable scales in the occupationally related item material of the TOP (see Table 3). In other words, the desired multidimensional measurement of the Dark Triad is possible with the TOP.

Table 3 presents the factors of the TOP and their origin. The scales of the TOP research version or the original constructs from which the new factor is derived are shown in the left-hand column of the predecessor column for the final version (if different from the original construct, this is indicated in brackets).

Table 3: TOP-60: Factors, origin, and assignment to theoretical bases

<table>
<tr><th></th><th colspan="2">Original scales and constructs</th><th>TOP research version</th><th>TOP</th></tr>
<tr><td rowspan="5">Narcissism</td><td>Emmons (1984, 1987):</td><td>Raskin & Terry (1988), Schütz et al. (2004):</td><td></td><td></td></tr>
<tr><td>Exploitativeness/ Entitlement</td><td>Entitlement/ Dominance, Exploitiveness, Entitlement</td><td>Authority/ Dominance</td><td>Need for Authority</td></tr>
<tr><td>Leadership/ Authority</td><td>Leadership Personality; Authority, Ambition/Leadership</td><td>Leadership Capacities</td><td>Claim to Leadership</td></tr>
<tr><td>Self-Absorption/ Self-Admiration</td><td>Independence/ Influence, Self-Sufficiency, Physical vanity, Vanity</td><td>Admiration</td><td rowspan="2">Sense of Superiority</td></tr>
<tr><td>Superiority/ Arrogance</td><td>Arrogance/Superiority, Sense of Superiority, Superiority, Exhibitionism</td><td>Grandiosity</td></tr>
<tr><td rowspan="4">Machiavellianism</td><td colspan="2">Christie & Geis (1970), Jones & Paulhus (2009):</td><td></td><td></td></tr>
<tr><td>Views</td><td></td><td>Mistrust/Cynicism</td><td>Skepticism</td></tr>
<tr><td rowspan="2">Tactics</td><td></td><td>Toughness (psychopathy)/ Results Oriented</td><td rowspan="2">Assertiveness</td></tr>
<tr><td></td><td>Strategic Contact Behavior</td></tr>
</table>

Table 3: Continued

	Original scales and constructs		TOP research version	TOP
Psychopathy	Cooke & Michie (2001):	Hare (2003):		
	Arrogant and Deceitful Interpersonal Style	Cunning-manipulative, Glibness/Superficial Charm, Grandiose Sense of Self-Worth	Manipulative Charm	Belief in Persuasive Power
		Pathological Lying	Willingness to Lie	Extenuation
	Deficient Affective Experience	Shallow Affect	Flat Affective Life	Unsentimentality
		Callous/Lack of Empathy	Emotional Coldness	
	Impulsive and Irresponsible Behavioral Style	Irresponsibility, Failure to Accept Responsibility, Lack of Remorse/Guilt	Irresponsibility	Flexibility
		Parasitic Lifestyle, Lack of Realistic, Long Term Goals	Lack of Career Goals	
		Need for Stimulation	Appetite for Risk	Appetite for Risk
		Impulsivity	Impulsivity	Impulsivity

Note. Reprinted with permission from *Dark Triad of Personality at Work* (TOP) (UK/US Adaptation) by D. Schwarzinger & H. Schuler, 2019, p. 29.© Hogrefe.

The Structure of the TOP

To clarify which structure underlies the scales and thus what the internal structure of TOP is, ML and PAF were calculated for the scales, in this case also with a constraint on three factors. For PAF and ML, both with the criterion eigenvalue >1 and with a constraint on three factors, the initial eigenvalues (3.8; 2.3; 1.0; 0.7), scree plot, and parallel analysis indicate three factors. The same three factors can be meaningfully interpreted. The MAP test in both versions indicates only two factors. The decision was made in favor of the ML solution because, on the one hand, it has fewer cross-loadings than the PAF and, on the other hand, the loadings of the scales on the factors are somewhat higher.

The first factor found in the TOP is made up of the three scales theoretically associated with the construct narcissism, namely, the claim to leadership, the need for authority, and the feeling of superiority as well as the "psychopathy scales" of belief in persuasive power and appetite for risk. Regarding the belief in persuasive power, this can be explained theoretically quite well: Individual items of the underlying scale grandiosity have "migrated" from psychopathy to narcissism in previous reduction steps, which explains the connection statistically. The great similarity in the content of the first psychopathy factor with narcissism has also often been discussed in the literature (see Chapters 3 and 4). In particular, the superficial charm and exaggerated self-esteem of the psychopath, which are captured by the belief in persuasive power scale, represent narcissistic aspects. On the second scale, appetite for risk, there is also evidence of an increased risk appetite among narcissists, which was also demonstrated regarding the profession (Campbell et al., 2004; Emmons, 1981; Foster et al., 2009). Since the factor contains related content of a different construct, it was not referred to as narcissism, but as Self-Centered Work Approach – a specific work-related variant of narcissism – not the least to emphasize the specific occupational background of the procedure.

For the same reasons, the second factor, which is a broad professional representation of the Machiavellianism construct, was named Enforcement-Focused Work Attitude. In addition to the theoretically expected scales of skepticism and assertiveness – of which the latter in turn has received "psychopathy items" in previous steps – that comprise most of the items initially written for Machiavellianism, it also contains the "psychopathy scale" of unsentimentality. This empirical assignment can be explained since emotional coldness or detachment from the beginning of scientific research are emphasized aspects of the Machiavellianism construct ("cool-syndrome") and empirically show a close relationship to it (see Chapters 3 and 4).

Finally, the psychopathic core characteristics of the third factor Lifestyle according to Hare (2003) and Impulsive and Irresponsible Behavior Style according to Cooke and Michie (2001) remained for the third factor. It was therefore named Uncommitted-Impulsive Work Style. It comprises work-related items that tap the impulsivity and other aspects of the psychopath's irresponsible lifestyle (lack of goal orientation, irresponsibility, nonplanfulness), i.e., contents that are hardly associated with the other Triad constructs and are seen as distinguishing features from them (Mathieu & Babiak, 2016a; see also Section 3.3.3). In addition, it contains the scale extenuation, the content of which – "lies" – is a well-established part of psychopathy, located on the first factor Interpersonal in the Hare model. This classification can be explained both content-wise and empirically. The willingness to lie and cheat classically has high correlations to aspects of the factor Lifestyle in the common psychopathy models. In the work-related item material, lying is more likely to be associated with the other rule-breaking aspects of the factor Uncommitted-Impulsive Work Style than with the contents of Self-Centered Work Approach.

Thus, both statistical and logical reasons speak for the solution found, which, however, represents an empirical factorial delimitation of the Triad constructs but not completely and purely theory-conforming factors. The empirical factorial solution for the Dark Triad thus differs from standard Dark Triad factor solutions, but it can be explained in terms of content and described as a mapping of its central core content in the form of occupationally relevant excerpts of the constructs.

The TOP scales are thus based on three factors that can be described as occupational variants of narcissism, Machiavellianism, and subclinical psychopathy. However, the first two have broader content than theoretically expected and Uncommitted-Impulsive Work Style represents only a subset of psychopathy, namely, the third factor Lifestyle. Table 4 shows the empirical Dark Triad solution of the TOP scales.

Table 4: TOP-60 Scales 3-Factor Solution

	Self-centered work approach	Enforcement-focused work attitude	Uncommitted-impulsive work style
Claim to leadership	.95	–.07	–.24
Belief in persuasive power (psychopathy)	.81	–.17	.06
Need for authority	.70	.13	.05
Appetite for risk (psychopathy)	.64	.09	–.21
Sense of superiority	.60	.03	.25
Unsentimentality (psychopathy)	–.11	.94	–.23
Assertiveness	.06	.69	.16
Skepticism	.01	.51	.22
Flexibility	–.23	–.12	.61
Impulsivity	.05	.17	.44
Extenuation	.11	.21	.42

Note. Reprinted with permission from *Dark Triad of Personality at Work* (TOP) (UK/US Adaptation) by D. Schwarzinger & H. Schuler, 2019, p. 32. © Hogrefe.

Based on the two explorative analysis steps described above, a structure is assumed for the TOP which consists of the 11 subscales found and the three factors above them: Self-Centered Work Approach, Enforcement-Focused Work Attitude, and Uncommitted-Impulsive Work Style (Dark Triad model). Its structure is empirically derived and well illustrates the theoretical expectations of the Dark Triad characteristics, which is why this model was tested for its fit. For purposes of comparison, the further theoretical suggestions on the Dark Triad structure discussed in Section 3.3.1 were considered, which seem possible for the TOP scales. Accordingly, the structure above the scales could be described by a latent factor (dark g-factor model) or two factors (dark dyad model) – the latter when Machiavellianism and psychopathy are combined into one factor.

Following Fabrigar et al. (1999), this was carried out on a dataset independent of the exploratory analysis (N=263). For the model, the recommended fit indices are given: χ^2 with p-value, CFI (comparative fit index), RMSEA (root mean square error of approximation), and SRMR (standardized root mean residual) (see Beauducel & Wittmann, 2005; Bühner, 2011).

First, the Dark Triad model was tested, in which the 60 items in the 11 scales found are based on three latent factors. As expected, the Chi-square value is very high at χ^2=2909.802

(df=1697; χ^2/df=1.71), indicating that the model does not fit the data (p=.000; Bollen-Stine corrected p=.001). However, the RMSEA of .052 is below the maximum limit of .06 for the sample size, the 90% confidence interval does not include 0, and the upper limit of .055 is within the specified range. The probability p=.127 also indicates that the RMSEA does not deviate significantly from a value of .05. The CFI of .825 is slightly below the required minimum limit of "by .95." The SRMR of .0901 is within the desired range mentioned by Hu and Bentler (1999) of<.11 and close to the value of .08 often mentioned for a good fit.

With two out of four limits met, the global fit measures of the model are not fully satisfactory. However, all variables have significant relationships to the latent factors. Furthermore, no standardized regression weight is much above 1, which would indicate estimation problems. The error variances are also all significantly different from 0. In principle, this speaks in favor of a local model fit (see Bühner, 2011).

Next, the models with two factors (dark dyad) and one factor (dark g-factor) were modeled on the same dataset and using the same procedure. The dark dyad model has almost the same fit as the Dark Triad model, each with slightly weaker fit values: χ^2 (1699)=2937.819 (p=.000; Bollen-Stine corrected p=.001; χ^2/df=1.73); RMSEA=.053 (CI 90: .050–.056), p=.079; SRMR=.0922; CFI=.821. The dark g-factor model has worse fit values than the other two. With χ^2 (1700)=3112.966 (p=.000; Bollen-Stine corrected p=.001; χ^2/df=1.83); RMSEA=.056 (CI 90: .053–.059), p=.001; SRMR=.1109; CFI=.796 it can only be considered a good fit according to one of the fit indices. Although the RMSEA range is below .06, the p-value of .001 indicates that it deviates significantly from an RMSEA=.05.

The Dark Triad model with a three-factor structure above the scales, which was explored for the TOP, has the best fit values in comparison, almost identical to the two-factor model (dark dyad). The Dark Triad model has a significantly better fit than the single factor model with $\Delta\chi^2$ (3)=203.164 (p=.001) and than the two-factor model with $\Delta\chi^2$ (2)=28.017 (p=.001). A three-factor structure thus explains the data better than is possible with one or two factors.

However, two of the fit indices of this model are considered too low by current standards, which is why the structure cannot be considered fully confirmed from a confirmation point of view. In addition to the content reasons known from research on the Triad constructs, such as the high intercorrelation of the scales within but also across construct boundaries (see Chapter 3), it should be noted – with limitations on the method used – that models from multi-item questionnaire studies are difficult to confirm with strict test procedures, such as the Chi-square statistics. Marsh et al. (2004), for example, point out that in questionnaire studies with many individual items the cut-off values are usually hard to meet. Hu and Bentler (1999) state that the cut-off values of fit indices are probably better understood as rules of thumb, which in some cases lead to incorrect estimates.

A modification of the model based on existing modification indices, by establishing further relationships between variables, makes no sense in the present case of testing the structure of a test procedure, since test items or scales can only be assigned to one scale or factor in this case. According to Bühner (2011, p. 429), this "purely statistical approach" is merely an exploratory approach to a suitable structure and should therefore be rejected. For this reason, other possible approaches, such as ESEM or B-ESEM (see Section 3.3.1) shown by McLarnon and Tarraf (2017), which aim to explain as much variance as possible, were not considered appropriate for the present case.

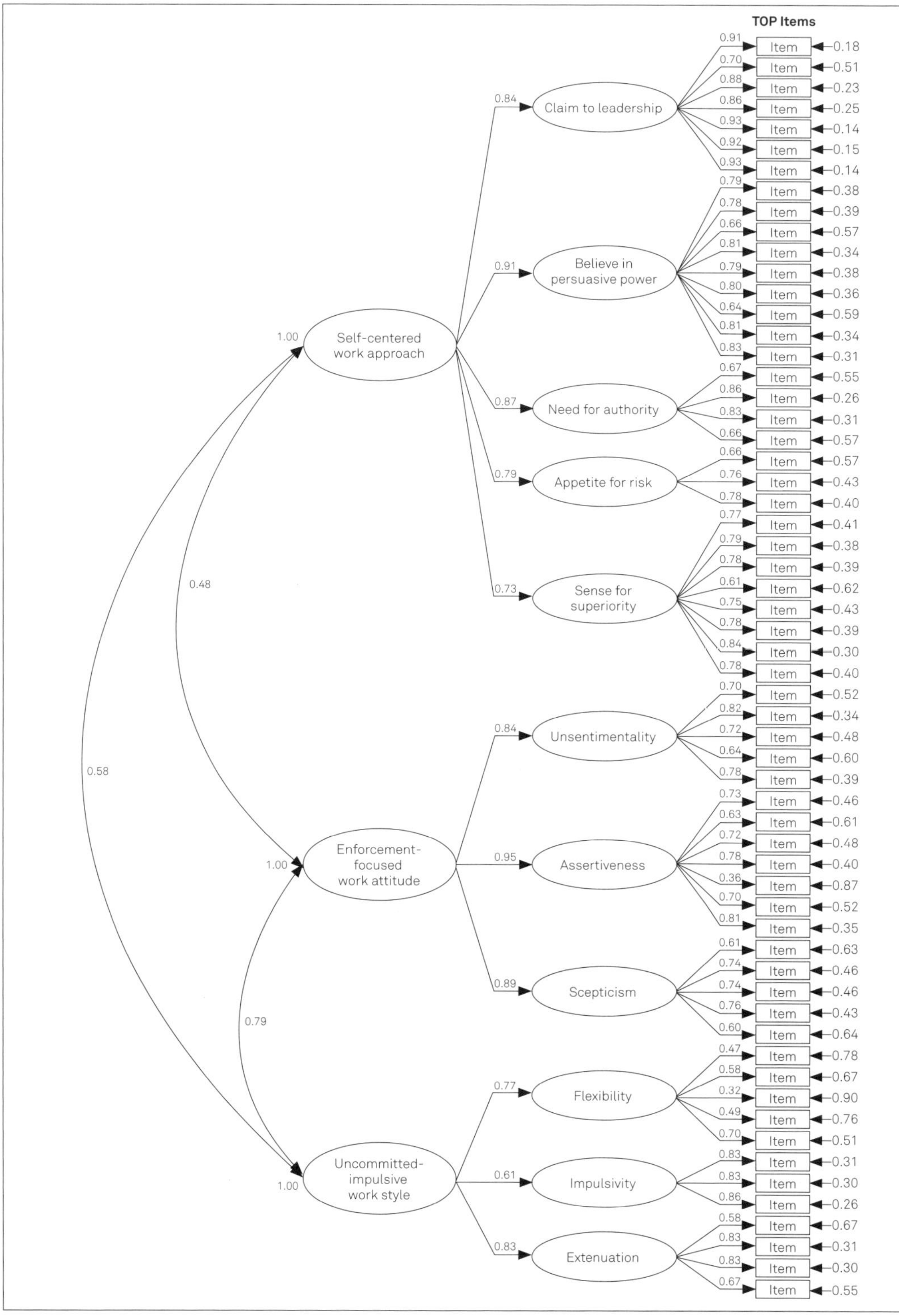

Figure 4: TOP-60: Structural model of 60 items and the latent scales and factors in the pilot 2 study sample ($N = 369$). Reprinted with permission from *Dark Triad of Personality at Work* (TOP) (UK/US Adaptation) by D. Schwarzinger & H. Schuler, 2019, p. 58, Hogrefe. © Hogrefe 2019.

From the theoretical as well as the empirical work on the Dark Triad, we know that there is a large number of shared contents and common variance of the features and their scales, which suggests that further covariance and potential paths between the variables of the model can be modeled (and possibly further variance explanation can be achieved by establishing a bifactor). For a test procedure, however, one should check whether the assumed main structure, i.e., the central relationships between the scales and factors, can be confirmed and whether empirical data can be described with the structure that a test intends and purports to measure. In the present case, the focus thus lies on proving the structural construct-related validity of a procedure for concrete use cases – not on examining the general structure of the Triad characteristics. In operative use, results are calculated for concrete scales and constructs and used and reported accordingly. In test development, it must therefore be demonstrated that these are suitable for validly describing the data structure. The fact that other structures can be modeled for the Triad constructs themselves, measured with any Triad method and thus also the TOP – and that these may have better fit values – remains unaffected.

It can therefore be stated that, from a confirmatory point of view, the theoretically well-fitting solution, determined empirically via three steps of exploratory factor analyses, cannot be fully confirmed but has acceptable fit dimensions. Against the background of the complexity of the model and the synopsis of all indices and the discussion about them, one can assume that the three-factor model represents a largely meaningful representation of the data. Therefore, this model is assumed to be the best possible structural description of the item contents of the TOP for practical purposes and thus "the structure of the TOP." This has since also been replicated with essentially the same fit-index pattern in the English version and several additional language versions (see Schwarzinger & Schuler, 2016, 2019, 2020, 2021a, b, c, 2022a, b). Figure 4 shows the Dark Triad model with 60 items, the 11 scales, and the three factors latently behind them of the UK/US adaptation.

6.2 Reliability, Validity, and Standardization

This section presents data from the TOP test manuals (Schwarzinger & Schuler, 2016, 2019) and intends to show the extent to which a reliable and valid measurement of the Dark Triad is fundamentally possible with a work-related procedure, and which considerations and analyses are relevant if characteristics of the Dark Triad are to be used for operative personnel work. The general discussion is therefore based mainly on the German original development, though the most important psychometric properties of the UK/US adaptation are also presented alongside to highlight the psychometric quality of the English version of TOP and its suitability for occupational aptitude diagnostics.

6.2.1 Objectivity, Reliability, and Distributional Characteristics

The quality criterion of objectivity requires that the test results be independent of the test user in their execution, evaluation, and interpretation (Lienert & Raatz, 1994). These requirements relate primarily to the application of a test, which is why ensuring objectivity in practical use is of decisive importance. The TOP test manual contains all the necessary instructions for the objectively correct administration, evaluation, and interpretation of the procedure (see Schwarzinger & Schuler, 2016, 2019). An objective recording of the Dark Triad is therefore basically possible with the TOP. Particularly in the case of characteristics such as narcissism, about which, on the one hand, there are common concepts that are complex and multilayered, a high degree of objectivity in recording and interpretation should be ensured in any use of personnel psychology, primarily through the construction of suitable procedures and scales, such as behavior-based grading scales in interviews or assessment center exercises (see Schuler, 2004).

For any scale, but especially for test development, the question of reliability, i.e., measurement accuracy or freedom from measurement errors, is crucial (Bühner, 2011). There are various approaches to this, and for the investigation of the TOP several were used to ensure the most multifaceted consideration possible. As one measure for the internal consistency of the scales, the value of Cronbach's alpha as well as the mean correlations between the items (MIC) and split-half reliabilities were calculated. These measures indicate how closely the items or contents of a scale correspond and are, for example, strongly dependent on the length of the scale (Schmitt, 1996). Jonason and Webster (2010) describe an alpha of less than .70 as acceptable for a scale with only 4 items, for example. According to Schmitt (1996), however, the brevity of a scale is not an argument or even a cure for lack of alpha reliability, whereas low alphas are legitimate if the scale justifies it in terms of its content. A scale should be neither too homogeneous nor too heterogeneous, and deviations should be judged against the background of the content and the length of the scale. In most cases, a Cronbach's alpha of .70 to .80 is considered good; the split-half reliability should be in a similar range, and the mean item intercorrelation should lie between .20 and .40 (Bühner, 2011).

Both the Spearman-Brown formula and the Guttman formula, the latter of which is considered more conservative, were used to determine the split-half reliability. Scales with an odd number of items lead to unequal subscales in the case of splits, which is why a Spearman-Brown formula specific to this purpose was used. The test stability or retest reliability was determined for a short period of time (2 to 4 weeks) and for half a year. The retest reliability depends on the stability of the feature and the timespan of the measurement. It should be as high as possible: For personality tests, it is .79 on average, and in a comparative study of several personality tests, for half of all the methods examined it was between .71 and .86 (Amelang & Schmidt-Atzert, 2006).

To assess the distributional properties of the TOP scales and factors, their mean value, standard deviation, skewness, and kurtosis were tested. These measures allow a statement to be made about the response behavior of the subjects regarding the items on the underlying scale and thus an assessment of whether the responses are scattered over the entire scale width and all value ranges are present, i.e., whether the required subclinical, normally distributed measurement of the Dark Triad is possible with the TOP. Not necessary for a normal distribution, but desirable for practical purposes, are mean values in the theoretical middle of the scale and, in the case of a 7-step scale, operationally well-applicable standard deviations around the value $SD=1$. Such a normal distribution around the center of the scale describes a suitable scattering on both sides of the distribution and is thus able to make differences between persons visible. The normal distribution property of a scale can be assessed with appropriate tests or, in the case of samples larger than $N=400$ – as is here the case and therefore used – also using skewness in the range −0.5 to +0.5 and kurtosis values between −1 and +1 (see Lienert & Raatz, 1994).

The factor Self-Centered Work Approach consists of 31 items, and its contents are most widely represented in the TOP with five subscales. In the German normative sample (N = 1,318), this yielded a mean value at the midpoint of the 7-point scale (M = 4.08) and a standard deviation of close to 1, good kurtosis, and skewness – very good distributional properties. Alpha, split-half, and retest reliability values of around or above .90 indicate high homogeneity and measurement stability. This pattern applies in a slightly weakened form to all subscales except appetite for risk, which, despite a high inter-item correlation, shows a low Cronbach's alpha and a rather weak retest reliability; one reason could be the brevity of the scale of only 3 items. This interpretation is supported by the fact that the scale need for authority, with 4 items, also consistently shows the second-worst values. The MIC values are high on all subscales and indicate that the items are rather close in terms of content.

The Enforcement-Focused Work Attitude factor can be considered stable and sufficiently homogeneous, with slightly weaker but consistently similar values to Self-Centered Work Approach. All subscale values lie within the required ranges. The only exception to this, for which no explanation can be offered, is the retest reliability over half a year for unsentimentality, which is clearly too low (in the UK/US-adaptation, for example, it is .73, thus at an acceptable level). Their Enforcement-Focused Work Attitude is rated by the test subjects on average lower than the middle of the scale (M = 3.37), but the values still follow a normal distribution. This also applies to the factor Uncommitted-Impulsive Work Style, which, with an average scale value of just over three (M = 3.17) and a slightly left-steep distribution, is the part of the TOP for which the test subjects give the lowest values. Alpha, split-half, and retest reliability values of more than .70 to mostly around .80 prove its good reliability; the comparatively low long-term measurement stability of the subscales is a weakness of the German version. During the adaptation to UK–US, therefore, also new items were tested to optimize psychometric properties. Table 5 shows the reliability of the English version of TOP.

In summary, the TOP has the necessary reliability for a suitability diagnostic use, in both language versions. Most of the various reliability parameters were met to the required extent. This applies unreservedly to the factors.

Distribution characteristics indicate a normal distribution of values that produces sufficient variance. Thus, TOP enables a dimensional, subclinical measurement of the Dark Triad, and the value distributions also reflect respondents' response behavior, which makes it seem possible to collect useful data in occupational contexts using TOP (in high-stakes settings, the distribution characteristics remain pretty much the same, see below). Thus, not only are very negative answers given (indicated, e.g., by low mean values around 2, which would indicate a negative attitude toward and potential problems with the items), but also those that are scattered across the entire scale width. As a practical recommendation for the development of further methods and scales for the Dark Triad, one should therefore aim for a normal distribution of the values. The highest possible reliability must be ensured in any case, just like the objectivity discussed at the beginning of this section.

Table 5: Reliability of TOP scales

Factor/subscale	Items	r_{tt}	Mean IC	α	$α_{uk}$	$α_{us}$	$α_{mgt}$
Self-centered work approach	31	0.93	0.42	.96	.96	.95	.95
Claim to leadership	7	0.90	0.69	.94	.94	.93	.90
Belief in persuasive power	9	0.86	0.53	.91	.92	.91	.89
Need for authority	4	0.85	0.50	.80	.79	.81	.76
Appetite for risk	3	0.79	0.49	.74	.77	.73	.76
Sense of superiority	8	0.86	0.52	.90	.90	.89	.88
Enforcement-focused work attitude	17	0.85	0.26	.86	.86	.86	.87
Unsentimentality	5	0.73	0.28	.65	.65	.66	.68
Assertiveness	7	0.81	0.32	.77	.79	.75	.76
Skepticism	5	0.79	0.37	.75	.73	.76	.76
Uncommitted-impulsive work style	12	0.84	0.24	.79	.75	.80	.84
Flexibility	5	0.71	0.19	.52	.41	.55	.62
Impulsivity	3	0.78	0.60	.82	.82	.81	.84
Extenuation	4	0.81	0.40	.73	.73	.71	.76

Note. Items: number of items on the scale; *rtt:* test-retest reliability estimated in the pilot 2 research sample, n = 335; Mean IC = average item intercorrelation in the combined UK and US standardization sample (N = 2,001); α = Cronbach's Alpha estimated in the combined UK and US standardization sample (N = 2,001); $α_{uk}$ = Cronbach's Alpha estimated in the UK working population (N = 1,001); $α_{us}$ = Cronbach's alpha estimated in the US working population (N = 1,000); αmgt: Cronbach's alpha estimated in the managerial population (N = 435). Reprinted with permission from "*Dark Triad of Personality at Work* (TOP)" (UK/US Adaptation) by D. Schwarzinger & H. Schuler, 2019, p. 56. © Hogrefe AG.

6.2.2 Construct-Related Validity: Standard Scales, Personality Models, and Relationships to Procedures and Constructs Used in Aptitude Diagnostics

In the context of construct-related validation, the aim is to investigate the extent to which a test measures the property it claims to measure (as is a common, concise definition of construct validity, see Bühner, 2011). There are various strategies for this purpose (see Box 5).

Box 5: Strategies for Checking the Construct-Related Validity

- One of these can be seen in the already described investigations of the *factorial structure* of the TOP, by which the Dark Triad constructs and their partial aspects were delimited.
- The most important approach, however, is to examine the relationships of a procedure to other, similar constructs. From the comparison with procedures that adequately represent the construct, it can be deduced – if there is a sufficiently high degree of agreement – that the test is *convergently valid for the construct.*
- There is also the question of the *discriminatory construct-related validity of* a test, i.e., its differentiability from other related constructs or procedures. Ideally, all constructs to be investigated are covered by several methods.
- The results can then be summarized in a *multitrait-multimethod matrix*, where the same constructs should be linked as closely as possible across methods, but it should be possible to distinguish between different constructs within a method.

As explained in Section 5.1.2, at the time of test development, apart from self-assessments, no demonstrably valid methods for recording the Dark Triad, such as third-party assessments or interviews, were available. Therefore, the TOP was examined only regarding its construct-related validity in comparison to other test procedures. Future studies on the Dark Triad in the occupational context should ideally include additional procedures and diagnostic approaches to examine not only the construct validity of the individual procedures but also the incremental benefit of different modes of aptitude diagnostics in the measurement and use of the Dark Triad in personnel work.

In the present case, three questions were of particular importance which have been discussed and therefore examined many times in the history of research on the Dark Triad. For a procedure for the combined measurement of characteristics, such as the TOP, its internal validity should be examined, i.e., how high the characteristics, operationalized as scales of the test, are themselves related. In addition, relationships with standard procedures for measuring the Dark Triad are reported to assess the extent to which the Dark Triad is measured, albeit concerning the profession. Also examined were the position of the TOP scales in general, broad personality models, and the validity of the TOP regarding constructs that are demonstrably significant in their later target field, the professional and especially the personnel-selection context: cognitive abilities, professional interests, performance motivation, and social competence as well as political skills.

Among the most valid "criteria" for testing what a method measures are the standard procedures that have been used to obtain most of the information on the constructs in question (see Section 5.2.2). The findings obtained by these scales not only represent large parts of the state of research on the constructs, in the case of narcissism and Machiavellianism even the initial (subclinical) construct was explicitly seen in the manifest results on the NPI and Mach IV scales (see Section 3.1). Therefore, in the present case, the German-language procedures were used for construct-related validation, from which the greatest possible comparability with the standard procedures was expected. The relationship of the TOP to narcissism was assessed using the German-language version of the NPI by Schütz et al. (2004). Of the various translations of the Mach IV into German, the scale M of the MK (Machiavellianism/Conservatism) by Cloetta (1972) shows the greatest agreement in terms of content with the original Mach IV. To measure psychopathy, the KPI of Köhler et al. (in preparation) was used, which is an original development but was constructed according to the concept of psychopathy by Hare. The first part of the KPI was used to measure the three core characteristics of personality psychology or the first three factors of psychopathy. In the KPI they are called Superficial Charm/Grandiosity, Coldhearted/Unemotional, and Manipulative/Impulsive Lifestyle. In addition, the relationships of the TOP to the widely used short scales for the Dark Triad DD and SD 3 were surveyed (discussed in Section 5.2.2).

To assess the construct validity of a scale, it is useful to take a closer look at its "location" in the reference model of empirical personality research – the FFM. In addition, the connections of the TOP with the scales of the HEXACO model are reported, since this model, as explained in Section 2.1.2, contains a promising additional factor (especially for research into the Dark Triad), the "H-factor" or Honesty-Humility (Ashton & Lee, 2007). The NEO Five Factor Inventory (NEO-FFI; official German version by Borkenau & Ostendorf, 2008) was used to measure the Big Five. The HEXACO factors according to Lee and Ashton were recorded with the HEXACO-60 Personality Inventory (HEXACO-60; Ashton & Lee, 2009). Table 6 presents the central relationships of the TOP factors to each other and to related scales and general personality models.

Self-Centered Work Approach and Enforcement-Focused Work Attitude are related at r=.26, Enforcement-Focused Work Attitude and Uncommitted-Impulsive Work Style at r=.53, and Self-Centered Work Approach and Uncommitted-Impulsive Work Style at r=.22. Thus, the first two relationships are somewhat less close in the TOP but about the same amount as found in three meta-analyses for the Dark Triad (see Section 3.3.1). The latter relationship (narcissism and psychopathy) is the weakest in the TOP and differs the most from meta-analytical results. In O'Boyle et al. (2012), the characteristics relate at r=.51, the other two meta-analyses, in contrast, come at r=.38 (Muris et al., 2017; Vize, Lynam et al., 2018). The weaker relationship in the TOP is because of the "empirical conception" of its psychopathy scale, which does not measure the full psychopathy construct but only the contents of the third factor Lifestyle.

The factor Self-Centered Work Approach has reasonable convergent validity with the NPI and the corresponding factor of SD 3, but low (r=.24) with that of DD. There is very good discriminant validity with the MK and the Machiavellianism and psychopathy scales of the short procedures (expressed by the closeness of the correlation being even less than that found meta-analytically for the characteristics). On the other hand, there is a connection to the KPI at r=.64, which is closer than meta-analyses suggest (there it is between .53 and .59), and on the TOP side again can be explained with psychopathy characteristics, such as superficial charm and need for stimulation (TOP scales belief in persuasive power and appetite for risk), on the TOP factor Self-Centered Work Approach. Enforcement-Focused Work Attitude has a good convergent validity to the corresponding factor in SD 3 and MK, but not in the DD with r=.34. Differentiation from the other characteristics is successful against the background of the existing overlapping of the characteristics and the relationships expected according to the meta-analyses. Uncommitted-Impulsive Work Style shows both discriminant and convergent validity compared to the standard procedures, but to a lesser extent (e.g., r=.50 for the KPI), which can be explained by the limitations of the empirical concept of the factor Uncommitted-Impulsive Work Style. This is not the case with the short scales. The TOP "psychopathy scale" has a slightly higher correlation with the Machiavellianism factor than with the psychopathy factor of the short scales, though the level corresponds roughly to that which has been meta-analytically proven (see Section 3.3.1).

Table 6: Relationships of the TOP Factors to Standard, Short, and Personality Procedures

	Self-centered work approach	Enforcement focused work attitude	Uncommitted-impulsive work style
Self-centered work approach	–	.26**	.22**
Enforcement-focused work attitude	–	–	.53**
NPI	.59**	.23*	.19
MK	.29**	.69**	.53**
KPI	.64**	.47**	.50**
SD 3 Narcissism	.56**	.27**	.42**
SD 3 Machiavellian-ism	.18*	.64**	.56**
SD 3 Psychopathy	.12	.28**	.53**
DD Narcissism	.24**	.35**	.61**
DD Machiavellianism	.22*	.34**	.52**
DD Psychopathy	.09	.28**	.43**
NEO_Neuroticism	–.29**	.27**	.38**
NEO_Extraversion	.40**	–.13	–.03
NEO_Openess	.04	–.21*	–.09
NEO_Agreeableness	–.54**	–.57**	–.56**
NEO_Conscientious-ness	.04	–.02	–.34**
Honesty-Humility	–.47**	–.44**	–.52**
Emotionality	–.35**	.00	.15
Extraversion	.36**	–.33**	–.17
Agreeableness	–.38**	–.32**	–.44**
Conscientiousness	–.07	–.02	–.32**
Openness	.18	–.15	–.07

Note. Internal validity: N = 1,318; standard procedures: N = 55-80; short measures: N = 128; personality models: N = 112. **p < .01, *p < .05.

In summary, the shift in the content of aspects in the TOP primarily leads to a narrowing of the psychopathy factor, which is responsible for the generally weaker convergent relationships of Uncommitted-Impulsive Work Style. On the other hand, the absence of the "more positive" aspects (often more related to narcissism) results in a nuanced depiction of the psychopathy construct regarding those personality aspects that are not appreciated in employees (see the "NEO profile" from Table 6: "neurotic, not conscientious, disagreeable"). The other two factors show adequate convergent validity. The discriminant validity of the TOP is given regarding SD 3 and standard procedures to the extent that can be expected based on meta-analytical findings. Primarily regarding the relationship of the TOP factors to the DD, a few unsatisfactory convergent and discriminatory relationships arise, the cause of which, in addition to the reasons mentioned on the TOP side, can also be found in the DD. The procedure has been heavily criticized and demonstrably measures incomplete or even theory-consistent construct contents (see Section 5.2.2).

To further examine which individual aspects of the Dark Triad are related to the TOP factors, respectively, their relationships to the subscales of the NPI and KPI were calculated (not included in the table). The factor Self-Centered Work Approach is substantially related to all subscales of the NPI, moreover to all of the factor Interpersonal of psychopathy, very high with self-esteem and charm; also, with lack of conscience and superficial feelings of the factor Affective, but apart from impulsiveness with none of the scales of the factor Lifestyle. Enforcement-Focused Work Attitude is related only to the antagonistically connoted factors of narcissism, such as Exploitativeness/Entitlement, not to the more self-inflated, such as Grandiosity, nor to their counterparts in the KPI. Enforcement-Focused Work Attitude and Uncommitted-Impulsive Work Style correlate with the aspects of the factor Interpersonal – fraudulent/manipulative, need for stimulation, and pathological lying – that are closer to the constructs, not with the narcissism-related scales of the factor (charm and self-esteem); but both correlate with the expected aspects of the factor Affective (superficial feelings and lack of empathy) as well as with those of the factor Lifestyle (lack of responsibility, low behavioral control, and impulsiveness). The latter relationships run contrary to the theoretical expectations of the Machiavellianism construct, though, empirically, connections between Machiavellianism and impulsiveness have been found repeatedly (see Section 3.2). Uncommitted-Impulsive Work Style shows almost the same pattern as Enforcement-Focused Work Attitude, with one accentuation: While for Enforcement-Focused Work Attitude (according to the scale Unsentimentality contained therein) the relationships to affective aspects are closer, this is true for Uncommitted-Impulsive Work Style and the scales of the factor Lifestyle – low behavioral control, impulsiveness, and lack of goals. Based on the subscales of the standard procedures, convergent validity can be assumed for all TOP factors, but not sufficient discriminant validity of Enforcement-Focused Work Attitude and Uncommitted-Impulsive Work Style.

In summary, the data show that there is convergent validity of the TOP to such an extent that one can speak of measurement of the target constructs, but there is sometimes too little discriminant validity between the TOP factors and the constructs far removed from the profession. As a qualification, note that almost all the correlations concerned exist at a level that meta-analytically has been shown for the characteristics. Machiavellianism and psychopathy are, as often noted in research on the Triad, closely related in terms of content, difficult to separate empirically, and therefore probably not discriminantly valid as constructs in principle (see Section 3.3). In the TOP, too, Enforcement-Focused Work

Attitude and Uncommitted-Impulsive Work Style show a substantial relationship, despite factorial demarcation and the resulting clearly divergent contents.

All TOP scales are (strongly) negatively correlated with Agreeableness (in both models) and, as expected, Honesty-Humility is also clearly negatively correlated with the Triad components in the TOP. Thus, the central expectations for the TOP regarding broad personality models are fulfilled. For Uncommitted-Impulsive Work Style, the expected negative correlation to Conscientiousness can be shown, but not for Enforcement-Focused Work Attitude. Moreover, Self-Centered Work Approach is, as expected, associated with Extraversion and with Emotional Stability in both models, but not correlated with Openness.

Relationships to Methods and Constructs Used in Aptitude Diagnostics

In the context of construct validation, a procedure should be distinguished from constructs that capture content differing from it. For example, of interest in the context of test development for a job-related personality test are relationships to procedures from the areas of interests, traits, or abilities commonly considered in this field. Section 4.3 explained which representatives of these characteristic groups can potentially be used together with the Triad components for aptitude-diagnostic questions. The most important predictor of occupational performance – intelligence (see Schmidt & Hunter, 1998) – should also be considered solely because personality tests should be as free as possible from intelligence components. The relationships of the TOP to cognitive abilities, interests, performance motivation, political skills, and social skills were examined to clarify these questions.

Self-estimated intelligence was measured with Self-IQ (Self-IQ Scale of Intelligence of S & F Personnel Psychology, S & F Personalpsychologie, n.d.a), intelligence test scores with KAPPA (Short Scale of General Intelligence of S & F Personnel Psychology, S & F Personalpsychologie, n.d.b). The test procedure KAPPA is web-based, consists of classical intelligence tasks, and also allows the separate identification of numerical and verbal abilities. A combination of personality traits, interests, and cognitive aspects is represented by the framework model Intellect by Mussel (2013), which uses a self-assessment questionnaire to measure personality-related basics of cognitive operations of searching and processing problems and learning content. Related to this is also the concept of occupational curiosity (recorded with the Work-Related Curiosity Scale; Mussel et al., 2012).

Based on the considerations often made in research on the Dark Triad about typical occupational fields that attract those with high characteristics and the interests that distinguish them, the TOP scales were examined to determine which specific occupational environments or areas of interest are related to them. For this purpose, the procedure INTEREST (Vocational Interests test of S & F Personnel Psychology, S & F Personalpsychologie, n.d.c) was used, which records the six interests of the Holland hexagonal RIASEC model using one self-description item each (according to the definition of Holland) on a 10-level scale.

The typical job-related behavior and motives of bearers of Triad characteristics were related to the TOP using procedures developed for the target context and proven to be valid there. In detail, these were the concept of performance motivation with the BMT (Occupational Motivation test of S & F Personnel Psychology, S & F Personalpsychologie, n.d.d) method, a short variant of the Achievement Motivation Inventory (LMI) by Schuler and Prochaska (2001), political skill with the Political Skill Inventory (PSI; Blickle & Gläser,

2009), and social skills with the Social Skills Inventory (ISK; Kanning, 2009). Table 7 presents the results.

Regarding cognitive abilities, it can be confirmed for the TOP that the Triad characteristics are independent of intelligence. In addition, high scorers on Self-Centered Work Approach overestimate their intelligence; high self-assessments in this regard are associated with objectively nonexistent higher cognitive performance. The unexpected negative correlation of Enforcement-Focused Work Attitude with numerical intelligence stems from the skepticism scale, which is significantly correlated at $r = -.13$. No convincing explanation can be offered for the negative assessment and thus underestimation of one's own intelligence at elevated values of Uncommitted-Impulsive Work Style. Regarding the concepts of intellect and curiosity, however, there may be a potential indication of this in the main scales and subscales. Especially Uncommitted-Impulsive Work Style, but also Enforcement-Focused Work Attitude, are related to a rejection of intellectual content and activities, whereas Self-Centered Work Approach is related to a positive relationship with them and also generally greater professional curiosity.

Table 7: The TOP and Interests as well as Cognitive, Social, and Motivational Aspects

	Self-centered work approach	Enforcement-focused work attitude	Uncommitted-impulsive work style
Self-rated intelligence	.55**	−.06	−.31**
General intelligence	.04	−.04	.04
Numerical intelligence	−.02	−.12*	−.02
Verbal intelligence	.04	−.02	.05
Intellect	.38**	−.20**	−.47**
Curiosity	.37**	−.08	−.12
Realistic interest	.13*	.20**	.16**
Intellectual interest	.18**	.08	−.02
Artistic interest	.02	−.13*	−.08
Social interest	−.03	−.27**	−.22**
Enterprising interest	.35**	−.01	−.18**
Conventional interest	−.04	−.16*	−.24**
Achievement motivation	.39**	.37**	.23*
Social skills	.38**	−.08	−.29*
Political skill	.85**	.20	.20

Note. Cognitive skills: $N = 317$; Curiosity: $N = 197$; Interests: $N = 293$; Achievement motivation and social skills: $N = 78$; Political skills: $N = 59$; $^{**}p < .01$, $^{*}p < .05$.

In the TOP, all Triad components are associated with a tendency toward realistic activities, which are seen as typically "masculine" (Holland, 1997). Self-Centered Work Approach is also related to intellectual interests and entrepreneurial orientation but not to artistic interests. Uncommitted-Impulsive Work Style is associated with realistic activities but negatively associated with entrepreneurial orientation. This unexpected finding for Uncommitted-Impulsive Work Style can possibly be explained with the empirical conception in the TOP – the scales that load on the "narcissism factor" in the TOP would accordingly be responsible for the entrepreneurial orientation of the original psychopathy construct. Indeed, all Self-Centered Work Approach scales are positively associated with entrepreneurial orientation. Enforcement-Focused Work Attitude and Uncommitted-Impulsive Work Style are also, as expected, negatively related to social interests. A conventional orientation associated with recurring, structured processes is also negatively associated with Enforcement-Focused Work Attitude and Uncommitted-Impulsive Work Style and almost all subscales. In addition, there is a negative relationship of Enforcement-Focused Work Attitude to artistic interests, which is because of the scale of unsentimentality – a flat emotional life apparently does not demand artistic expression.

All Triad traits are positively associated with the overall value of achievement motivation. The reason for this lies primarily in individual performance goals or those that include social comparison or competition, for example, the subscales dominance, pride of achievement, status aspiration, and competitive attitude are related to the three TOP scales, each between $r=.30$ and $r=.50$. Aspects that are oriented toward concrete work and persistent willingness to make efforts, such as endurance, flexibility, flow, motivation to learn, and self-discipline or self-responsibility, have no connection with the Triad characteristics.

Self-Centered Work Approach has a positive relationship to the overall value of social skills, Enforcement-Focused Work Attitude has none, and Uncommitted-Impulsive Work Style is negatively related to social skills. The positive relationship of Self-Centered Work Approach is based on the Offensivity factor, with a correlation of $r=.54$, which includes contents such as assertiveness, Extraversion, and decisiveness; also, on the Reflexivity factor, which includes self-expression and self-attention (see Kanning, 2009). Enforcement-Focused Work Attitude and Uncommitted-Impulsive Work Style are primarily negatively related to Social Orientation ($r=-.25$ and $-.37$, respectively), which includes prosociality, for example, through the willingness to compromise and to accept perspectives. Uncommitted-Impulsive Work Style is also negatively related to Self-Control, which includes aspects such as self-control and emotional stability.

All subscales of Self-Centered Work Approach are highly positively correlated with one's attribution of political skill, correspondingly strongly at $r=.85$ of the total value. In contrast, only the Enforcement-Focused Work Attitude and Uncommitted-Impulsive Work Style scales skepticism and extenuation are related to political skills, so there are weak and nonsignificant relationships for these factors.

6.2.3 Relationships to Integrity, Prosocial, and Counterproductive Behavior

In the previous sections, the findings on the assessment of the construct-related validity of the TOP were described in terms of correlations with other characteristics of the person, such as their cognitive abilities, i.e., a more individual perspective was chosen. In the following, the focus is on the effects that increased Triad values have on third parties at the workplace. The constructs considered here, Organizational Citizenship Behavior (OCB) and Counterproductive Behavior at Work (CWB), can be understood as personality-based constructs; at the same time, OCB, as an operationalization of contextual performance, represents a component of occupational performance, and CWB quite explicitly describes possible harmful effects that can be considered clear criteria of negative "performance" at work (see Sections 2.2.1 and 4.1). Accordingly, the main justification for the use of the Dark Triad in aptitude testing was the likelihood of showing counterproductive behavior associated with high levels of the characteristics. To investigate the relationships of the TOP to this, correlations to OCB and CWB were examined at the main and subscale levels and by regression analysis. In addition, the proportion of CWB that the TOP scales can explain beyond integrity and broad personality models is determined.

Initially, the TOP was related to Organizational Citizenship Behavior (OCB), as recorded with the FELA-S scale by Staufenbiel and Hartz (2000). It provides a total of five factors of organization-compliant behavior – four classic OCB dimensions and a scale for "in-role" or task performance. The scales can be used to calculate the two dimensions individual-related (OCB-I) and organization-related OCB (OCB-O). For the measurement of CWB, the scale of Bennett and Robinson (2000) was used, which, in addition to the total value (CWB-BR), allows a distinction between individual-related (CWB-I) and organization-related (CWB-O) counterproductive behavior. For the analysis of CWB at the facet level, 11 distinguishable dimensions of counterproductive behavior according to Gruys and Sackett (2003) were recorded additionally, and these were also aggregated to a total value (CWB-GS). Table 8 presents the results.

Both Uncommitted-Impulsive Work Style and Enforcement-Focused Work Attitude are negatively related to OCB. Self-Centered Work Approach, on the other hand, has no relationship to OCB, because of the contents of the factor Deployment, which is substantially positively correlated. It captures individual proactive behavior at work, which primarily serves one's advancement and advantage but does not include concrete help for other people or the organization (see Staufenbiel & Hartz, 2000). The other two TOP factors indicate problematic attitudes toward voluntary, non-task-related work for colleagues or the organization, expressed by a negative relationship to the Helpfulness and, above all, to the Uncomplicatedness factor, which records a very problematic attitude toward work critical of tasks or colleagues and the only one also negatively correlated with Self-Centered Work Approach (the items are inverted). Only for Uncommitted-Impulsive Work Style do additional problematic relationships to Conscientiousness and Work behavior (i.e., factors that are closely related to the classical components of task-related performance) become apparent.

Self-Centered Work Approach is positively related to CWB, which is almost exclusively because of person-related counterproductive behavior (CWB-I); there is no relationship to CWB-O (except for the subscale theft). Enforcement-Focused Work Attitude is not associated with any CWB aspect except inappropriate verbal acts and misuse of information,

Table 8: TOP and Organizational Citizenship Behavior (OCB) and Counterproductive Work Behavior (CWB)

	Self-centered work approach	**Enforcement-focused work attitude**	**Uncommitted-impulsive work style**
OCB-individual	−.14	−.38**	−.32**
OCB-organizational	.05	−.25**	−.42**
OCB (total value)	−.01	−.33**	−.44**
• Helpfulness	−.08	−.23*	−.20*
• Conscientiousness	−.07	.09	−.19*
• Uncomplicatedness	−.20*	−.46**	−.42**
• Deployment	.38**	−.12	−.11
• Work behavior	−.05	−.14	−.36**
CWB-BR	.26*	.11	.37**
CWB-individual	.28**	.13	.36**
CWB-organizational	.16	.07	.27**
CWB-GS	.26*	.18	.42**
• Inappropriate verbal actions	.28**	.31**	.45**
• Inappropriate physical actions	.28**	.15	.31**
• Misuse of information	.16	.19*	.37**
• Misuse of time and resources	.19	.10	.25*
• Theft and related behavior	.21*	.09	.32**
• Poor attendance	.10	.09	.17
• Poor quality work	.08	.13	.20*
• Destruction of property	.03	.05	.19*
• Unsafe behavior	.04	−.11	.11
• Alcohol and drug use	−.05	−.01	.24*

Note. $N = 112$; $^{**}p < .01$, $^{*}p < .05$. The CWB scales had to indicate the actual frequency with which given counterproductive behavior was shown in the last year. Seven response alternatives were available, from *never* to *daily*.

therefore not with the aggregated variables. Uncommitted-Impulsive Work Style, on the other hand, is associated with almost all CWB subaspects and, of the three TOP factors, most strongly with CWB-I and CWB-O. Uncommitted-Impulsive Work Style is unrelated only to the scale's poor attendance and unsafe work behavior. This may be an effect of the sample, which is mainly composed of well-educated university graduates from the management sector, whose workplaces are presumably rarely known to have a timeclock and safety shoes. A sampling effect can also be offered as an explanation for the findings on Enforcement-Focused Work Attitude: A cool-rational, realistic orientation of the Machiavellian can be deduced (see Section 3.1.2) from the theoretical description of the construct and empirical findings on typical behavior patterns. Acts against individuals driven by a lack of self-control and an interpersonal drive for recognition, but above all behavior targeted against the organization that are severely criminally counterproductive may be deliberately omitted because of a lack of expectation of benefit or the probability of being discovered.

To clarify how much variance the results of the TOP can explain in OCB and CWB, multiple regression of these values to the TOP scales was performed. This procedure, which is frequently used in the literature on the Dark Triad, is suitable for investigating the individual explanatory contributions of the characteristics. The sole execution on the global factor level was criticized because the characteristics have shared or related contents, so it is unclear in individual cases what was excluded or what remains in the considered residual (see Section 3.3.2). For this reason, a regression was carried out at the TOP subscale level to clarify to which typical, individual aspects of the Dark Triad this attitude is attributable. In the regression analyses reported in the following, first models were calculated with sex as an additional variable. Sex was always a very low influence factor (usually beta weights around 0), never a significant predictor, or even resulted in increases in R^2 when included in the model or a change in the beta weights of the Triad scales (which would indicate mediating or suppression effects; see Bühner, 2011), which is why sex was not considered further.

No distinction was made between OCB-I and OCB-O, as the TOP scales have a virtually identical relationship to both subsectors. The model for the explanation of the OCB total value with $F(11/100)=3.773$, $p=.000$ shows a significant explanatory contribution of the TOP. The TOP scales explain 29% of the variance in OCB. According to the β-weights, it becomes clear that, although all subscales of Uncommitted-Impulsive Work Style have a negative relationship, the explanation of variance is mainly because of flexibility, which is the only one to show a very significant explanatory contribution ($\beta=-.34$). Also, the scale skepticism from Enforcement-Focused Work Attitude is with $\beta=-.24$ a significantly negative predictor for OCB. The latter relationship is obvious in terms of content; a general disregard for others should not lead to helpfulness and commitment toward colleagues or the organization. The influence of flexibility can be explained by the fact that an unplanned and aimless completion of one's work probably does not go hand in hand with additional, out-of-job commitment to others. At this point, I should point out once again that flexibility, like the designations of the other TOP scales, is a euphemistic paraphrase of the contents of the scale. Its original, phenomenologically more accurate designation was "irresponsibility/lack of career goals."

To test how much variance in CWB can be explained by the TOP scales, multiple regressions of CWB-I and CWB-O, each according to Bennett and Robinson (2000), were calculated on the TOP scales; in this case, separately for the variables, since relevant differences of the TOP factors to these are visible in the bivariate relationships. The model for CWB-I shows a significant explanatory contribution of the TOP with $F(11/97)=3.319$, $p=.001$, and 27% explanation of variance. The model for CWB-O also shows a significant explanatory contribution of TOP with $F(11/90)=1.954$, $p=.043$, and 19% variance explanation.

The β-weights indicate that, in the model for CWB-I, only impulsivity and extenuation of Uncommitted-Impulsive Work Style make an independent explanatory contribution. In the model for CWB-O, mainly also extenuation and flexibility from Uncommitted-Impulsive Work Style are effective, in addition to the skepticism scale from Enforcement-Focused Work Attitude. These characteristics or attitudes are classic aspects of integrity scales and those of psychopathy, which are also related to extraoccupational antisocial behavior (see Sections 2.2 and 3.2).

It can thus be stated that, on the whole, the results of the TOP can explain substantial proportions (20% to 30%) of (lack of) helpful behavior or contextual performance, on the one hand, and of increased counterproductive behavior toward individuals and the organization, on the other hand. The latter, with the exception of Enforcement-Focused Work Attitude, to the extent that they could be meta-analytically proven for the Dark Triad in its original operationalization (see Section 4.1).

The research on personnel determinants of CWB has focused primarily on general personality models and the variable integrity – the latter, since it has emerged from the very tests that are designed to predict counterproductive behavior (see Marcus, 2000; Sackett et al., 2017). The characteristic integrity has a negative relationship to the Dark Triad (see Section 4.1). Possible incremental validity to broad personality models (and integrity) is a central interest of further research on dark personality traits (e.g., LeBreton et al., 2018; Wu & LeBreton, 2011) and is relevant for the decision on the use of appropriate procedures in practice. Therefore, CWB was regression-analytically traced back to the personality models FFM and HEXACO as well as integrity and the incremental explanatory contribution of the TOP to these variables was determined.

First, the relationships of the TOP with integrity were examined, compared on two different samples, and each recorded via the PIA (Personality Inventory for Integrity Assessment of S & F Personnel Psychology, S & F Personalpsychologie, n.d.e). The procedure that emerged from the Hohenheim project on integrity research is the most frequently used integrity test in German companies. All factors and scales of the TOP are negatively related to integrity, except for the scales claim to leadership and belief in persuasive power among trainees. Almost identical correlations are found in both samples (see Table 9).

To test the incremental validity of the TOP (indicated by significant changes in R^2), the personality models were included in regression analyses in the first step, followed by the TOP factors or integrity. The CWB scale according to Gruys and Sackett (2003) was used as the criterion variable for the broadest possible representation of the phenomenon.

As a first model, a regression of CWB on the five major personality factors was calculated; then, as a second model, it was tested how much incremental validity the TOP scales explain beyond these factors. The second model clarifies 6% additional variance ($\Delta R^2=.06$), with $F(3/86)=2.179$, $p=.096$ but not significantly more. Using the identical procedure, the incremental validity of the TOP was checked using the HEXACO model. Again, with $\Delta R^2=.03$, $F(3/85)=1.384$, $p=.253$ an increase, but no statistically significant increase in R^2

Table 9: Relationship of TOP to Integrity in Two Samples

	Integrity	
	Apprentices/students	Senior employees
Self-centered work approach	−.16**	−.36**
Claim to leadership	−.01	−.20*
Belief in persuasive power	−.01	−.32**
Need for authority	−.28**	−.39**
Appetite for risk	−.23**	−.24*
Sense of superiority	−.24**	−.32**
Enforcement-focused work attitude	−.55**	−.55**
Unsentimentality	−.23**	−.34**
Assertiveness	−.53**	−.57**
Skepticism	−.54**	−.42**
Uncommitted-impulsive work style	−.67**	−.69**
Flexibility	−.52**	−.46**
Impulsivity	−.48**	−.44**
Extenuation	−.56**	−.59**

Note. N Trainees = 317, *N* Senior Employees = 112. $^{**}p < .01$, $^{*}p < .05$.

can be achieved. Of the TOP factors, only Uncommitted-Impulsive Work Style has an explanatory contribution in this model. Compared to the FFM, Conscientiousness has no explanatory contribution from the major personality factors, but the factor Honesty-Humility – a scale that measures integrity – does (Lee et al., 2005). Finally, a model consisting of the HEXACO factors, integrity, and the TOP was tested. By including all three test procedures, a total of 42% of the variance in CWB can be explained. The TOP in the model with $\Delta R^2 = .04$, $F(3/84) = 2.110$, $p = .105$ again provides a small additional explanatory contribution of 4%, which is not significant. This results in additional explanatory contributions of the TOP on broad personality models and integrity, but these are consistently low and not significant in the present case.

6.2.4 Criterion-Related Validity: Relationships to Job Performance and Success

The ultimately interesting and thus probably most important main quality criterion of a test is its validity in predicting criteria; for a procedure for the assessment of occupational aptitude, it is primarily the criteria of job performance, professional success, or failure. The most frequent, albeit problematic, criterion of a person's occupational performance is the performance assessment by the direct supervisor. For the TOP, assessments of supervisors were collected using various scales that allow distinctions to be made between task-, team- and organization-related performance, in addition to the global assessment of job performance (see Section 2.2). For selected performance criteria, curvilinear relationships of the TOP were examined in addition to simple correlations and whether the person's intelligence or integrity play a moderating role.

One of the studies on the relationship between TOP scores and job performance assessments was conducted as part of the validation of a job-related test battery for personnel selection. As part of that larger online-test battery, the test persons, trainees and dual students of a large German financial institution filled out TOP and at the end of the second year of apprenticeship were assessed by their supervisors regarding their job performance. The $N=226$ supervisor assessments were made on the Work Role Behavior Scale (WRBS; Griffin et al., 2007), which enables the separate assessment of general task-related performance (proficiency) and contextual performance. The latter is reported separately as team member and organization member performance. The proficiency dimensions are differentiated from the degree of adaptivity and proactivity shown for task and contextual performance. In addition, an overall value of "Work Role Behavior" is calculated.

The sample showed correlations neither with any of the TOP factors (all "zero correlations") for any of the dimensions of performance nor with the overall value. Thus, in accordance with the results of the meta-analysis by O'Boyle et al. (2012), there was no linear correlation of the Dark Triad with occupational performance evaluations. One possible explanation lies in the potential curvilinear effects that exist, for example, for narcissism and Machiavellianism (see Section 4.2), which is why the quadratic effects of the TOP factors on the criterion of occupational performance were examined. The findings are presented below in the section entitled "Curvilinearity and Moderation Effects as Explanations."

Another possible explanation for the absence of a linear relationship of TOP factors to occupational performance is the sample. The persons considered are at the beginning of their professional careers. Moreover, possible situational conditions discussed in Triad research do not affect the specific situation (see Chapter 4). For example, how tasks are completed and how performance goals are pursued cannot be controlled autonomously. Because of the age of the subjects and the associated low level of professional experience, the behavior shown and assessed is not fully representative of longer-term professional behavior and corresponding performance.

Therefore, the question of the relationship of the TOP factors to occupational performance was investigated in further samples, also to other criteria of interest. First, in a second sample ($N=34$), which shows a significantly higher average age, hierarchical positions, autonomy, and complexity of work tasks, again supervisor assessments, were recorded on the WRBS scale described above according to Griffin et al. (2007). In this case, only the proficiency dimensions were assessed, i.e., the fulfillment of clearly describable performance requirements, without adaptivity or proactivity. In addition, a global external assessment of occupational performance was recorded using a sequential percentile rank scale (SPRS; see Brandstätter & Schuler, 1974). Table 10 presents the results.

This sample shows a clear positive relationship to job performance for Self-Centered Work Approach on both assessment scales and especially for contributions as an

Table 10: Correlations of the TOP with the Assessments of Supervisors

	Self-centered work approach	Enforcement-focused work attitude	Uncommitted-impulsive work style
Global professional performance (SPRS)	.50**	−.10	.04
Proficiency (aggregated)	.45**	−.13	−.11
Individual task proficiency	.34*	−.02	−.13
Team member proficiency	.26	−.21	−.07
Organization member proficiency	.54**	−.09	−.09

Note. $N = 34$, $n = 31$ (SPRS). $^{**}p < .01$, $^{*}p < .05$.

organizational member; for the other two TOP factors, however, there are weakly negative relationships, which are more pronounced here than in the other sample but also not significant.

Several explanations can be given for this: It could be that a stronger Self-Centered Work Approach leads to better performance but only becomes apparent over time or with appropriate tasks and conditions. Another explanation is that there is less direct and frequent cooperation and thus a limited observability of the behavior of those being evaluated. In addition, work tasks such as performance targets are more heterogeneous, i.e., performance can be assessed far less clearly and objectively than in the case of trainees. In this case, the effects of classic narcissistic self-portrayal could have influenced the evaluators and led to better assessments, although objectively there is no better performance. Given the meta-analytically confirmed zero correlation to work performance per se (the sample selection of which does not, however, include any higher hierarchical levels from the business sector, see Section 4.2.2), the results from the sample of trainees and students and the other reported findings for narcissism and performance, the level of the correlation argues more in favor of the second interpretation. However, this question must be pursued (for the TOP as well as the Dark Triad in general) with further studies on larger datasets comparing objective and externally assessed data (above all also by systematic comparisons across job levels).

Curvilinearity and Moderation Effects as Explanations

The findings on the effects of the Dark Triad on job performance are inconclusive (except for the negative effects of increased counterproductive behavior). This is reflected in meta-analyses of the Triad and many of the proposed moderators, some of whom I discussed in Chapter 4. At the same time, inverse U-shaped relationships to performance assessments were shown for the characteristics narcissism and Machiavellianism (see Section 4.2). Thus, the best performance ratings are associated with average values for the trait in question as well as low or high values with poorer performance. The TOP data also showed different and sometimes contradictory relationships to criteria of occupational performance. According to the explanatory approaches in Triad research, the possible effects of moderators and the existence of curvilinear relationships were therefore examined.

For the TOP, the dataset from $N=226$ persons was used containing the assessments by supervisors of the vocational performance of trainees and students and their TOP values, in which no linear relationship of predictors and criteria exists. In a first step (Model 1), the characteristic to be examined was included in the regression analyses, and in a second step (Model 2), the squared term (of the *z*-standardized variable) was included in addition to the predictor. If the β-weight of the squared term is significant, there is a curvilinear effect; if the sign is negative, it is inversely U-shaped. Incremental validity via the linear effect exists with significant changes in R^2 (see Grijalva et al., 2015).

The expected inverse U-shaped relationship of Self-Centered Work Approach and externally assessed occupational performance can be confirmed with $F(1/223)=3.962$, $p=.048$; $\Delta R^2=.017$. Low values are not associated with good performance assessments, medium values with the highest assessments. Persons with the most pronounced values in Self-Centered Work Approach receive the worst supervisor ratings.

Figure 5 shows the course of this relationship. Here, the averaged performance assessments of the subjects per category of minus two to plus two standard deviations in Self-Centered Work Approach are plotted as points.

Using the same procedure, an inverse U-shaped relationship could also be demonstrated for Enforcement-Focused Work Attitude and externally assessed job performance with $F(1/223)=5.146$, $p=.024$; $\Delta R^2=.022$. Figure 6 presents the results.

For Uncommitted-Impulsive Work Style, however, no such relationship can be found with $F(1/223)=0.369$, $p=.544$; $\Delta R^2=.002$. Slightly above-average values negatively affect

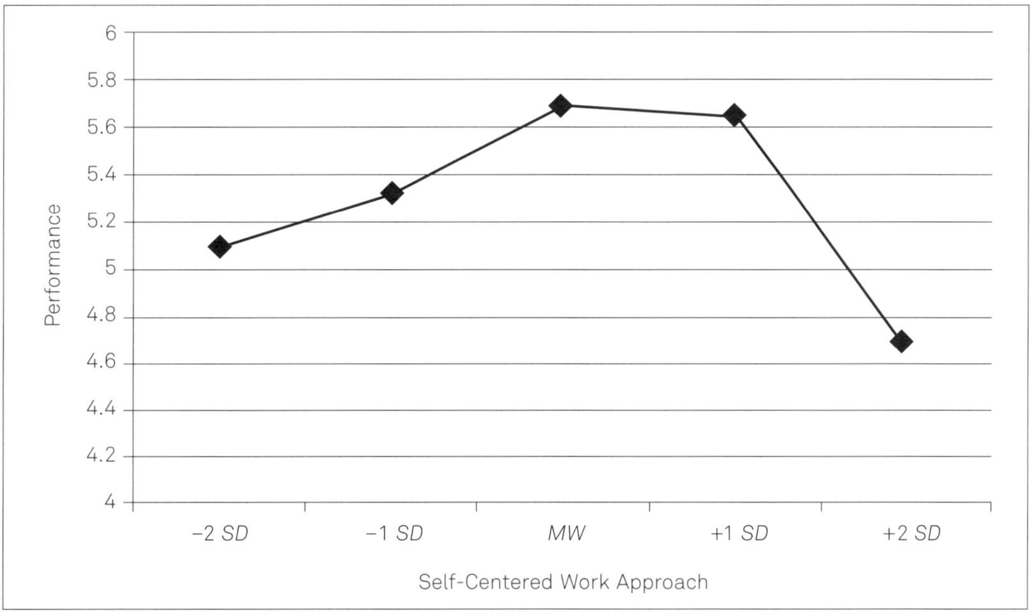

Figure 5: Curvilinear relationship between Self-centered work approach and job performance. Reprinted with permission from *TOP: Dark Triad of Personality at Work* (UK/US adaptation) by D. Schwarzinger & H. Schuler, 2019, Figure 7.1, p. 44. © Hogrefe AG.

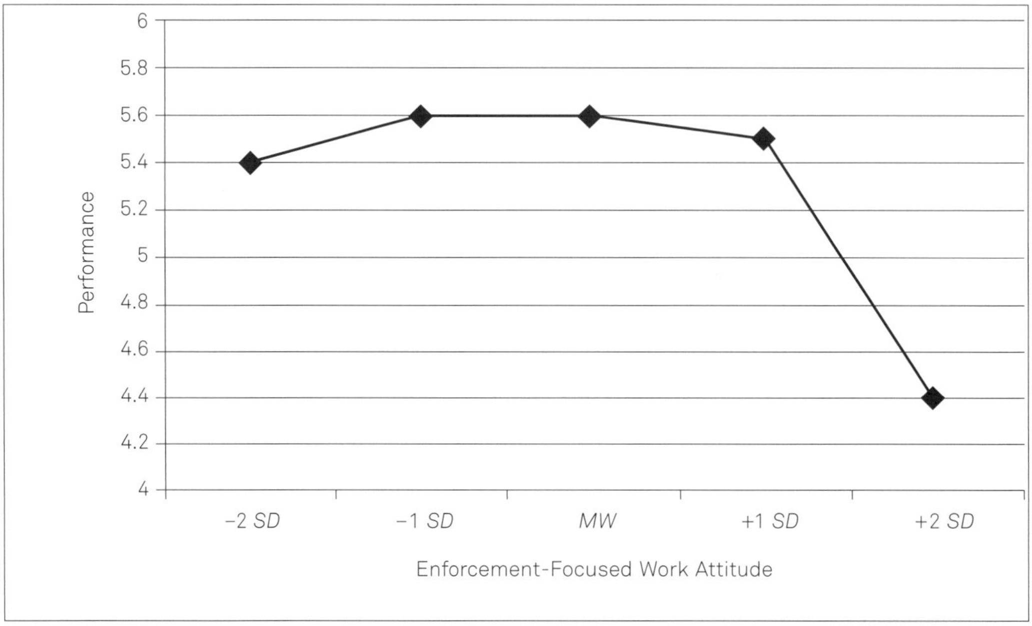

Figure 6: Curvilinear relationship between Enforcement-focused work attitude and job performance. Reprinted with permission from *TOP: Dark Triad of Personality at Work* (UK/US adaptation) by D. Schwarzinger & H. Schuler, 2019, Figure 7.2, p. 44. © Hogrefe AG.

performance assessments, but in the range of plus two standard deviations above the mean, the subjects receive the best performance assessments.

Another hypothesis put forward for the relationship between the Dark Triad and job performance is that of a moderating effect of integrity or intelligence (see Section 4.2). It is assumed that a positive relationship with occupational performance exists when these characteristics are strong and the Triad values are high.

To investigate a moderation effect, the regression analyses in the second step (Model 2) included the TOP factor to be investigated and the moderator intelligence or integrity as well as the interaction effect of the two predictors. Significant β-weights of the interaction indicate an existing moderating effect, a significant R^2 indicates an improvement of the prediction model by considering the moderator.

With $F(1/222)=2.972$, $p=.086$; $\Delta R^2=.013$, no moderating effect of integrity on the relationship of Self-Centered Work Approach with job performance or model improvement through its inclusion can be demonstrated in the dataset (moderating effect and model improvement are significant only on $p<.10$). The results are shown in Figure 7.

In contrast, with $F(1/222)=5.230$, $p=.023$; $\Delta R^2=.022$, there is a moderating effect of integrity on the relationship between Enforcement-Focused Work Attitude and job performance; both interaction effect and change in R^2 are significant. Figure 8 presents the results.

Integrity moderates the relationship between Enforcement-Focused Work Attitude and job performance. A similar effect exists for Self-Centered Work Approach but cannot be sufficiently verified against chance. For Uncommitted-Impulsive Work Style, the hypothesis of a moderating effect of integrity with $F(1/222)=0.064$, $p=.801$; $\Delta R^2=.000$, must be rejected.

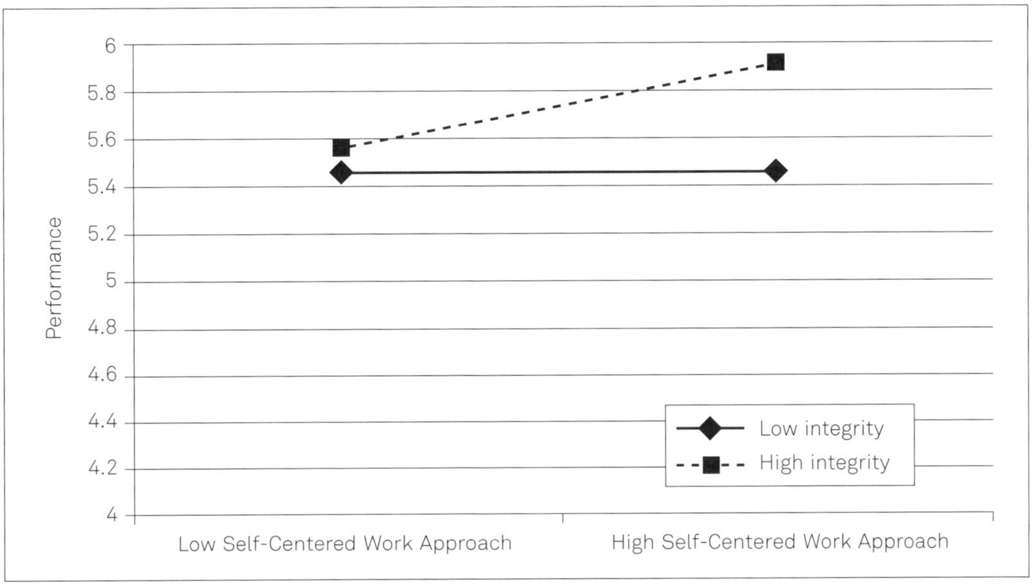

Figure 7: Moderating effect of integrity on the relationship between Self-centered work approach and job performance. Reprinted with permission from *TOP: Dark Triad of Personality at Work* (UK/US adaptation) by D. Schwarzinger & H. Schuler, 2019, Figure 7.3, p. 45. © Hogrefe AG.

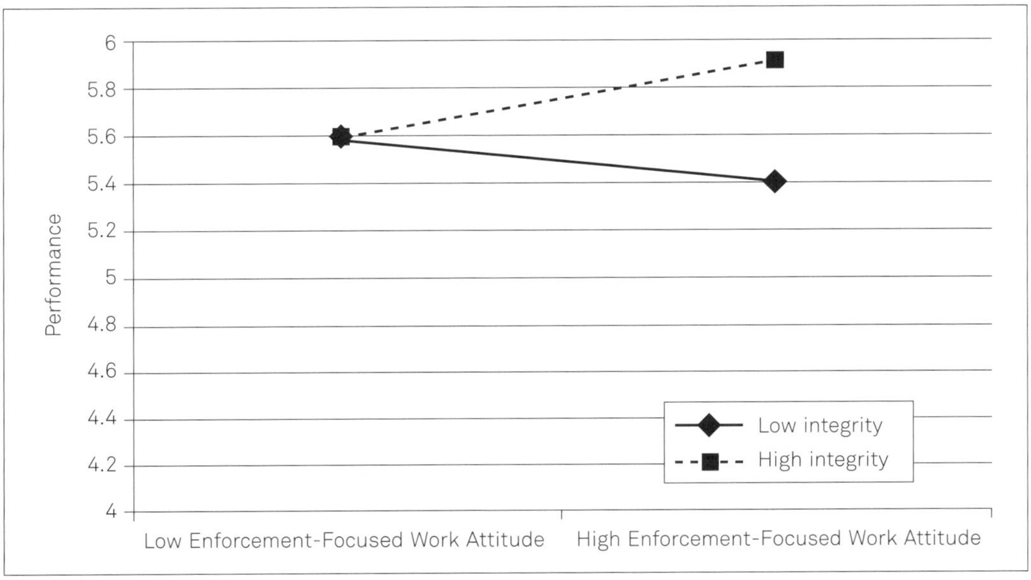

Figure 8: Moderating effect of integrity on the relationship between Enforcement-Focused work attitude and professional performance. Reprinted with permission from *TOP: Dark Triad of Personality at Work* (UK/US adaptation) by D. Schwarzinger & H. Schuler, 2019, Figure 7.4, p. 45. © Hogrefe AG.

Potential moderating effects of intelligence on the relationship of TOP factors to occupational performance were examined using the same approach and dataset. For Self-Centered Work Approach, this results in $F(1/222)=1.914$, $p=.168$; $\Delta R^2=.008$. Also, for

Enforcement-Focused Work Attitude with $F(1/222)=0.039$, $p=.844$; $\Delta R^2=.000$ and Uncommitted-Impulsive Work Style with $F(1/222)=0.665$, $p=.416$; $\Delta R^2=.003$, no moderating effect of intelligence on the relationship of TOP factors to job performance can be proven in the dataset.

Conclusion
No Better Performance by Dark Triad Personalities

Based on all results in this section, there is no linear relationship between the TOP factors and professional performance. For Self-Centered Work Approach there seems to be a curvilinear effect, one that is effective depending on the sample and the type of workplace, or one that is only existing in the assessments by superiors. For Enforcement-Focused Work Attitude, there is a moderating effect of integrity and a curvilinear relationship to job performance. The bivariate, linear results for Enforcement-Focused Work Attitude and Uncommitted-Impulsive Work Style from two samples also confirm for the TOP factors the meta-analytically found slightly negative relationship of Machiavellianism and psychopathy with superior assessments. Thus, the TOP factors are also rather weak predictors of professional performance across all groups of people, as is the case for the Dark Triad in general, as O'Boyle et al. (2012) found in their meta-analysis.

In conjunction with the findings on OCB as an aspect of contextual performance, a negative influence on professional performance in the sense of an overall contribution to organizational value must be expected, at least in the case of high values of Enforcement-Focused Work Attitude or Uncommitted-Impulsive Work Style. The contribution is likely to become negative in particular if the connections with counterproductive behavior and the costs of the resulting damage described in Section 6.2.3 are included in the calculation.

Professional Success

In accordance with the relationships shown for the TOP and the findings for the Dark Triad in general presented in Chapter 4, there is no evidence of overall better occupational performance of people with high levels on any of the Dark Triad traits as well as TOP factors. However, such values are associated with negative effects on the organization through counterproductive behavior. Therefore, individuals with high TOP scores are unlikely to have greater overall professional success. However, good or bad job performance does not automatically lead to success or failure. Individual success is also measured according to criteria other than the performance contributions made to an organizational goal and depends on many basic conditions not inherent in the person with the characteristic. The criteria of occupational success are therefore contaminated and deficient (see Section 2.2.1).

To provide the most versatile approach possible to the hypothetical construct of overall success, this section reports on the relationship of the TOP to self-assessments of professional success, personal job satisfaction, commitment to organization, assessments of managed teams, and objective success data. In addition, performance assessments and well-being values of teams are used as indicators of success for their managers.

Table 11: Relationships Between TOP and the Self-Assessment Scale of Professional Success (SBE)

	Self-centered work approach	Enforcement-focused work attitude	Uncommitted-impulsive work style
SBE total value	.51**	−.20**	−.14**
I am professionally more successful than colleagues who work in a similar position.	.45**	.02	−.07
I fulfill all work tasks to the fullest satisfaction.	.24**	−.16**	−.13**
My professional development has been successful.	.34**	−.12**	−.06
I am often asked for advice from colleagues.	.43**	−.18**	−.05
All in all, I am professionally successful.	.35**	−.29**	−.17**

Note. $n = 683$. $^{**}p < .01$, $^{*}p < .05$.

Self-evaluated occupational success was operationalized utilizing the Self-Evaluation Scale of Occupational Success (SBE; see Mussel et al., 2011). One of the questions contained in this scale deals with the perception of one's task-related work performance; the other items concern professional success in the narrower sense regarding one's professional development, integration in teams, and comparison with colleagues. Furthermore, an overall value for success can be calculated. The scale has been included in most online studies on the TOP, so the values thus represent a broad representation of self-assessments of one's success across several samples, age, and occupational groups. Table 11 shows the results.

A higher Self-Centered Work Approach is accompanied by positive self-assessments of one's performance and all partial aspects that relate to an assessment of one's success. Since this assessment of success (especially at this level) cannot be objectively confirmed for this factor, either from theoretical and empirical perspective (see Chapter 4) or from the results of the TOP reported above, there is also an overestimation of one's success: An increased Self-Centered Work Approach manifests itself in high estimations and an overestimation of one's own professional achievements and success. Negative relationships to assessments of job performance as well as the overall value for success and most partial aspects are found for Uncommitted-Impulsive Work Style and Enforcement-Focused Work Attitude. These self-assessments of both direction and level are therefore consistent with the external assessments of performance reported above as well as with the meta-analytic values determined by O'Boyle et al. (2012) and are even slightly stronger and thus presumably somewhat too pessimistic.

As explained in Section 2.2.1, in addition to broadly operationalized and usually deficient success indicators (I report on these later in this section), measures of one's own “well-being at work” are also available as criteria for individual success. As a further self-assessment, therefore, $N = 50$ managers of a bank were surveyed to assess their job satisfaction and commitment to the organization. The Job Satisfaction Scale used by Baillod and Semmer (1994) consists of a total of 8 items, the first of which measures global job satisfaction. This global satisfaction question and 3 further items of the scale were added to the “job satisfaction” indicator by Lais (2013), who collected the data in a joint study and subsequently made them available. The organizational commitment of managers was assessed in the study via the Commitment Questionnaire of Felfe et al. (2010; see also Felfe & Franke, 2012). In addition, Lais (2013) assessed the perceived effectiveness of the managed team in the areas of work quality, customer friendliness, timely completion of tasks, profit-oriented thinking and acting, rapid processing of customer inquiries/problems, flexibility in dealing with unexpected changes, achievement of objectives, and overall performance, and aggregated these to form the indicator “overall performance of the team.” The effectiveness value thus reflects the perceived performance of the team by the manager, especially regarding the quality of the work performed and the goals achieved. It could therefore be seen as an (albeit deficient and contaminated) indicator of success in the management role, as the manager steers his team toward achieving the goals. Table 12 shows the results.

According to the results, there is no negative correlation between the Dark Triad characteristics in the TOP and commitment to the organization. Own job satisfaction is assessed consistently negative, most strongly for Uncommitted-Impulsive Work Style and substantially negative also for Enforcement-Focused Work Attitude. There is no connection to Self-Centered Work Approach. Only Enforcement-Focused Work Attitude has a significant value for the effectiveness of the managed team, to which there is a negative correlation for all Triad characteristics. The managers scoring high on TOP were particularly critical of too little profit-oriented thinking and acting, low flexibility in dealing with new requirements, and the general achievement of objectives.

Table 12: TOP and self-assessment of satisfaction, commitment, and effectiveness of the managed team

	Self-centered work approach	**Enforcement-focused work attitude**	**Uncommitted-impulsive work style**
Commitment	.04	–.12	.04
Job satisfaction	–.27	–.32*	–.40**
Team effectiveness	–.21	–.34*	–.25

Note. $N = 50$. $^{**}p < .01$, $^{*}p < .05$.

As measured by the criterion of team effectiveness, people with high scores on TOP scales tend to rate their leadership success less highly. However, in line with the typically Machiavellian attitude of cynicism toward others or narcissistic motives of devaluation or disdain for others, such motives may also have played a role in the assessment.

A further central issue of occupational research on Dark Triad characteristics relates to the effects people with elevated values have on employees and teams in their function as managers. In addition to the performance values of teams or their members, the well-being of the employees managed is primarily considered (see Section 4.2.1). To examine these relationships, the TOP values of the managers were assigned to the self-assessments of the managed teams regarding job satisfaction and commitment. In addition, the effectiveness of the team was again assessed – in this case from the perspective of the team members, i.e., their perceived team performance. The values recorded can in this case thus be used as externally assessed success or failure indicators for leadership: Successful leadership should contribute to more positive assessments of the variables, while poor or even destructive, abusive leadership should result in negative assessments.

The same scales, which were also filled out by the managers, were used for this purpose. In addition, the leadership style of the managers was assessed by the *Multifactor Leadership Questionnaire* (MLQ) by Bass and Avolio (1994), translated into German by Felfe and Goihl (2002). According to the results, increased values of managers on a TOP factor are not accompanied by negative evaluations of the team regarding their job satisfaction, commitment, or estimated effectiveness. On the contrary, teams of managers with elevated values in Self-Centered Work Approach show a higher commitment to the organization (r=.32). No TOP factor is associated with a particular leadership style in the study; Self-Centered Work Approach tends to be associated with transformational leadership.

Objective Performance Indicators

In addition to self-assessments of one's own professional success and evaluations by supervisors, objective criteria are primarily used to examine professional success. In the TOP validation studies, the criteria of hierarchical position, promotions received, leadership span, and salary were also surveyed (in the relevant analysis, only full-time employees were considered, and a correction for years of professional experience was applied). The results (criteria group 1 in Table 13) were to be assessed in the form of a self-assessment on anchored scales with up to ten categorical gradations each. In addition, performance indicators from organizational controlling could be assigned to the TOP values of the discussed sample of managers and their teams (criteria group 2): These were achievement of sales KPI, absence rate per team, and contributions to the company suggestion scheme per team. The objective data at the team level can be regarded as "hard" data for assessing the success of the manager – if the values achieved by the managed team are understood in the sense of the above explanations as a criterion of the professional success of the team leader. Like the other criteria used, these are contaminated and deficient. In contrast, directly assignable, objective personal success criteria are the grades recorded in the sample used to examine the vocational performance of trainees and dual students (criteria group 3); they reflect success in school and in-company training in the form of averaged school-leaving certificates (certificate section) and the Chamber of Commerce intermediate examination. The results are shown in Table 13.

Higher scores on Self-Centered Work Approach are accompanied by positive assessments of all criteria in group 1. This is in line with the findings of Paleczek et al. (2018) on salary and leadership position; the value for salary is also similar to that Spurk et al. (2016) found. A higher Self-Centered Work Approach is associated with higher (self-reported)

Table 13: TOP factors and objective success data

		Self-centered work approach	Enforcement-focused work attitude	Uncommitted-impulsive work style
1	Hierarchical position	.14**	−.11	−.02
	Promotions	.20**	−.09	−.07
	Leadership span	.28**	−.13**	−.06
	Salary	.19**	.05	.10*
2	Achievement rate of led team	−.13	−.30	.01
	Absenteeism managed team	.05	.23	−.07
	Improvement suggestions	.52*	.18	.15
3	Chamber of Commerce grade	.01	−.20**	−.06
	School grades	−.03	−.34**	−.14

Note. N Chamber of Commerce grade = 262, n School grades = 69, n Achievement of objectives, absenteeism, and suggestions for improvement = 50, n Hierarchical position, promotions, leadership span, salary = 459. $^{**}p < .01$, $^{*}p < .05$.

salary and hierarchy levels, more promotions, and a greater leadership span. On the other hand, there is no relationship to the performance indicator grades (criteria group 3), nor are the team's performance values better (except for a higher number of suggestions for improvement submitted).

For Uncommitted-Impulsive Work Style, there is almost always zero correlation with professional success measures and only slightly higher salaries. Enforcement-Focused Work Attitude is negatively related to operational and educational success operationalized by grades. Teams led by people with a higher Enforcement-Focused Work Attitude show higher absenteeism and tend to have lower goal attainment (both relationships exist to a moderate extent but are not significant). Persons with a higher Enforcement-Focused Work Attitude also indicate a lower leadership span and tend to have lower levels of hierarchy attained. Enforcement-Focused Work Attitude is not positively related to higher hierarchical positions. Spurk et al. (2016) found a positive relationship with the criterion leadership position. Their study, however, included only people with a few years of work experience and dichotomously tested them for the achievement of a leadership position. In the scale used in the TOP studies, the assessment had to be made on a multilevel scale regarding hierarchical level, ranging from simple worker/employee to managing director/board member; the sample also represented a larger age range and different lengths of employment.

Conclusion
Relationships to Professional Success

In summary, there is little evidence of relationships between the TOP factors and professional success, and the evidence is also differentiated. Self-Centered Work Approach is associated with a higher self-assessment of professional success and with positive evaluations of self-rated objective criteria. There is no connection to hard success data and evaluations of guided employees. Self-experienced professional success in the sense of high job satisfaction or commitment cannot be confirmed either; on the contrary, there tend to be negative relationships with these criteria. Uncommitted-Impulsive Work Style has no relation to professional success; there are zero correlations with virtually all the criteria examined, except for personal job satisfaction. A higher Enforcement-Focused Work Attitude seems to be the least conducive to professional success. Own job satisfaction and the effectiveness of the team are lower in self- and team-assessment, also other objective success data tend to be negatively correlated – for grades there is even a substantially negative correlation.

6.3 Evaluation of the TOP

Section 6.2 presented the findings on the psychometric characteristics of TOP and its possibilities for predicting criteria relevant to aptitude diagnostics. This can be used to check compliance with common quantitative criteria of psychological test theory, which must also be present in occupational aptitude diagnostics in practice according to professional standards. As explained in Chapter 5, however, these psychometric requirements are only one component of the overall statement on the actual applicability of a personnel-selection procedure. For this to be present, further fundamental requirements must be fulfilled, some of which require special attention in the case of dark personality traits. Therefore, in the following sections, I discuss the suitability of the TOP regarding legal specifications and requirement reference, social validity, acceptance by the test persons, and standardization, as derived in Chapter 5.

6.3.1 Legal and Professional Requirements

In accordance with the comments on the legal requirements for a procedure, the areas of the legality of individual questions, potential clinical measurement or interpretation of the results, development and standardization in the target population, and the professional and requirement reference established must be considered.

The TOP development formulated only occupational items to capture aspects of the characteristics relevant to this target context. Potentially legally or invasively questionable contents of the Triad constructs were not transferred to the occupational context to avoid inappropriate personality intrusion, e.g., the scales on sexual behavior from the psychopathy construct promiscuity and many marital-like relationships as well as the contents of factor four according to Hare "Antisocial," which depicts concretely committed antisocial and mostly criminally relevant behavior – even retrospectively in the sense of querying previous convictions. Thus, the TOP items do not contain any legally questionable content.

As the theoretical preparatory work and the validation results for the items reported in Section 6.2 have shown, the behaviors and attitudes depicted in the items are work-related and connected to criteria of general professional success or failure, and were validated against specific constructs and criteria relevant in the target context that were obtained from representative samples. This means that values on TOP factors are fundamentally related to occupations for which the use of the TOP is possible, and the content measured with the TOP is related to the requirements at the corresponding workplaces. Thus, the TOP can be related to occupations and requirements and can be used in fully compliant HR processes. As these sometimes need to be checked and assessed anew for the individual case, the TOP, in form of its manuals in multiple languages, can proof its formal legalty and professional standards compliance using available documentation, validation, and user instructions. The TOP test manuals provide all the necessary instructions for carrying out and interpreting the Dark Triad by TOP nonclinical, merely job-related, aided by reports to feedback candidates, and cover a wide range of findings on its psychometric properties and validity for criteria of organizational interest (see Schwarzinger & Schuler, 2016, 2019, 2020, 2021a, b, c, 2022a, b).

As the illustrations in Section 6.2.1 on the distribution of the TOP values show, the TOP can be used to perform the required normally distributed, dimensional measurement. The evaluation notes provided in the manual and the evaluation and profile sheets available separately are used to classify and interpret the results accordingly. From an empirical point of view, the requirement that only a subclinical measurement with the TOP should be possible is thus fulfilled. The explanations in Chapter 5 on the potential misuse of personality inventories through unintentional categorization and interpretation of the results are explicitly addressed in the manual to give a "notice of possible misuse." It is pointed out, regarding the range and context of measurement, that no complete and certainly no clinical recording of the constructs can be made, so "mental health diagnoses" are not possible with TOP.

6.3.2 Feedback of Results and Social Validity

The notes on the feedback of results in the TOP manuals call for a renunciation of clinically connoted attributions; they also provide suggestions for socially valid application. Among other things, it is emphasized that only work-related characteristics are recorded in isolation, and therefore no general personality traits or private information or behavior can be assessed.

A personal meeting is recommended for feedback, in which only work-related interpretations of the results should be made. Depending on the type of application (classic paper-pencil or online in the Hogrefe Test System HTS 5), either simple paper-based feedback forms with short scale descriptions and standard values obtained or more detailed narrative reports in PDF format are provided. For each scale and each factor, depending on the characteristic value, these provide the test participant with a detailed statement about what the concrete value can mean practically in professional life as well as information about possible consequences and suggestions for reflection. Such feedback and the information conveyed increase the transparency and support the creation of a socially valid application. To steer clear away of any clinical interpretations and ensure best possible acceptance by candidates the TOP holds rather euphemistic scale descriptions, e.g., extenuation instead of pathological lying. Such an approach – euphemistic and generally understandable naming of the scales – was also chosen for the HDS method (Hogan & Hogan, 2009), which is established on the market and accepted by users and applicants alike – which is why it was decided to offer this option for the TOP as well. From its first application projects in practice, it became clear that test materials without the explicit naming of the Triad properties are urgently needed for organizational purposes, since any proximity to the original constructs should be avoided.

In accordance with the explanations in this section, it can be stated that the TOP meets the established requirements regarding legal aspects, and that the foundations for a job-related, socially valid recording of the Dark Triad with the TOP are given.

6.3.3 Acceptance

As the comments on social validity have further shown, a desirable consequence of a socially valid selection process is better acceptance by the tested persons. The pure acceptance of the procedure used was tested for the TOP in comparison with the short procedures DD and SD 3 as well as the bright personality traits OCB (OCB; Lee & Allen, 2002) and work commitment (Utrecht Work Engagement Scale (UWES); Schaufeli & Bakker, 2003). The German TOP short form (TOP-K) was used, which contains a total of 9 items from 9 of the 11 TOP scales and thus represents a broad and representative representation of the item contents of the TOP. The assessments obtained for this procedure can thus be considered a good illustration of the acceptance of the contents of the TOP standard version. The TOP-K was selected because it shows a higher equivalence in the number of items with the compared procedures than the full version, which means that the additional situation-related influencing factor test length did not affect the ratings.

The study was carried out on employed part-time students of industrial and organizational psychology, in other words, on people who have a basic understanding of the terms and requirements surrounding valid and accepted job-related diagnostics, in some cases even relevant professional experience. The sample used is the subset of $n = 55$ for which acceptance assessments could be assigned. These were recorded with the two areas of the AKZEPT-P questionnaire (Kersting, 2005): privacy and face validity. Each of these two areas is based on several items, each of which covers aspects of invasiveness or perceived invasion of privacy and the lack of apparent validity of a test for personnel selection, which are summed up to a scale. In addition, a self-formulated single item was used to ask how the appropriateness of the procedure is assessed for personnel-selection purposes. Controlled by a random mechanism, the test subjects worked through bright and dark procedures, each followed directly by an assessment of its acceptance. Table 14 shows the mean values of the assessments.

Table 14: Mean values in acceptance of TOP and other procedures

	TOP-K	DD	SD 3	OCB	UWES
Protection of privacy	5.5	5.1	4.0	6.1	6.2
Face validity	4.0	3.5	3.1	4.1	4.0
The procedure is appropriate for use in personnel selection	3.6	2.7	2.4	3.5	3.6

Note. $n = 55$. The mean values are shown on a 7-point scale from *does not apply* to *fully applies*.

Privacy of TOP-K was lower than the scales for OCB ($t(54)=3.10$, $p<.00$; $d_{\text{Cohen}}=.456$) and work engagement ($t(54)=3.61$, $p<.00$; $d_{\text{Cohen}}=.532$); compared to the other Triad methods SD 3 ($t(54)=-6.91$, $p<.00$; $d_{\text{Cohen}}=-.822$) and DD ($t(54)=-1.91$, $p<.06$; $d_{\text{Cohen}}=-.241$); however, it was considered better in this respect, that is, not invading the private sphere as much as standard Dark Triad procedures do.

The TOP-K face validity was also higher than that of DD ($t(54)=-2.78$, $p<.01$; $d_{\text{Cohen}}=-.385$) and SD 3 ($t(54)=-5.63$, $p<.00$; $d_{\text{Cohen}}=-.692$), and assessed as given to the same extent as the OCB ($t(54)=0.51$, $p<.61$; $d_{\text{Cohen}}=.083$) and work engagement scale ($t(54)=-0.25$, $p<.81$; $d_{\text{Cohen}}=.004$). In summary, the adequacy of the TOP-K for personnel-selection purposes was also assessed to the same extent as for the OCB ($t(54)=0.09$, $p<.93$; $d_{\text{Cohen}}=-.061$) and work engagement scale ($t(54)=0.00$, $p<1.00$; $d_{\text{Cohen}}=.000$) and as given to a higher extent than for DD ($t(54)=3.22$, $p<.00$; $d_{\text{Cohen}}=-.545$) and SD 3 ($t(54)=4.69$, $p<.00$; $d_{\text{Cohen}}=-.727$).

The positive assessments of the TOP – better than the Triad short procedures regarding each area covered and in some cases just as good as the bright procedures – indicate that contextualized formulations have succeeded in increasing the requirement reference and thus the relevance and face validity of the Dark Triad for the selection context in the eyes of the test persons, at least in comparison to the measurement of the constructs in their original, distant conceptualization. The TOP method, which considers the pure test material, therefore meets the requirement to capture the Dark Triad in organizations in an acceptable form.

6.3.4 Standardization

A further central requirement, which was clarified for the assessment of the applicability of TOP for practical personnel-psychological questions, is the provision of suitable standard values for a procedure. Based on these, individual participant values can be set concerning a representative sample, which is why the standard must be up to date and above all suitable for the target context. The reference group from which the standard data are obtained should correspond in key characteristics such as age, educational level, and professional experience to those for whom the use of the aptitude diagnostic instrument is planned according to the procedural instructions.

Diverse language norms were calculated for the TOP from representative samples regarding several demographic criteria according to the national census of the different countries and provided in the test manuals. Also, in the adaptation and standardization of the

TOP, only persons with professional experience were included in the analyses. The samples for the initial German test development were taken from studies in occupational contexts or companies/organizations, which meant that the TOP was initially developed and standardized in the target area. As the sample descriptions in the test manuals show, the norms were applied to persons who largely correspond to the target population of the TOP in terms of age, educational background, and areas of professional activity. This is seen in the working general population with a tendency toward slightly higher educational levels in business-related occupations.

For the TOP, in accordance with theoretical expectations, there are higher mean values for men for all scales, though statistically significant differences were found in Germany only for Self-Centered Work Approach. The same is true for the UK/US adaptation and all yet existing language versions: small to moderately higher scores for men on Self-Centered Work Approach, but not for the other two factors and respective scales because of small, insignificant gender differences. Taking into consideration the factual nonbinarity of gender and personal identification, it was decided to have one unisex norm for both UK (N=1,000) and US (N=1,001) population, both sampled according to the national census on ethnic background, age, and work type. For a detailed description of the standardization process, please see Schwarzinger and Schuler (2019).

Apart from sex, there are no explicit theoretical expectations regarding group differences, such as age or educational level, as is common in cognitive testing. Nevertheless, exploratory tests were carried out during test development to examine various age and educational group differences, but, as expected, none were found that would have allowed the identification of further separate norms (see Schwarzinger & Schuler, 2016). Exceptions are persons in managerial positions; higher values in Self-Centered Work Approach were also found for this group ($t(54)=3.22, p<.00; d_{Cohen}=-.545$). The norm group of managers consists of n=258 persons, 58% male, with an average age of 42 years (SD=10.5). In the UK/US-adaptation, the same effect was found, resulting in a separate norm group for managerial positions (N = 435). In a sample of managers, there were no differences between men and women on the factors of the TOP (Mai et al., 2017).

6.3.5 Research-Practice Effects

One, if not the main application of the TOP is for personnel selection. This special situation traditionally influences the respondents' response behavior. In the selection situation, persons generally tend to present themselves in a positive light, which is reflected in higher values for positively associated procedures or constructs such as Conscientiousness (Marshall et al., 2005; see also the comments on faking in Section 5.1.1). Lower values are therefore expected for dark procedures in the selection situation, as is the case for TOP.

To get an impression of the strength of this effect, the TOP items were presented in a selection situation. This was an online preselection test of applicants for all vacant positions in a medium-sized technical company, i.e., a very broad mix of different educational levels and fields. Their scores were compared with the overall research sample. The effect strengths were determined as Hedge's g (or Cohen's d) for samples of different sizes.

For the scales and factors of the TOP, unexpectedly mostly small or no effects as well as medium-strong effects appeared. The largest effects, with two-thirds of a standard deviation, are for Uncommitted-Impulsive Work Style, but none for Enforcement-Focused Work Attitude. On average, a small effect of g=–.30 resulted. Table 15 presents the results.

Thus, the TOP procedure was developed and standardized on the target population, and the norms are accessible to users. That several foreign-language adaptations of TOP are now being published or in the process of validation will also enable comparative cultural studies of the Dark Triad of personality in the professional context.

Table 15: Effect sizes research vs. selection

	Research		Selection					
	M	*SD*	*M*	*SD*	t (1 454)	*p*	Hedges g	Effect according to Cohen
Self-centered work approach	4.08	0.86	3.72	1.08	4.56	.00	–.41	Small
Claim to leadership	4.44	1.27	4.24	1.34	1.75	.08	–.16	Small
Belief in persuasive power	4.54	0.90	4.07	0.90	5.84	.00	–.52	Medium
Need for authority	3.37	1.19	2.90	1.20	4.41	.00	–.40	Small
Appetite for risk	4.55	1.13	4.58	1.08	0.30	.77	.03	No effect
Sense of superiority	3.45	1.13	2.80	0.89	6.55	.00	–.59	Medium
Enforcement-focused work attitude	3.37	0.94	3.35	1.00	0.24	.81	–.02	No effect
Unsentimentality	3.57	1.11	4.08	1.10	5.14	.00	.46	Small
Assertiveness	3.35	1.12	3.25	0.97	1.01	.31	–.09	No effect
Skepticism	3.20	1.15	2.72	0.91	4.75	.00	–.43	Small
Uncommitted-impulsive work style	3.17	0.93	2.53	1.08	7.57	.00	–.68	Medium
Flexibility	3.12	1.02	2.44	0.82	7.58	.00	–.68	Medium
Impulsivity	3.28	1.40	2.51	1.19	6.23	.00	–.56	Medium
Extenuation	3.15	1.32	2.64	1.23	4.35	.00	–.39	Small

Note. Research N = 1,318, Selection setting N = 138. A negative sign for effect sizes indicates that lower values were obtained in the selection situation. Hedges g interpretation according to Cohen (1988): $<.20$ = no effect, .20–.50 = small effect, .50–.80 = moderate effect, $>.80$ = strong effect.

7 Recommendations for Practice and Further Research

This book aimed to clarify the extent to which the consideration of the personality traits narcissism, Machiavellianism, and psychopathy can make a meaningful contribution to the diagnosis of aptitude for a profession. I discussed whether the characteristics can be validly recorded in the occupational context and whether they are related to criteria of occupational success or job performance. In addition, I examined whether the Dark Triad can be used for personnel selection in compliance with professional ethical, legal, and operative requirements, i.e., whether its application in practice appears possible. In the following, I summarize the contents and results of the theoretical and methodological foundation and the findings on the validity and operative applicability of the Dark Triad in personnel selection and link them with each other to derive further research needs and practical recommendations for action.

7.1 Recommendations for Research

7.1.1 The Need for Further Theoretical Foundation and Methodological Consolidation

The Dark Triad of personality belongs to a larger group of traits grouped under the umbrella category of dark-side personality traits. These are characterized by the fact that they are dimensional or subclinical concepts, mostly originally of clinical personality disorders. In addition to narcissism, Machiavellianism, and psychopathy, these primarily include the characteristics based on the DSM or the scales of HDS (Spain et al., 2014), but there are also many others. They represent mixtures of individual, delimitable aspects and thus are so-called compound traits (Dilchert et al., 2014). They do not necessarily have negative consequences; positive ones are also discussed and proven, especially for the trait carrier (Wille et al., 2013). The relationships of the various dark concepts to each other have not yet been sufficiently researched. Rather, there are several parallel proposals for content-related "cores," and the individual traits cannot be clearly distinguished from each other – a clear taxonomy of dark traits has been lacking so far (Spain et al., 2014) and is still missing. Such an integrating function could be performed by the maladaptive trait model of the new DSM-5 (APA, 2013), which has an empirically definable, hierarchical structure similar to that of the FFM (Guenole, 2014). Research in the area of connecting or unifying all dark-side traits in one model is promising and urgently needed.

The Dark Triad itself is also a group of overlapping traits that share content (Furnham, Richards et al., 2013) and common genetic foundations (Vernon et al., 2008), but also in some cases they show considerable differences in their relationship to external criteria, which differ in trait-specific terms, for example, regarding overestimating oneself

(Jonason, Abboud et al., 2017), emotional aspects (Jonason & Kroll, 2015), impulsiveness (Jones & Paulhus, 2011), or antisocial behavior (Baughmann et al., 2012). All Triad components are associated with several interpersonally negative behaviors, but psychopathy is the most problematic feature of the Dark Triad in terms of its effects on others (Muris et al., 2017). The characteristics also differ in their relationship to general personality models (O'Boyle et al., 2015) and regarding the maladaptive trait model (Grigoras & Wille, 2017).

On the other hand, as argued by Muris et al. (2017), the Triad as a whole could be a redundant concept, since its variance can be explained almost entirely by the FFM (O'Boyle et al., 2015) as well as in part also by the core of the Triad disagreeableness (Vernon et al., 2008) and the H-factor of the HEXACO model (Hodson et al., 2018) or main components of the psychopathy construct (Book et al., 2015). However, neither psychopathy nor the H-factor nor the FFM can explain the entire variance of the Dark Triad (see Book et al., 2015; Hodson et al., 2018). Because of the large overlaps, in some cases, a better model fit was found for the modeling of one factor and including a bifactor (Bertl et al., 2017; McLarnon & Tarraf, 2017; Volmer et al., 2019) or the combination of Machiavellianism and psychopathy as one factor (Miller et al., 2017) than for the assumption of a three-factor structure of the Dark Triad. Accordingly, it has repeatedly been pointed out that Machiavellianism and psychopathy are difficult to distinguish and share considerable variance (e.g., Vize, Collison et al., 2018).

For this reason, regression analyses have often been used methodically or as an analytical strategy to investigate the relationships of the Dark Triad to external variables. This has been criticized for the fact that partialing out shared variance leads to considerable changes in the original constructs under consideration, so it is no longer clear what the residuals represent in terms of content (Sleep et al., 2017). Another prominent approach of Triad research, the use of composite scores, was particularly critically evaluated, since by combining the multilayered features, considerable portions of variance are lost, which can even lead to a leveling of existing relationships to external criteria (Watts et al., 2017). The use of different techniques such as composite scores, SEM, or regressions was therefore viewed critically – or at least called for a clear statement of the method used and proof of its suitability (Vize, Collison et al., 2018).

The reason for the theoretical and methodological problems of Triad research is primarily seen in the construct creep (Furnham, Richards et al., 2013). Decades of isolated research led to an expansion and overlapping of the considered feature areas, which now, when measured in combination, result in content redundancy and statistically in common variance. Even more so because of the widespread analytical methods of partialization of shared variance or the formation of composite scores, it became unclear what exact relationships individual features, or their partial aspects, have to external variables. For this reason, the conception and use of the Dark Triad constructs as one-dimensional monoliths have been criticized, making the multidimensional consideration of the Dark Triad the most reasonable approach (Miller et al., 2019; Watts et al., 2017). Furthermore, a corresponding recording is postulated as a basis for any analytical strategy and an essential prerequisite for its improved future exploration.

As a conclusion to the theoretical and measurement methodological issues surrounding the Triad, it can be said that there is a need for a critical examination of what constitutes the properties in terms of content, what their differences are, and to what extent they can be delimited with the measurement and calculation methods available. If necessary, new procedures should be developed (and the further use of unsuitable ones refrained from), to further pursue the questions of the structure of the Dark Triad and the taxonomy of the entire "dark side" of the personality on an improved data basis. To clarify the nomological network of dark traits and the (statistical) search for empirical or content-related cores, the broadest possible standard procedures should be used, including all known dark concepts, i.e., not applying too narrow a preselection regarding content.

For the investigation of the relationship of the Dark Triad to criteria variables, it is also fundamentally advisable to orient the chosen methodology more strongly than before to the question posed and, following the symmetry hypothesis, to the level of consideration of the criteria. In exceptional cases, this can mean calculating a composite score; structural equation models or multiple regressions are often better. As a data basis for this, and in many cases probably exclusively, the use of procedures with as many facets as possible is recommended, with the possibility of displaying bivariate correlations of factor and subscale scores.

For further research and personnel practice, this results in the recommendation to take a multidimensional view of the Dark Triad properties, i.e., to collect as many specific, theoretically clearly derivable contents as possible. In this way, associated behaviors can be placed in a clear relationship to aspects of a work activity based on the requirements. Analytically, the use of basic procedures and the interpretation of the results of those subscales or factor values for which bivariate relationships to relevant criteria have been proven are thus initially suitable. If appropriate statistical knowledge and skills are present, the results of such procedures could also be reduced to their most significant influencing factors using regression analytical or structural modeling methods, and then these values could be used for aptitude diagnostics (before this, however, the predictors generated in this way would have to be tested for predictive validity for the specific application).

7.1.2 The Need for Further Practical Research and Practical Experience

Regardless of the unresolved conceptual and analytical questions, the explicitly job-related consideration of narcissism, Machiavellianism, and psychopathy is growing rapidly, as evidenced by a meta-analysis of the Dark Triad and work behavior (O'Boyle et al., 2012) and a review of the Dark Triad in the workplace (LeBreton et al., 2018). As practiced for the DSM-based dark-side traits for over 15 years, the use of the Dark Triad for personnel selection is obvious but is not yet carried out much, at least not to a broadly noticeable extent. For the justification of such use, formal basic conditions must be given; but above all the characteristics, if they are to offer a benefit for corresponding questions, must be able to predict criteria relevant to aptitude diagnostics, and this ideally better or with an additional explanatory contribution to procedures or constructs usually used in personnel work.

The long disregard for the dark side and excessive focus on the bright side in research on personality and profession has been criticized as a limitation (Guenole, 2014; Kaiser et al., 2015). As the comments on dark personality traits have shown, these extend the range of traits to include aspects of personality that are not or insufficiently included in general personality models, such as the Big Five, and corresponding inventories (Spain et al., 2014). They mark areas that lie outside of normal and everyday, but above all outside the publicly revealed part of personality.

Dark-side traits from the DSM tradition are often decidedly associated with problems concerning oneself or functioning in normal social life, often combined with a withdrawal from interpersonal exchange, competition, and sometimes even job performance. Other dark-side traits, like the Triad, focus on antagonistic traits, which are offensively directed against others and are sometimes morally reprehensible but are also associated with a better "functioning" in terms of one's progress. For narcissism, for example, this is the belief, which is exposed to the outside world but is socially little accepted that one is something very special and better than others and strives for corresponding confirmation. In the case of Machiavellianism, it is rather the hidden attitudes of disdain and a readiness to engage in the cool-rational exploitation of others to achieve one's own goals. In psychopathy, openly antisocial behavior such as lying, erratic and impulsive behavior with a lack of consideration for or compassion for others, up to criminal offenses, emerge to satisfy individual needs.

The dark side and especially the Dark Triad thus actually represent an extension of the range of characteristics on the predictor side. However, this is relevant only for the diagnosis of occupational aptitude if it also allows for an increased explanation of variance in criteria. The question is therefore whether the dark, hidden traits of people are effective at work, and if so, how strong their effects are.

The dark side of personality has been researched for a long time and has been proven to be very useful, especially in predicting counterproductive behavior (Sackett et al., 2017). Nowadays, dark-side traits are mostly used for research in the leadership context, primarily to explain the "derailment" of leaders (Dalal & Nolan, 2009). For DSM-based dark traits and indicators of disorders calculated with the so-called count technique from normal personality inventories, mostly negative correlations to criteria of professional or leadership success and professional development could be shown, but there are individual positive relationships, often for the narcissism-associated Bold scale of the HDS. Regarding individual questions, additional contributions to classical predictors or selection procedures could be shown, with the HDS, for example, for predicting the development of leadership (Harms et al., 2011), and with some FFM PD Counts incremental variance to the Big Five for objective performance criteria, but above all for subjective ones such as job satisfaction, could be explained (Wille et al., 2013).

Meta-analytically, a small negative relationship of Machiavellianism and psychopathy to job performance was demonstrated for the Dark Triad, but no connection was found for narcissism (O'Boyle et al., 2012), while a curvilinear relationship to leadership effectiveness was shown for the latter characteristic (Grijalva et al., 2015). The Dark Triad is associated with less voluntary commitment to others or the organization and less commitment to it (Sanecka, 2013). All Triad characteristics are associated with a greater degree of counterproductive behavior in the workplace, primarily toward individuals (O'Boyle et al., 2012). Leadership by individuals with elevated levels of Dark Triad traits can be expected to have negative effects on employee well-being and performance (Volmer et al., 2016). Positive effects are present only to a very small extent, primarily for individual success indicators such as salary (Spurk et al., 2016). There are usually negative correlations with criteria of subjective success, such as job satisfaction (Bruk-Lee et al., 2009).

The relationships of dark characteristics depend on the individual characteristic under consideration as well as moderators such as the autonomy of the activity, the sector, the corporate culture, or the specific profession, and in some cases, these are not linear (Harms & Spain, 2015). Moderators also play a major role in the Dark Triad in understanding their work and relationships in the occupational context and feature-specific differences (Smith et al., 2016). Particularly when bearers of the Triad traits have room for maneuver or feel restricted or competitive situations or opportunities for self-expression exist, trait-typical behavior and its effects become more apparent. In addition, in some cases, curvilinear relationships to criteria of job performance exist (Zettler & Solga, 2013).

The picture of the effect of dark characteristics in professional life is thus complex and not unequivocal, but, in any case, it could be proven that dark characteristics can in principle explain occupation-related questions. Narcissism, Machiavellianism, and psychopathy have no positive connection to job performance and success; on the contrary, they are associated with negative effects, especially on managed employees. Thus, the Dark Triad is demonstrably related to job and leadership performance-relevant variables and is a concept that promises fundamentally useful applications in vocational-aptitude diagnostics. In accordance with the shared variance with the Big Five described earlier in this section, incremental validity could be proven only in a few cases for questions relevant to aptitude diagnostics (e.g., Jonason & O'Connor, 2017; Paleczek et al., 2018; Scherer et al., 2013; Schneider et al., 2017), but corresponding studies are rare so far, and therefore further studies are urgently needed.

The central limitation in the use of dark personality traits and especially of the Dark Triad for aptitude-diagnostic purposes is therefore (besides application-related questions discussed below) the lack of more varied evidence of their incremental usefulness for aptitude diagnostics. This is needed to investigate which specific components of the multidimensional constructs are related to which professional (mis)behaviors and criteria, and which moderators or mediators play a role in this, and to which criteria curvilinear relationships exist. These questions need to be clarified in the use case and with occupational samples, ideally in a selection context, to allow more specific predictions of occupational behavior, experience, or performance. On this basis, studies with other common predictors of occupational performance and the investigation of incremental validity of the Dark Triad on them are also possible.

Regarding the aptitude-diagnostic usefulness of the Dark Triad, it can be stated that it exists in principle, both theoretically based and proven by empirical findings, but that much further research is needed to clarify in detail which narrow subfacets have an effect and in what combination. These can then be used for narrow occupational criteria or combined to predict broad criteria, perhaps to sometime obtain a dark Criterion-Focused Occupational Personality Scale compiled according to criteria-related validity – a "dark COPS."

7.2 Recommendations for Practice

7.2.1 Requirements and Recommendations for the Practical Application of the Dark Triad

Despite the limitations shown, the Dark Triad of personality is related to (mis)behavior relevant to professional success and is basically suitable for predicting criteria of job performance and success. It is, therefore, possible to apply the concept in practical personnel work. Primarily intended for personnel-selection procedures, there are various legal and professional requirements as well as considerations concerning the reaction of the applicants and the ethical justifiability of the assessment.

The question of legal admissibility can be answered by saying that there are no legal provisions or restrictions on the dimensional coverage of narcissism, Machiavellianism, and subclinical psychopathy. However, individual items, especially from psychopathy inventories, seem too invasive for the selection context or legally questionable. According to the prevailing opinion, genuine clinical diagnoses are not permitted in personnel selection; in some countries, this is also regulated by law. The use of, say, the PCL or a clinical interview for the diagnosis of narcissistic personality disorder would therefore not be appropriate in personnel selection. The situation is similar to methods that calculate indicators for disorders based on "normal" personality. Such analytical techniques and the conclusions drawn from them are not affected by the guidelines for clinical diagnosis (i.e., they are no official diagnosis), but they appear to be ethically questionable, especially if they are not applied transparently or even retrospectively.

As for all other methods of aptitude diagnostics, the standards of psychological test theory can be applied as technical requirements for the use of the Dark Triad in the occupational context, extended by relevant aspects from practice, such as the availability of user information and the occupational and requirement reference as well as the proven criterion-related validity of the procedures used. As the observations have shown, the common psychometric quality criteria for the standard procedures for the Dark Triad are largely met, even for the short procedure SD 3. The Dirty Dozen, on the other hand, must be described as less suitable for aptitude-diagnostic purposes (Spain et al., 2014). External assessments and proxies, especially IT- or even AI-supported ones based on personal information in social media, are not suitable for operative personnel work from a psychometric point of view according to the current state of data, and there are considerable practical difficulties and ethical concerns.

The requirements for personnel practice of job-relatedness and requirement reference, the documentation of a procedure, and the existence of user instructions are also not met for the new measurement approaches mentioned and the common standard and short procedures. The commercially distributed psychopathy scales SRP 4 and PPI comply with the documentation requirements but do not have any job-relatedness.

In connection with the occupational relevance of a procedure, social validity was discussed as a further aspect that urgently needs to be considered when assessing the applicability of the Dark Triad in aptitude diagnostics. The standard and short procedures were found to be possibly too invasive regarding their contents; FFM PD Counts were criticized for lack of transparency and their proximity to clinical disorders; and novel methods were rejected because of the lack of control over the diagnostic situation. A socially valid application of the Dark Triad can generally succeed if it is recorded in an ethically acceptable manner, that is, when the professional relevance of the characteristics is communicated transparently and appropriate feedback is given.

The investigation of the applicability of the Dark Triad in real personnel-selection processes or in executive coaching has only just begun. In addition, there are reservations on the part of users because of the background and designation of the three characteristics and an assumed rejection on the part of applicants – or at least an increased need for explanations of the characteristics in practice. There is still too little experience available about how the characteristics can be integrated into selection processes and results can be reported back as well as what effects there are on reliability and validity in selection situations. These questions are accordingly the most relevant future field of research for practice and should be examined in detail by science, but above all by human resource managers in organizations for their concrete application.

In summary, the Dark Triad of personality can be applied like any other trait in practical means of vocational-aptitude diagnostics, provided the legal guidelines and professional requirements applicable to the field are met. This is not the case for the alternative measurement approaches presented or at least this cannot yet be assessed based on the data available. Therefore, the use of these techniques and methods for recording the Triad for personnel psychological purposes must be urgently advised against.

Self-evaluation procedures have been identified as the only type of procedure that currently meets the requirements of an instrument for operational personnel selection. In addition, other promising measurement procedures have been proposed and should be further researched to introduce them into organizational use and research. These include conditional reasoning tests (CRT), digital work simulations, and forced-choice procedures. In the sense of multimodal personnel selection, the consideration of other diagnostic approaches, such as those of the simulation approach, situational interview questions or role-plays, also promises great knowledge gain and potential incremental benefits.

7.2.2 Personnel Selection with the TOP – Possibilities and Limitations

Using the personality test TOP as an example, it was examined to what extent a measurement of the Dark Triad is validly possible in a professional context, and to what extent a procedure of this kind is practically applicable. Within the framework of test development, it was possible to transfer numerous individual aspects of the characteristics to the occupational context. From a pool of occupationally formulated items, 11 scales were extracted that depict central contents of narcissism, Machiavellianism, and psychopathy in a work-related variant. The 11 scales are based on three factors that can be described as the Dark Triad to a large extent. The "psychopathy factor" represents a content-restricted form of the complete original construct, which only covers occupationally related aspects of the psychopath's lifestyle. This limits the possibility of direct comparison with common Triad methods. The complex structural model of the TOP with 11 scales and three latent factors does not show a perfect but acceptable fit to the data concerning all fit indices in confirmatory testing. As for the English version and several other language adaptations of the procedure, quasi-identical fit values could be found so at least the structure was confirmed across languages (Schwarzinger & Schuler, 2019, 2020, 2021a, b, c, 2022 a, b).

The psychometric properties of the TOP are generally satisfactory to good, and an objective and reliable measurement of the Dark Triad can be assumed. The distribution properties of the TOP scales are good and allow the subclinical, normally distributed measurement of the characteristics. Construct-related validity of the TOP could be proven in several aspects. For example, the Triad properties are related to each other and convergent to the factors of standard and short procedures to an extent that can generally be expected for the Triad according to meta-analytical results.

Using general personality models, a pattern for the TOP factors that is considered typical for the Dark Triad could be confirmed, primarily their common core of "disagreeableness" and low Honesty-Humility and expected differences, for example, for Extraversion. Specific differences between the TOP factors are also found concerning the characteristics of the maladaptive trait model. The relationship of the TOP to the new DSM-5 model is a field to be explored in more detail in the future to clarify the taxonomic classification of the TOP and the other dark traits.

With the TOP scales, it was possible to demonstrate to a large extent the professional interest structures for Triad factors known from the literature, such as the negative correlations of Machiavellianism and psychopathy to social interests and the positive correlations of narcissism to entrepreneurial orientation. The Triad characteristics are also measured with the TOP independently of intelligence, the expected overestimations of cognitive performance for Self-Centered Work Approach occur. All TOP factors show a positive relationship to achievement motivation. Upon closer examination, almost exclusively correlations are found with aspects of motivation oriented toward social comparison and individual status. Regarding such concepts that depict interpersonal influence, considerable differences between the factors can be identified. Self-Centered Work Approach is positively associated with social competence and political skill, whereas the other two factors are not or, in the case of Uncommitted-Impulsive Work Style and social competence, even negatively.

The TOP factor Uncommitted-Impulsive Work Style is negatively associated with OCB and positively with more CWB, both for the two targets – individuals and organizations – and with almost all subaspects of CWB. Self-Centered Work Approach has a relationship with CWB toward individuals, but not with CWB toward organizations and not with OCB. Enforcement-Focused Work Attitude is related to less OCB but unexpectedly not to CWB. Using the TOP scales, a substantial proportion of the variance in OCB and CWB can be explained, but there is little incremental contribution to explain counterproductive behavior beyond personality models and the composite characteristic of integrity.

Regarding criteria of job performance and professional success, the TOP largely follows the relationships derived from the literature. In one sample, for Self-Centered Work Approach, there is no linear relationship to job performance in supervisor assessment but a curvilinear relationship. In a further study, however, there are strong correlations, which may have arisen because of the specific sample and the relationship to the assessor. Assessments of managed employees also show no evidence of better performance or leadership or a particular management style. In self-assessment, on the other hand, Self-Centered Work Approach gives very positive evaluations of one's own performance and success, especially about objective criteria that one has stated oneself. The two other TOP factors, on the other hand, are related to tendentially rather negative evaluations of one's performance, success, and objective criteria, but the connections are usually weak. Teams that are subordinate to managers with higher values in Enforcement-Focused Work Attitude tend to have worse objective success indicators, and their job satisfaction is also rather low. A more pronounced Enforcement-Focused Work Attitude is associated with poorer grades in school and vocational training. All TOP factors are associated with low job satisfaction and tend to show less commitment to the organization.

The difference between Enforcement-Focused Work Attitude and Uncommitted-Impulsive Work Style seems to be that the former is the least conducive to individual performance and success criteria as well as leadership performance, and Uncommitted-Impulsive Work Style, even in the workplace, has the strongest negative correlation with interpersonally negative criteria. Of all the TOP factors, Self-Centered Work Approach is the least problematic, with, in some cases, even positive effects on individual performance and professional success (in line with the literature on narcissism at work).

The requirements and expectations for a test derived for a practical application of Dark Triad characteristics can be described as largely fulfilled. As the explanations have shown, the TOP has acceptable psychometric quality and shows good distributional characteristics that allow for a subclinical measurement of the Dark Triad. The development was carried out on the working general population and in professional contexts, and norms and user information are available. As far as items and documentation are concerned, the test material can be described as suitable for the target context. Initial studies on the acceptance of the procedure and the explanations in the manual on the intended application also suggest that a socially valid application that is accepted by applicants is possible. Thus, the prerequisites are given for the use of the procedure for operative personnel selection according to legal and professional aspects as well as regarding the acceptance of applicants.

From seminars on the TOP with test users, it became clear that the described steps for contextualization are very much welcomed by practitioners, but that there are concerns because of the background of the features and the common understanding of their contents, especially regarding communication and justification of the use and feedback of the results. In contrast, initial practical projects are very optimistic: The items and the procedure have been assessed as "relatively normal" and suitable for the purpose, and respondents from the top management of a large financial group have attested the procedure a high degree of face validity and basic applicability in the executive assessment of their organization – and there has been no explicit criticism from applicants from real life. It should be noted that the introduction of the TOP in the practical example described was accompanied by careful communication and training of the participants, and that care was taken to establish a clear requirement reference to the mission statement and the Code of Conduct of the company. All persons and organizations interested in using the Dark Triad in operational personnel selection – with any procedure or diagnostic approach – must be strongly recommended to take similar steps.

Summarizing the results of the test design and validation, the development of TOP and the "small migration" of the Dark Triad to the occupational context have largely succeeded. This makes a published procedure available whose use in a socially valid selection process according to professional standards is basically possible. However, the communication of the application and the results must be planned very carefully, and the decision to use the TOP for personnel-psychological purposes must be made only after weighing the expected benefits and the effort required for this. Its use is potentially worthwhile in any case.

7.3 Conclusion: The Dark Triad of Personality in Personnel Selection

The Dark Triad of personality is a group of characteristics related in many ways to criteria of professional success and job performance. The measurement of narcissism, Machiavellianism, and psychopathy thus promises to be useful for professional aptitude diagnostics. Because of the "grand migration" (Furnham, Richards et al., 2013, p. 200) to the subclinical sphere, the characteristics can be used without legal problems, even for personnel-selection purposes. With the TOP, an explicitly work-related procedure is now available for practical purposes; regarding documentation, theoretical foundation, psychometric characteristics, and available user information, it enables a socially valid application that is accepted from a professional point of view and by the applicants. The last couple of years have seen additional job-related procedures that also seem promising to potentially fulfill the requirements explained and set throughout this book. The Dark Triad of personality can thus be used as a concept, especially measured with the TOP and embedded in a diagnostic process according to the field standards, for practical personnel selection or related application purposes. It promises to contribute to the clarification of a person's professional suitability or fit.

Nevertheless, there are still some unresolved theoretical and analytical questions about the Dark Triad and practical reservations about the background and "branding" of the features. And central to the assessment of the usefulness of their use, the relationships to criteria of professional success are usually weak, or at least the incremental validity to common predictors of job performance or misconduct is small according to previous findings. The question is thus less whether narcissism, Machiavellianism, and psychopathy *can be* used to select personnel, but rather whether it *should be* done at all, i.e., whether it makes sense in that environment.

The use of such explanatory features for personnel selection must be well justified, and there must be sound arguments speaking in its favor. One would be a distinct aptitude to predict job performance, yet this is rather not the case, as meta-analytical findings on the Dark Triad in general and data on the TOP suggest that the Dark Triad traits show virtually no linear relationship to task-related performance. For some criteria curvilinear relationships have been shown, and further investigation of these is promising. The findings on contextual performance, on the other hand, are clearer: People with high scores on the Triad traits are, to put it nicely, not very kind to colleagues and are unwilling to commit themselves to others or the organization if it does not promise them individual benefit. According to their background and typical motivation and behavioral patterns known from studies outside of the workplace, Triad traits are associated with an increased tendency toward counterproductive behavior, especially against individuals. The greatest danger in this respect is probably posed by managers with high scores on one of the three characteristics.

Numerous reliable findings reveal an expectation of destructive, abusive leadership behavior with considerable consequences for the performance and well-being of subordinates, including dismissal or depression. Thus, contrary to the expectations partially formulated at the beginning of the study, which lie primarily outside of science, the Dark Triad of personality proves to be unsuitable for finding successful future *leaders*, but it is useful for *stopping the wrong people* on their way to leadership, for mirroring people who act from improper motives, or for giving behavioral feedback with the goal of desired behavioral change.

In conclusion, if suitable procedures and appropriate actions are applied, the Dark Triad of personality can indeed be implemented in personnel work without further ado. In this context, its primary applications in personnel preselection lie in identifying highly problematic persons at an early stage. Even in more extensive test batteries for personnel selection and for advisory purposes, such as the analysis of the potential for career path planning, career guidance, or in the context of coaching, the Dark Triad characteristics can contribute valuable additional information that cannot be provided by any of the common job-related test procedures. Although this does not justify any hype about these characteristics from a personnel-psychological point of view, it does justify further research and, in many cases, the practical application of the Dark Triad of personality in personnel selection.

References

Ackerman, R.A., Witt, E.A., Donnellan, M.B., Trzesniewski, K.H., Robins, R.W., & Kashy, D.A. (2011). What does the Narcissistic Personality Inventory really measure? *Assessment, 18*, 67–87. https://doi.org/10.1177/1073191110382845

Adam, D. (2019, March 12). Does a "Dark Triad" of personality traits make you more successful? *Science*. https://www.sciencemag.org/news/2019/03/does-dark-Triad-personality-traits-make-you-more-successful https://doi.org/10.1126/science.aax3078

Aghababei, N., & Błachnio, A. (2015). Well-being and the Dark Triad. *Personality and Individual Differences, 86*, 365–368. https://doi.org/10.1016/j.paid.2015.06.043

Ahmetoglu, G., Dobbs, S., Furnham, A., Crump, J., Chamorro-Premuzic, T., & Bakhshalian, E. (2016). Dark side of personality, intelligence, creativity, and managerial level. *Journal of Managerial Psychology, 31*, 391–404. https://doi.org/10.1108/JMP-03-2013-0096

Akhtar, R., Ahmetoglu, G., & Chamorro-Premuzic, T. (2013). Greed is good? Assessing the relationship between entrepreneurship and subclinical psychopathy. *Personality and Individual Differences, 54*, 420–425. https://doi.org/10.1016/j.paid.2012.10.013

Akhtar, S. (2006). Deskriptive Merkmale und Differenzialdiagnose der Narzisstischen Persönlichkeitsstörung [Descriptive characteristics and differential diagnoses of narcisstic personality disorder]. In O.F. Kernberg & H.-P. Hartmann (Eds.), *Narzissmus. Grundlagen, Störungsbilder, Therapie* (pp. 231–262). Schattauer.

Aktas, N., de Bodt, E., Bollaert, H., & Roll, R. (2016). CEO narcissism and the takeover process: From private initiation to deal completion. *Journal of Financial and Quantitative Analysis, 51*, 113–137. https://doi.org/10.1017/S0022109016000065

Ali, F., Amorim, I.S., & Chamorro-Premuzic, T. (2009). Empathy deficits and trait emotional intelligence in psychopathy and Machiavellianism. *Personality and Individual Differences, 47*, 758–762. https://doi.org/10.1016/j.paid.2009.06.016

Ali, F., & Chamorro-Premuzic, T. (2010). The dark side of love and life satisfaction: Associations with intimate relationships, psychopathy, and Machiavellianism. *Personality and Individual Differences, 48*, 228–233. https://doi.org/10.1016/j.paid.2009.10.016

Allport, G.W., & Odbert, H.S. (1936). Trait-names: A psycho-lexical study. *Psychological Monographs, 47*, i–171. https://doi.org/10.1037/h0093360

Amelang, M., & Bartussek, D. (1997). *Differentielle Psychologie und Persönlichkeitsforschung* [Differential psychology and personality research]. Kohlhammer.

Amelang, M., & Schmidt-Atzert, L. (2006). *Psychologische Diagnostik und Intervention* [Psychological diagnostic and intervention] (4th ed.). Springer. https://doi.org/10.1007/3-540-28507-5

Amelang, M., & Zielinski, W. (2002). *Psychologische Diagnostik und Intervention* [Psychological diagnostic and intervention] (3rd ed.). Springer. https://doi.org/10.1007/978-3-662-09578-2

American Educational Research Association, American Psychological Association, National Council on Measurement in Education (NCME). (2014). *Standards for educational and psychological testing*. American Educational Research Association.

American Psychiatric Association. (2000). *Diagnostic and Statistical Manual of Mental Disorders – DSM-IV* (4th ed.). American Psychiatric Association.

American Psychiatric Association. (2013). *Diagnostic and Statistical Manual of Mental Disorders – DSM-5* (5th ed.). American Psychiatric Association.

American Psychological Association. (2018). Professional practice guidelines for occupationally mandated psychological evaluations. *American Psychologist, 73*, 186–197. https://doi.org/10.1037/amp0000170

ADA. (1990). *Americans with Disabilities Act of 1990. Pub. L. No. 101–336, § 12101, 104 Stat. 327 (1990, 2008)*. US Government Publishing Office. https://www.govinfo.gov/content/pkg/STATUTE-104/pdf/STATUTE-104-Pg327.pdf

Ames, A., & Kidd, A. H. (1979). Machiavellianism and women's grade point average. *Psychological Reports, 44*, 223–228. https://doi.org/10.2466/pr0.1979.44.1.223

Anderson, N., Salgado, J. F., & Hülsheger, U. R. (2010). Applicant reactions in selection: Comprehensive meta-analysis into reaction generalization versus situational specificity. *International Journal of Selection and Assessment, 18*, 291–304. https://doi.org/10.1111/j.1468-2389.2010.00512.x

Andrea, R. K., & Conway, J. A. (1982). Linear and curvilinear considerations of Machiavellianism and school leader effectiveness. *School Psychology International, 3*, 203–212. https://doi.org/10.1177/014303438200300404

Andreassen, C. S., Ursin, H., Eriksen, H. R., & Pallesen, S. (2012). The relationship of narcissism with workaholism, work engagement, and professional position. *Social Behavior and Personality: An International Journal, 40*, 881–890. https://doi.org/10.2224/sbp.2012.40.6.881

Arvan, M. (2013). A lot more bad news for conservatives, and a little bit of bad news for liberals? Moral judgments and the Dark Triad personality traits: A follow-up study. *Neuroethics, 6*, 51–64. https://doi.org/10.1007/s12152-012-9155-7

Asendorpf, J. B. (2009). *Persönlichkeitspsychologie* [Personality psychology]. Springer.

Ashton, M. C., & Lee, K. (2007). Empirical, theoretical, and practical advantages of the HEXACO model of personality structure. *Personality and Social Psychology Review, 11*, 150–166. https://doi.org/10.1177/1088868306294907

Ashton, M. C., & Lee, K. (2008). The HEXACO model of personality structure. In G. J. Boyle, G. Matthews, & D. Saklofske (Eds.), *Handbook of personality theory and assessment: Volume 2 – Personality measurement and testing* (pp. 239–260). Sage.

Ashton, M. C., & Lee, K. (2009). The HEXACO-60: A short measure of the major dimensions of personality. *Journal of Personality Assessment, 91*, 340–345. https://doi.org/10.1080/00223890902935878

Austin, E. J., Farrelly, D., Black, C., & Moore, H. (2007). Emotional intelligence, Machiavellianism and emotional manipulation: Does EI have a dark side? *Personality and Individual Differences, 43*, 179–189. https://doi.org/10.1016/j.paid.2006.11.019

Azizli, N., Atkinson, B. E., Baughman, H. M., Chin, K., Vernon, P. A., Harris, E., & Veselka, L. (2016). Lies and crimes: Dark Triad, misconduct, and high-stakes deception. *Personality and Individual Differences, 89*, 34–39. https://doi.org/10.1016/j.paid.2015.09.034

Babiak, P. (1995). When psychopaths go to work: A case study of an industrial psychopath. *Applied Psychology, 44*, 171–188. https://doi.org/10.1111/j.1464-0597.1995.tb01073.x

Babiak, P. (1996). Psychopathic manipulation in organizations: Pawns, patrons, and patsies. In D. J. Cooke, A. E. Forth, J. P. Newman, & R. D. Hare (Eds.), *Issues in criminological and legal psychology, No. 24: International perspectives on psychopathy* (pp. 12–17). British Psychological Society.

Babiak, P. (2007). From darkness into the light: Psychopathy in industrial and organizational psychology. In H. Hervé, & J. C. Yuille (Eds.), *The psychopath: Theory, research, and practice* (pp. 411–428). Erlbaum.

Babiak, P., Neumann, C. S., & Hare, R. D. (2010). Corporate psychopathy: Talking the walk. *Behavioral Sciences & the Law, 28*, 174–193. https://doi.org/10.1002/bsl.925

Bachrach, Y., Kosinski, M., Graepel, T., Kohli, P., & Stillwell, D. (2012). Personality and patterns of Facebook usage. *Proceedings of the 4th Annual ACM Web Science Conference* (pp. 24–32). ACM. https://doi.org/10.1145/2380718.2380722

Back, M. D., Schmukle, S. C., & Egloff, B. (2010). Why are narcissists so charming at first sight? Decoding the narcissism-popularity link at zero acquaintance. *Journal of Personality and Social Psychology, 98*, 132–145. https://doi.org/10.1037/a0016338

Baillod, J., & Semmer, N. (1994). Fluktuation und Berufsverläufe bei Computerfachleuten [Turnover and career development of IT professionals]. *Zeitschrift für Arbeits- und Organizationspsychologie, 38*, 152–163.

Baloch, M. A., Meng, F., Xu, Z., Cepeda-Carrion, I., Danish, & Bari, M. W. (2017). Dark Triad, perceptions of organizational politics and counterproductive work behaviors: The moderating effect of political skills. *Frontiers in Psychology, 8*, Article 1972. https://doi.org/10.3389/fpsyg.2017.01972

Baron, R. A. (2004). Workplace aggression and violence. In R. W. Griffin, & A. M. O'Leary-Kelly (Eds.), *The dark side of organizational behavior* (pp. 23–26). Jossey-Bass.

Barrick, M.R., & Mount, M.K. (1991). The Big Five personality dimensions and job performance: A meta-analysis. *Personnel Psychology, 44*, 1–26. https://doi.org/10.1111/j.1744-6570.1991.tb00688.x

Barrick, M.R., Mount, M.K., & Judge, T.A. (2001). Personality and performance at the beginning of the new millennium: What we do know and where do we go next? *International Journal of Selection and Assessment, 9*, 9–30. https://doi.org/10.1111/1468-2389.00160

Bartlett, C.J., Quay, L.C., & Wrightsman Jr, L.S. (1960). A comparison of two methods of attitude measurement: Likert-type and forced-choice. *Educational and Psychological Measurement, 20*, 699–704. https://doi.org/10.1177/001316446002000405

Basler, H. (2007). *Psychopathie und das Fünf-Faktoren-Modell der Persönlichkeit* [Psychopathy and the five-factor model of personality]. Unpublished diploma thesis, Christian Albrechts University of Kiel.

Bass, B.M., & Avolio, B.J. (1994). Transformational leadership and organizational culture. *The International Journal of Public Administration, 17*, 541–554. https://doi.org/10.1080/01900699408524907

Baughman, H.M., Dearing, S., Giammarco, E., & Vernon, P.A. (2012). Relationships between bullying behaviors and the Dark Triad: A study with adults. *Personality and Individual Differences, 52*, 571–575. https://doi.org/10.1016/j.paid.2011.11.020

Baughman, H.M., Jonason, P.K., Lyons, M., & Vernon, P.A. (2014). Liar liar pants on fire: Cheater strategies linked to the Dark Triad. *Personality and Individual Differences, 71*, 35–38. https://doi.org/10.1016/j.paid.2014.07.019

Baughman, H.M., Jonason, P.K., Veselka, L., & Vernon, P.A. (2014). Four shades of sexual fantasies linked to the Dark Triad. *Personality and Individual Differences, 67*, 47–51. https://doi.org/10.1016/j.paid.2014.01.034

Beauducel, A., & Wittmann, W.W. (2005). Simulation study on fit indexes in CFA based on data with slightly distorted simple structure. *Structural Equation Modeling, 12*, 41–75. https://doi.org/10.1207/s15328007sem1201_3

Becker, J.A., & O'Hair, D.H. (2007). Machiavellians' motives in organizational citizenship behavior. *Journal of Applied Communication Research, 35*, 246–267. https://doi.org/10.1080/00909880701434232

Bennett, R.J., & Robinson, S.L. (2000). Development of a measure of workplace deviance. *Journal of Applied Psychology, 85*, 349–360. https://doi.org/10.1037/0021-9010.85.3.349

Bensch, D., Maaß, U., Greiff, S., Horstmann, K.T., & Ziegler, M. (2019). The nature of faking: A homogeneous and predictable construct? *Psychological Assessment, 31*, 532–544. https://doi.org/10.1037/pas0000619

Benson, M.J., & Campbell, J.P. (2007). To be, or not to be, linear: An expanded representation of personality and its relationship to leadership performance. *International Journal of Selection and Assessment, 15*, 232–249. https://doi.org/10.1111/j.1468-2389.2007.00384.x

Benz, S.M. (2018). *Conditional Reasoning Test zur Erfassung der Dunklen Triade im beruflichen Kontext (CRT-DT)*. [Conditional Reasoning Test for assessing the Dark Triad in the professional context (CRT-DT)]. Unpublished master thesis, Zurich University of Applied Sciences.

Berry, C.M., Ones, D.S., & Sackett, P.R. (2007). Interpersonal deviance, organizational deviance, and their common correlates: A review and meta-analysis. *Journal of Applied Psychology, 92*, 410–424. https://doi.org/10.1037/0021-9010.92.2.410

Berry, C.M., Sackett, P.R., & Wiemann, S. (2007). A review of recent developments in integrity test research. *Personnel Psychology, 60*, 271–301. https://doi.org/10.1111/j.1744-6570.2007.00074.x

Bertl, B., Pietschnig, J., Tran, U.S., Stieger, S., & Voracek, M. (2017). More or less than the sum of its parts? Mapping the Dark Triad of personality onto a single dark core. *Personality and Individual Differences, 114*, 140–144. https://doi.org/10.1016/j.paid.2017.04.002

Bezdjian, S., Raine, A., Baker, L.A., & Lynam, D.R. (2011). Psychopathic personality traits in children: Genetic and environmental contributions. *Psychological Medicine, 41*, 589–600. https://doi.org/10.1017/S0033291710000966

Birkeland, S.A., Manson, T.M., Kisamore, J.L., Brannick, M.T., & Smith, M.A. (2006). A meta-analytic investigation of job applicant faking on personality measures. *International Journal of Selection and Assessment, 14*, 317–335. https://doi.org/10.1111/j.1468-2389.2006.00354.x

Blair, C.A., Hoffman, B.J., & Helland, K.R. (2008). Narcissism in organizations: A multisource appraisal reflects different perspectives. *Human Performance, 21*, 254–276. https://doi.org/10.1080/08959280802137705

Blickle, G., & Gläser, D. (2009). Politische Fertigkeiten und Arbeitsstile: Eine Feldstudie [Political skill and work styles: A field study]. *Zeitschrift für Arbeits- und Organisationspsychologie, 53*, 94–103. https://doi.org/10.1026/0932-4089.53.3.94

Blickle, G., Schlegel, A., Fassbender, P., & Klein, U. (2006). Some personality correlates of business white-collar crime. *Applied Psychology, 55*, 220–233. https://doi.org/10.1111/j.1464-0597.2006.00226.x

Blickle, G., & Schütte, N. (2017). Trait psychopathy, task performance, and counterproductive work behavior directed toward the organization. *Personality and Individual Differences, 109*, 225–231. https://doi.org/10.1016/j.paid.2017.01.006

Boddy, C.R. (2011). Corporate psychopaths, bullying and unfair supervision in the workplace. *Journal of Business Ethics, 100*, 367–379. https://doi.org/10.1007/s10551-010-0689-5

Boddy, C. R. (2017). Psychopathic leadership a case study of a corporate psychopath CEO. *Journal of Business Ethics, 145*, 141–156.

Boddy, C.R., Miles, D., Sanyal, C., & Hartog, M. (2015). Extreme managers, extreme workplaces: Capitalism, organizations and corporate psychopaths. *Organization, 22*, 530–551. https://doi.org/10.1177/1350508415572508

Book, A., Visser, B.A., & Volk, A.A. (2015). Unpacking "evil": Claiming the core of the Dark Triad. *Personality and Individual Differences, 73*, 29–38. https://doi.org/10.1016/j.paid.2014.09.016

Borkenau, P., & Ostendorf, F. (2008). *NEO Fünf Faktoren Inventar nach Costa and McCrae* (NEO-FFI; 2. Auflage.). [NEO Five Factor Inventory of Costa and McCrae (NEO-FFI; 2nd ed.)]. Hogrefe.

Borman, W.C., & Motowidlo, S.M. (1993). Expanding the criterion domain to include elements of contextual performance. In N. Schmitt, & W.C. Borman (Eds.), *Personnel selection in organizations* (pp. 71–98). Jossey-Bass.

Brandstätter, H., & Schuler, H. (1974). *Overcoming halo and leniency: A new method of merit rating.* Paper presented at the 18th International Congress of Applied Psychology, Montreal.

Braun, S. (2017). Leader narcissism and outcomes in organizations: A review at multiple levels of analysis and implications for future research. *Frontiers in Psychology, 8*, Article 773. https://doi.org/10.3389/fpsyg.2017.00773

Brown, A., & Maydeu-Olivares, A. (2013). How IRT can solve problems of ipsative data in forced-choice questionnaires. *Psychological Methods, 18*, 36–52. https://doi.org/10.1037/a0030641

Bruk-Lee, V., Khoury, H.A., Nixon, A.E., Goh, A., & Spector, P.E. (2009). Replicating and extending past personality/job satisfaction meta-analyses. *Human Performance, 22*, 156–189. https://doi.org/10.1080/08959280902743709

Brunell, A.B., Gentry, W.A., Campbell, W.K., Hoffman, B.J., Kuhnert, K.W., & DeMarree, K.G. (2008). Leader emergence: The case of the narcissistic leader. *Personality and Social Psychology Bulletin, 34*, 1663–1676. https://doi.org/10.1177/0146167208324101

Bühner, M. (2011). *Einführung in die Test- und Fragebogenkonstruktion* (3. Aufl.). [Introduction to test and questionnaire construction (3rd ed.)]. Pearson.

Bushman, B.J., Bonacci, A.M., van Dijk, M., & Baumeister, R.F. (2003). Narcissism, sexual refusal, and aggression: Testing a narcissistic reactance model of sexual coercion. *Journal of Personality and Social Psychology, 84*, 1027–1040. https://doi.org/10.1037/0022-3514.84.5.1027

Cairncross, M., Veselka, L., Schermer, J.A., & Vernon, P.A. (2013). A behavioral genetic analysis of alexithymia and the Dark Triad traits of personality. *Twin Research and Human Genetics, 16*, 690–697. https://doi.org/10.1017/thg.2013.19

Campbell, W.K., Goodie, A.S., & Foster, J.D. (2004). Narcissism, confidence, and risk attitude. *Journal of Behavioral Decision Making, 17*, 297–311. https://doi.org/10.1002/bdm.475

Campbell, W.K., Hoffman, B.J., Campbell, S.M., & Marchisio, G. (2011). Narcissism in organizational contexts. *Human Resource Management Review, 21*, 268–284.

Campbell, W.K., & Miller, J.D. (2011). *The handbook of narcissism and narcissistic personality disorder: Theoretical approaches, empirical findings, and treatments.* Wiley. https://doi.org/10.1002/9781118093108

Campbell, J., Schermer, J.A., Villani, V.C., Nguyen, B., Vickers, L., & Vernon, P.A. (2009). A behavioral genetic study of the Dark Triad of personality and moral development. *Twin Research and Human Genetics, 12*, 132–136. https://doi.org/10.1375/twin.12.2.132

Carey, A.L., Brucks, M.S., Küfner, A.C., Holtzman, N.S., große Deters, F., Back, M.D., Donnellan, M. B., Pennebaker, J. W., & Mehl, M. R. (2015). Narcissism and the use of personal pronouns revisited. *Journal of Personality and Social Psychology, 109*, e1–e15. https://doi.org/10.1037/pspp0000029

Carter, G.L., Montanaro, Z., Linney, C., & Campbell, A.C. (2015). Women's sexual competition and the Dark Triad. *Personality and Individual Differences, 74*, 275–279. https://doi.org/10.1016/j.paid.2014.10.022

Carton, H., & Egan, V. (2017). The Dark Triad and intimate partner violence. *Personality and Individual Differences, 105*, 84–88. https://doi.org/10.1016/j.paid.2016.09.040

Cascio, W.F., & Aguinis, H. (2008). Research in industrial and organizational psychology from 1963 to 2007: Changes, choices, and trends. *Journal of Applied Psychology, 93*, 1062–1081. https://doi.org/10.1037/0021-9010.93.5.1062

Castille, C.M., Kuyumcu, D., & Bennett, R.J. (2017). Prevailing to the peers' detriment: Organizational constraints motivate Machiavellians to undermine their peers. *Personality and Individual Differences, 104*, 29–36. https://doi.org/10.1016/j.paid.2016.07.026

Cattell, R.B. (1947). Confirmation and clarification of primary personality factors. *Psychometrika, 12*, 197–220. https://doi.org/10.1007/BF02289253

Chabrol, H., Bouvet, R., & Goutaudier, N. (2017). The Dark Tetrad and antisocial behavior in a community sample of college students. *Journal of Forensic Psychology Research and Practice, 17*, 295–304. https://doi.org/10.1080/24732850.2017.1361310

Chabrol, H., van Leeuwen, N., Rodgers, R., & Séjourné, N. (2009). Contributions of psychopathic, narcissistic, Machiavellian, and sadistic personality traits to juvenile delinquency. *Personality and Individual Differences, 47*, 734–739. https://doi.org/10.1016/j.paid.2009.06.020

Chatterjee, A., & Hambrick, D.C. (2007). It's all about me: Narcissistic chief executive officers and their effects on company strategy and performance. *Administrative Science Quarterly, 52*, 351–386. https://doi.org/10.2189/asqu.52.3.351

Cheung, M.W.L., & Jak, S. (2018). Challenges of big data analyses and applications in psychology. *Journal of Psychology, 226*, 209–211. https://doi.org/10.1027/2151-2604/a000348

Christiansen, N. D., Fisher, P. A., Robie, C., & Quirk, S. (2019). Tilting at windmills and improving personality assessment practices. *Industrial and Organizational Psychology, 12*, 177–183. https://doi.org/10.1017/iop.2019.35

Christiansen, N.D., Quirk, S.W., Robie, C., & Oswald, F.L. (2014). Light already defines the darkness: Understanding normal and maladaptive personality in the workplace. *Industrial and Organizational Psychology, 7*, 138–143. https://doi.org/10.1111/iops.12122

Christie, R. (1970a). Why Machiavelli? In R. Christie, & F.L. Geis (Eds.), *Studies in Machiavellianism* (pp. 1–9). Academic Press. https://doi.org/10.1016/B978-0-12-174450-2.50006-3

Christie, R. (1970b). Scale construction. In R. Christie, & F.L. Geis (Eds.), *Studies in Machiavellianism* (pp. 10–34). Academic Press. https://doi.org/10.1016/B978-0-12-174450-2.50007-5

Christie, R., & Geis, F.L. (1970). *Studies in Machiavellianism*. Academic Press.

Cleckley, H. (1941/1976). *The mask of sanity*. Mosby.

Cloetta, B. (1972). *MK: Fragebogen zur Erfassung von Machiavellismus und Konservatismus* [MK: Questionnaire to Assess Machiavellianism and Conservativism]. Zentrum I Bildungsforschung, Sonderforschungsbereich 23, Universität Konstanz.

Cohen, A. (2016). Are they among us? A conceptual framework of the relationship between the Dark Triad personality and counterproductive work behaviors (CWBs). *Human Resource Management Review, 2*, 69–85. https://doi.org/10.1016/j.hrmr.2015.07.003

Cohen, J. (1988). *Statistical power analysis for the behavioral sciences*. Erlbaum.

Colins, O.F., Fanti, K.A., Salekin, R.T., & Andershed, H. (2017). Psychopathic personality in the general population: Differences and similarities across gender. *Journal of Personality Disorders, 31*, 49–74. https://doi.org/10.1521/pedi_2016_30_237

Connelly, B.S., Lilienfeld, S.O., & Schmeelk, K.M. (2006). Integrity tests and morality: Associations with ego development, moral reasoning, and psychopathic personality. *International Journal of Selection and Assessment, 14*, 82–86. https://doi.org/10.1111/j.1468-2389.2006.00335.x

Cooke, D.J., & Michie, C. (2001). Refining the construct of psychopathy: toward a hierarchical model. *Psychological Assessment, 13*, 171–188. https://doi.org/10.1037/1040-3590.13.2.171

Cooke, D.J., Michie, C., & Hart, S.D. (2006). Facets of clinical psychopathy. In C.J. Patrick (Ed.), *Handbook of psychopathy* (pp. 91–106). Guilford.

Cooke, D.J., Michie, C., & Skeem, J. (2007). Understanding the structure of the Psychopathy Checklist-Revised. *The British Journal of Psychiatry, 190*, 39–50. https://doi.org/10.1192/bjp.190.5.s39

Corzine, J., Buntzman, G.F., & Busch, E.T. (1999). Machiavellianism in US bankers. *The International Journal of Organizational Analysis, 7*, 72–83. https://doi.org/10.1108/eb028895

Costa, P.T., Jr., & McCrae, R.R. (1985). *The NEO Personality Inventory manual.* Psychological Assessment Resources.

Cronbach, L.J. (1990). *Essentials of psychological testing.* Harper and Row.

Cronbach, L.J., & Gleser, G.C. (1965). *Psychological tests and personnel decisions.* University of Illinois Press.

Crossley, L., Woodworth, M., Black, P.J., & Hare, R. (2016). The dark side of negotiation: Examining the outcomes of face-to-face and computer-mediated negotiations among dark personalities. *Personality and Individual Differences, 91*, 47–51. https://doi.org/10.1016/j.paid.2015.11.052

Crotts, J.C., Aziz, A., & Upchurch, R.S. (2005). Relationship between Machiavellianism and sales performance. *Tourism Analysis, 10*, 79–84. https://doi.org/10.3727/1083542054547921

Crysel, L.C., Crosier, B.S., & Webster, G.D. (2013). The Dark Triad and risk behavior. *Personality and Individual Differences, 54*, 35–40. https://doi.org/10.1016/j.paid.2012.07.029

Dahling, J.J., Whitaker, B.G., & Levy, P.E. (2009). The development and validation of a new measure of Machiavellianism. *Journal of Management, 35*, 219–257. https://doi.org/10.1177/0149206308318618

Dahmen-Wassenberg, P., Kämmerle, M., Unterrainer, H.F., & Fink, A. (2016). The relation between different facets of creativity and the dark side of personality. *Creativity Research Journal, 28*, 60–66. https://doi.org/10.1080/10400419.2016.1125267

Dalal, D., & Nolan, K. (2009). Using dark side personality traits to identify potential failure. *Industrial and Organizational Psychology, 2*, 434–436. https://doi.org/10.1111/j.1754-9434.2009.01169.x

Dalal, R.S. (2005). A meta-analysis of the relationship between organizational citizenship behavior and counterproductive work behavior. *Journal of Applied Psychology, 90*, 1241–1255. https://doi.org/10.1037/0021-9010.90.6.1241

De Clercq, B., Hofmans, J., Vergauwe, J., De Fruyt, F., & Sharp, C. (2017). Developmental pathways of childhood dark traits. *Journal of Abnormal Psychology, 126*, 843–858. https://doi.org/10.1037/abn0000303

De Fruyt, F., De Clercq, B.J., Miller, J., Rolland, J.-P., Jung, S.-C., Taris, R., Furnham, A., & Van Hiel, A. (2009). Assessing personality at risk in personnel selection and development. *European Journal of Personality, 23*, 51–69. https://doi.org/10.1002/per.703

De Fruyt, F., Wille, B., & Furnham, A. (2013). Assessing aberrant personality in managerial coaching: Measurement issues and prevalence rates across employment sectors. *European Journal of Personality, 27*, 555–564. https://doi.org/10.1002/per.1911

De Hoogh, A.H., Den Hartog, D.N., & Nevicka, B. (2015). Gender differences in the perceived effectiveness of narcissistic leaders. *Applied Psychology, 64*, 473–498. https://doi.org/10.1111/apps.12015

Del Rosario, P.M., & White, R.M. (2005). The Narcissistic Personality Inventory: Test-retest stability and internal consistency. *Personality and Individual Differences, 39*, 1075–1081. https://doi.org/10.1016/j.paid.2005.08.001

Deluga, R.J. (1997). Relationship among American presidential charismatic leadership, narcissism, and rated performance. *The Leadership Quarterly, 8*, 49–65. https://doi.org/10.1016/S1048-9843(97)90030-8

Deluga, R.J. (2001). American presidential Machiavellianism: Implications for charismatic leadership and rated performance. *The Leadership Quarterly, 12*, 339–363. https://doi.org/10.1016/S1048-9843(01)00082-0

DeShong, H.L., Grant, D.M., & Mullins-Sweatt, S.N. (2015). Comparing models of counterproductive workplace behaviors: The Five-Factor Model and the Dark Triad. *Personality and Individual Differences, 74*, 55–60. https://doi.org/10.1016/j.paid.2014.10.001

DeShong, H.L., Helle, A.C., Lengel, G.J., Meyer, N., & Mullins-Sweatt, S.N. (2017). Facets of the Dark Triad: Utilizing the five-factor model to describe Machiavellianism. *Personality and Individual Differences, 105*, 218–223. https://doi.org/10.1016/j.paid.2016.09.053

DeYoung, C.G., Hirsh, J.B., Shane, M.S., Papademetris, X., Rajeevan, N., & Gray, J.R. (2010). Testing predictions from personality neuroscience: Brain structure and the Big Five. *Psychological Science, 21*, 820–828. https://doi.org/10.1177/0956797610370159

DeYoung, C.G., Peterson, J.B., & Higgins, D.M. (2002). Higher-order factors of the Big Five predict conformity: Are there neuroses of health? *Personality and Individual Differences, 33*, 533–552. https://doi.org/10.1016/S0191-8869(01)00171-4

DeYoung, C.G., Quilty, L.C., & Peterson, J.B. (2007). Between facets and domains: 10 aspects of the Big Five. *Journal of Personality and Social Psychology, 93*, 880–896. https://doi.org/10.1037/0022-3514.93.5.880

Dhanani, S., Kumari, V., Puri, B.K., Treasaden, I., Young, S., & Sen, P. (2017). A systematic review of the heritability of specific psychopathic traits using Hare's two-factor model of psychopathy. *CNS Spectrums, 23*, 29–38.

Diamond, D. (2006). Narzissmus als klinisches und gesellschaftliches Phänomen [Narcissism as clinical and societal phenomenon]. In O.F. Kernberg, & H.-P. Hartmann (Eds.), *Narzissmus. Grundlagen – Störungsbilder – Therapie* (pp. 171–204). Schattauer.

Digman, J.M. (1996). The curious history of the Five-Factor model. In J.S. Wiggins (Ed.), *The Five-Factor model of personality: Theoretical perspectives* (pp. 1–20). Guilford.

Digman, J.M. (1997). Higher-order factors of the Big Five. *Journal of Personality and Social Psychology, 73*, 1246–1256. https://doi.org/10.1037/0022-3514.73.6.1246

Dilchert, S., Ones, D.S., & Krueger, R.F. (2014). Maladaptive personality constructs, measures, and work behaviors. *Industrial and Organizational Psychology, 7*, 98–110. https://doi.org/10.1111/iops.12115

Donnellan, M.B., Trzesniewski, K.H., & Robins, R.W. (2009). An emerging epidemic of narcissism or much ado about nothing? *Journal of Research in Personality, 43*, 498–501. https://doi.org/10.1016/j.jrp.2008.12.010

Douglas, H., Bore, M., & Munro, D. (2012). Distinguishing the Dark Triad: Evidence from the Five-Factor model and the Hogan Development Survey. *Psychology, 3*, 237–242. https://doi.org/10.4236/psych.2012.33033

Dowgwillo, E.A., & Pincus, A.L. (2017). Differentiating Dark Triad traits within and across interpersonal circumplex surfaces. *Assessment, 24*, 24–44. https://doi.org/10.1177/1073191116643161

Dubbelt, L., Oostrom, J.K., Hiemstra, A.M., & Modderman, J.P. (2015). Validation of a digital work simulation to assess Machiavellianism and compliant behavior. *Journal of Business Ethics, 130*, 619–637. https://doi.org/10.1007/s10551-014-2249-x

DuBrin, A.J. (2012). *Narcissism in the workplace: Research, opinion and practice*. Edward Elgar Publishing. https://doi.org/10.4337/9781781001363

Dutton, K. (2012). *The wisdom of psychopaths: What saints, spies, and serial killers can teach us about success*. Macmillan.

Eaton, N.R., Krueger, R.F., South, S.C., Simms, L.J., & Clark, L.A. (2011). Contrasting prototypes and dimensions in the classification of personality pathology: Evidence that dimensions, but not prototypes, are robust. *Psychological Medicine, 41*, 1151–1163. https://doi.org/10.1017/S0033291710001650

Eisenbarth, H., Hart, C.M., & Sedikides, C. (2018). Do psychopathic traits predict professional success? *Journal of Economic Psychology, 64*, 130–139. https://doi.org/10.1016/j.joep.2018.01.002

Ellen, B.P., Kiewitz, C., Garcia, P.R.J.M., & Hochwarter, W.A. (2019). Dealing with the full-of-self-boss: Interactive effects of supervisor narcissism and subordinate resource management ability on work outcomes. *Journal of Business Ethics, 157*, 847–864. https://doi.org/10.1007/s10551-017-3666-4

Emmons, R.A. (1981). Relationship between narcissism and sensation seeking. *Psychological Reports, 48*, 247–250. https://doi.org/10.2466/pr0.1981.48.1.247

Emmons, R.A. (1984). Factor analysis and construct validity of the narcissistic personality inventory. *Journal of Personality Assessment, 48*, 291–300. https://doi.org/10.1207/s15327752jpa4803_11

Emmons, R.A. (1987). Narcissism: theory and measurement. *Journal of Personality and Social Psychology, 52*, 11–17. https://doi.org/10.1037/0022-3514.52.1.11

Equal Employment Opportunity Commission (EEOC). (2000). *Enforcement guidance: Disability-related inquiries and medical examinations of employees under the Americans with Disabilities Act (ADA).* https://www.eeoc.gov/policy/docs/guidance-inquiries.html#N_33_

Erdle, S., & Rushton, J.P. (2010). The general factor of personality, BIS-BAS, expectancies of reward and punishment, self-esteem, and positive and negative affect. *Personality and Individual Differences, 48*, 762–766. https://doi.org/10.1016/j.paid.2010.01.025

Fabrigar, L.R., Wegener, D.T., MacCallum, R.C., & Strahan, E.J. (1999). Evaluating the use of exploratory factor analysis in psychological research. *Psychological Methods, 4*, 272–299. https://doi.org/10.1037/1082-989X.4.3.272

Fehr, B., Samsom, D., & Paulhus, D.L. (1992). The construct of Machiavellianism: Twenty years later. In C.D. Spielberger & J.N. Butcher (Eds.), *Advances in personality assessment* (Vol. 9, pp. 77–116). Erlbaum.

Felfe, J., & Franke, F. (2012). *Commitment-Skalen* (COMMIT). [Commitment Scales (COMMIT)]. Huber.

Felfe, J., & Goihl, K. (2002). Deutsche überarbeitete und ergänzte Version des Multifactor Leadership Questionnaire (MLQ). [Revised German version of the Multifactor Leadership Questionnaire]. In A. Glöckner-Rist (Ed.), *ZUMA-Informationssystem. Elektronisches Handbuch sozialwissenschaftlicher Erhebungsinstrumente* (Version 5.00). Zentrum für Umfragen, Methoden und Analysen.

Felfe, J., Six, B., Schmook, R., & Knorz, C. (2010). Commitment gegenüber der Organization, dem Beruf/der Tätigkeit und der Beschäftigungsform (COBB). [Commitment toward the organization, the job, and the type of assignment]. In W. Sarges, H. Wottawa, & C. Roos (Eds.), *Handbuch wirtschaftspsychologischer Testverfahren, Band II: Organizationspsychologische Instrumente* (pp. 39–44). Pabst Science Publishers.

Ferris, G.R., Treadway, D.C., Kolodinsky, R.W., Hochwarter, W.A., Kacmar, C.J., Douglas, C., & Frink, D. (2005). Development and validation of the political skill inventory. *Journal of Management, 31*, 126–152. https://doi.org/10.1177/0149206304271386

Fiedler, P. (2001). *Persönlichkeitsstörungen* [Personality disorders]. Beltz.

First, M. B., Williams, J. B. W., Smith Benjamin, L., & Spitzer, R. L. (2019). *Structured Clinical Interview for DSM-5 Disorders – Personality Disorders (SCID-5-PD).* American Psychiatric Publishing.

Fisher, P.A., Robie, C., Christiansen, N.D., & Komar, S. (2018). The impact of psychopathy and warnings on faking behavior: A multisaturation perspective. *Personality and Individual Differences, 127*, 39–43. https://doi.org/10.1016/j.paid.2018.01.033

Fiske, D.W. (1949). Consistency of the factorial structures of personality ratings from different sources. *The Journal of Abnormal and Social Psychology, 44*, 329–344. https://doi.org/10.1037/h0057198

Foster, J.D., Shenesey, J.W., & Goff, J.S. (2009). Why do narcissists take more risks? Testing the roles of perceived risks and benefits of risky behaviors. *Personality and Individual Differences, 47*, 885–889. https://doi.org/10.1016/j.paid.2009.07.008

Freud, S. (1931). Über libidinöse Typen [On libidinious types]. In S. Freud (Ed.), *Gesammelte Werke* (Vol. XIV, pp. 507–513). Fischer.

Fritzon, K., Bailey, C., Croom, S., & Brooks, N. (2017). Problem personalities in the workplace: Development of the Corporate Personality Inventory. In P. A. Granhag, R. Bull, A. Shaboltas, & E. Dozortseva (Eds.), *Psychology and Law in Europe: When West Meets East* (pp. 139–166). CRC Press.

Furnham, A., Hughes, D.J., & Marshall, E. (2013). Creativity, OCD, narcissism and the Big Five. *Thinking Skills and Creativity, 10*, 91–98. https://doi.org/10.1016/j.tsc.2013.05.003

Furnham, A., Hyde, G., & Trickey, G. (2013). On-line questionnaire completion time and personality test scores. *Personality and individual differences*, *54*(6), 716–720. https://psycnet.apa.org/doi/10.1016/j.paid.2012.11.030

Furnham, A., Hyde, G., & Trickey, G. (2014). Do your dark side traits fit? Dysfunctional personalities in different work sectors. *Applied Psychology*, *63*(4), 589–606. https://psycnet.apa.org/doi/10.1111/apps.12002

Furnham, A., Richards, S.C., & Paulhus, D.L. (2013). The Dark Triad of personality: A 10-year review. *Social and Personality Psychology Compass, 7*, 199–216. https://doi.org/10.1111/spc3.12018

Furnham, A., Richards, S.C., Rangel, L., & Jones, D.N. (2014). Measuring malevolence: Quantitative issues surrounding the Dark Triad of personality. *Personality and Individual Differences, 67*, 114–121. https://doi.org/10.1016/j.paid.2014.02.001

Gable, M., & Dangello, F. (1994). Job involvement, Machiavellianism and job performance. *Journal of Business and Psychology, 9*, 159–170. https://doi.org/10.1007/BF02230634

Gable, M., Hollon, C., & Dangello, F. (1992). Managerial structuring of work as a moderator of the Machiavellianism and job performance relationship. *The Journal of Psychology, 126*, 317–325. https://doi.org/10.1080/00223980.1992.10543366

Gabriel, M. T., Critelli, J. W., & Ee, J. S. (1994). Narcissistic illusions in self-evaluations of intelligence and attractiveness. *Journal of Personality, 62*, 143–155. https://doi.org/10.1111/j.1467-6494.1994.tb00798.x

Gaddis, B. H., & Foster, J. L. (2015). Meta-analysis of dark side personality characteristics and critical work behaviors among leaders across the globe: Findings and implications for leadership development and executive coaching. *Applied Psychology, 64*, 25–54. https://doi.org/10.1111/apps.12017

Geis, F. L., & Christie, R. (1970). Overview of experimental research. In R. Christie, & F. L. Geis (Eds.), *Studies in Machiavellianism* (pp. 285–313). Academic Press. https://doi.org/10.1016/B978-0-12-174450-2.50020-8

Gerstenberg, F., Imhoff, R., Banse, R., & Schmitt, M. J. (2014). Discrepancies between implicit and explicit self-concepts of intelligence: Relations to modesty, narcissism, and achievement motivation. *Frontiers in Psychology, 5*, 85. https://doi.org/10.3389/fpsyg.2014.00085

Giammarco, E. A., Atkinson, B., Baughman, H. M., Veselka, L., & Vernon, P. A. (2013). The relation between antisocial personality and the perceived ability to deceive. *Personality and Individual Differences, 54*, 246–250. https://doi.org/10.1016/j.paid.2012.09.004

Gkorezis, P., Petridou, E., & Krouklidou, T. (2015). The detrimental effect of machiavellian leadership on employees' emotional exhaustion: Organizational cynicism as a mediator. *Europe's Journal of Psychology, 11*, 619–631. https://doi.org/10.5964/ejop.v11i4.988

Glenn, A. L., Raine, A., Yaralian, P. S., & Yang, Y. (2010). Increased volume of the striatum in psychopathic individuals. *Biological Psychiatry, 67*, 52–58. https://doi.org/10.1016/j.biopsych.2009.06.018

Glenn, A. L., & Sellbom, M. (2015). Theoretical and empirical concerns regarding the Dark Triad as a construct. *Journal of Personality Disorders, 29*, 360–https://doi.org/10.1521/pedi_2014_28_162. 377

Goldberg, L. R. (1993). The structure of phenotypic personality traits. *American Psychologist, 48*, 26–34. https://doi.org/10.1037/0003-066X.48.1.26

Gordon, D. S., & Platek, S. M. (2009). Trustworthy? The brain knows: Implicit neural responses to faces that vary in Dark Triad personality characteristics and trustworthiness. *Journal of Social, Evolutionary, and Cultural Psychology, 3*, 182–200. https://doi.org/10.1037/h0099323

Gottfredson, M. R., & Hirschi, T. (1990). *A general theory of crime*. Stanford University Press. https://doi.org/10.1515/9781503621794

Gough, H. G., & Bradley, P. (1992). Delinquent and criminal behavior as assessed by the revised California Psychological Inventory. *Journal of Clinical Psychology, 48*, 298–308. https://doi.org/10.1002/1097-4679(199205)48:3<298::AID-JCLP2270480306>3.0.CO;2-X

Griffin, M. A., Neal, A., & Parker, S. K. (2007). A new model of work role performance: Positive behavior in uncertain and interdependent contexts. *Academy of Management Journal, 50*, 327–347. https://doi.org/10.5465/amj.2007.24634438

Griffin, R. W., & O'Leary-Kelly, A. M. (2004). An introduction to the dark side. In R. W. Griffin & A. M. O'Leary-Kelly (Eds.), *The dark side of organizational behavior* (pp. 1–19). Jossey-Bass.

Griffith, R. L., Chmielowski, T., & Yoshita, Y. (2007). Do applicants fake? An examination of the frequency of applicant faking behavior. *Personnel Review, 36*, 341–355. https://doi.org/10.1108/00483480710731310

Grigoras, M., & Wille, B. (2017). Shedding light on the dark side: associations between the Dark Triad and the DSM-5 maladaptive trait model. *Personality and Individual Differences, 104*, 516–521. https://doi.org/10.1016/j.paid.2016.09.016

Grijalva, E., Harms, P. D., Newman, D. A., Gaddis, B., & Fraley, R. C. (2015). Narcissism and leadership: A meta-analytic review of linear and nonlinear relationships. *Personnel Psychology, 68*, 1–47. https://doi.org/10.1111/peps.12072

Grijalva, E., Maynes, T. D., Badura, K. L., & Whiting, S. W. W. (2020). Examining the "I" in team: A longitudinal investigation of the influence of team narcissism composition on team outcomes in the NBA. *Academy of Management Journal, 63*, 7–33. https://doi.org/10.5465/amj.2017.0218

Grijalva, E., & Newman, D.A. (2015). Narcissism and counterproductive work behavior (CWB): Meta-analysis and consideration of collectivist culture, Big Five personality, and narcissism's facet structure. *Applied Psychology, 64*, 93–126. https://doi.org/10.1111/apps.12025

Gruys, M.L., & Sackett, P.R. (2003). Investigating the dimensionality of counterproductive work behavior. *International Journal of Selection and Assessment, 11*, 30–42. https://doi.org/10.1111/1468-2389.00224

Guedes, M.J.C. (2017). Mirror, mirror on the wall, am I the greatest performer of all? Narcissism and self-reported and objective performance. *Personality and Individual Differences, 108*, 182–185. https://doi.org/10.1016/j.paid.2016.12.030

Guenole, N. (2014). Maladaptive personality at work: Exploring the darkness. *Industrial and Organizational Psychology, 7*, 85–97. https://doi.org/10.1111/iops.12114

Guenole, N. (2015). The hierarchical structure of work-related maladaptive personality traits. *European Journal of Psychological Assessment, 31*, 83–90. https://doi.org/10.1027/1015-5759/a000209

Guenole, N., Brown, A.A., & Cooper, A.J. (2016). Forced-choice assessment of work-related maladaptive personality traits: Preliminary evidence from an application of Thurstonian item response modeling. *Assessment, 25*, 1–14. https://doi.org/10.1177/1073191116641181

Guion, R.M., & Gottier, R.F. (1965). Validity of personality measures in personnel selection. *Personnel Psychology, 18*, 135–164. https://doi.org/10.1111/j.1744-6570.1965.tb00273.x

Gunnthorsdottir, A., McCabe, K., & Smith, V. (2002). Using the Machiavellianism instrument to predict trustworthiness in a bargaining game. *Journal of Economic Psychology, 23*, 49–66. https://doi.org/10.1016/S0167-4870(01)00067-8

Gustafson, S.B. (2000). Personality and organizational destructiveness: Fact, fiction, and fable. In L.R. Bergman, R.B. Cairns, L. Nilsson, & L. Nystedts (Eds.), *Developmental science and the holistic approach* (pp. 299–314). Erlbaum.

Gustafson, S.B., & Ritzer, D.R. (1995). The dark side of normal: A psychopathy-linked pattern called aberrant self-promotion. *European Journal of Personality, 9*, 147–183. https://doi.org/10.1002/per.2410090302

Hall, A.T., Hochwarter, W.A., Ferris, G.R., & Bowen, M.G. (2004). The dark side of politics in organizations. In R.W. Griffin, & A.M. O'Leary-Kelly (Eds.), *The dark side of organizational behavior* (pp. 237–261). Jossey-Bass.

Hare, R.D. (1980). A research scale for the assessment of psychopathy in criminal populations. *Personality and Individual Differences, 1*, 111–119. https://doi.org/10.1016/0191-8869(80)90028-8

Hare, R.D. (1985). Comparison of procedures for the assessment of psychopathy. *Journal of Consulting and Clinical Psychology, 53*, 7–16. https://doi.org/10.1037/0022-006X.53.1.7

Hare, R.D. (1996). Psychopathy: A clinical construct whose time has come. *Criminal Justice and Behavior, 23*, 25–54. https://doi.org/10.1177/0093854896023001004

Hare, R.D. (2003). *Hare Psychopathy Checklist-Revised (PCL-R): Technical manual* (2nd ed.). Multi-Health Systems.

Hare, R.D. (2005). *Gewissenlos. Die Psychopathen unter uns* [German edition of Without Conscience, Hare, 1999]. Springer.

Hare, R.D., & Neumann, C.S. (2006). The PCL-R assessment of psychopathy. In C.J. Patrick (Ed.), *Handbook of psychopathy* (pp. 58–88). Guilford.

Harms, P.D., Roberts, B.W., & Kuncel, N. (2004). *The mini-markers of evil: Using adjectives to measure the Dark Triad of personality.* Paper presented at the Meeting of the Society for Personality and Social Psychology, Austin, TX.

Harms, P.D., & Spain, S.M. (2015). Beyond the bright side: Dark personality at work. *Applied Psychology, 64*, 15–24. https://doi.org/10.1111/apps.12042

Harms, P.D., Spain, S.M., & Hannah, S.T. (2011). Leader development and the dark side of personality. *The Leadership Quarterly, 22*, 495–509. https://doi.org/10.1016/j.leaqua.2011.04.007

Harms, P.D., Wood, D., & DeSimone, J.A. (2019). Just because it's dark doesn't mean that we can't go there. *Industrial and Organizational Psychology, 12*, 206–210. https://doi.org/10.1017/iop.2019.40

Harpur, T.J., Hakstian, A.R., & Hare, R.D. (1988). Factor structure of the Psychopathy Checklist. *Journal of Consulting and Clinical Psychology, 56*, 741–747. https://doi.org/10.1037/0022-006X.56.5.741

Hart, S.D., & Hare, R.D. (1998). The association between psychopathy and narcissism: Theoretical views and empirical evidence. In E. Rooningstam (Ed.), *Disorders of narcissism: Theoretical, empirical, and clinical implications* (pp. 415–436). American Psychiatric Press.

Hartmann, H.-P. (2006). Narzisstische Persönlichkeitsstörungen: Ein Überblick [Narcissistic personality disorders: An overview]. In O.F. Kernberg, & H.-P. Hartmann (Eds.), *Narzissmus. Grundlagen – Störungsbilder – Therapie* (pp. 3–36). Schattauer.

Hathaway, S.R., & McKinley, J.C. (1943). *Manual for the Minnesota Multiphasic Personality Inventory*. Psychological Corporation.

Hausknecht, J.P., Day, D.V., & Thomas, S.C. (2004). Applicant reactions to selection procedures: An updated model and meta-analysis. *Personnel Psychology, 57*, 639–683. https://doi.org/10.1111/j.1744-6570.2004.00003.x

Heinze, P. E., Fatfouta, R., & Schröder-Abé, M. (2020). Validation of an implicit measure of antagonistic narcissism. *Journal of Research in Personality, 88*, 103993.

Heinzen, H., Seibert, M., Schulte Ostermann, M.A., Huchzermeier, C., & Eisenbarth, H. (2014). Diagnostische Verfahren zur Messung von psychopathischen Persönlichkeitsmerkmalen [Diagnostic procedures for the assessment of psychopathic personality traits]. *Praxis der Rechtspsychologie, 24*, 106–137.

Henslin, P.A. (2005). Conceptualizing and evaluating career success. *Journal of Organizational Behavior, 26*, 113–136. https://doi.org/10.1002/job.270

Hervé, H., & Yuille, J.C. (2007). *The psychopath: Theory, research, and practice*. Erlbaum.

Hicks, B.M., Carlson, M.D., Blonigen, D.M., Patrick, C.J., Iacono, W.G., & Mgue, M. (2012). Psychopathic personality traits and environmental contexts: Differential correlates, gender differences, and genetic mediation. *Personality Disorders: Theory, Research, and Treatment, 3*, 209–227. https://doi.org/10.1037/a0025084

Hirschi, A., & Jaensch, V.K. (2015). Narcissism and career success: Occupational self-efficacy and career engagement as mediators. *Personality and Individual Differences, 77*, 205–208. https://doi.org/10.1016/j.paid.2015.01.002

Hmieleski, K.M., & Lerner, D.A. (2016). The Dark Triad and nascent entrepreneurship: An examination of unproductive versus productive entrepreneurial motives. *Journal of Small Business Management, 54*, 7–32. https://doi.org/10.1111/jsbm.12296

Hodson, G., Book, A., Visser, B.A., Volk, A.A., Ashton, M.C., & Lee, K. (2018). Is the Dark Triad common factor distinct from low honesty-humility? *Journal of Research in Personality, 73*, 123–129. https://doi.org/10.1016/j.jrp.2017.11.012

Hodson, G., Hogg, S.M., & MacInnis, C.C. (2009). The role of "dark personalities" (narcissism, Machiavellianism, psychopathy), Big Five personality factors, and ideology in explaining prejudice. *Journal of Research in Personality, 43*, 686–690. https://doi.org/10.1016/j.jrp.2009.02.005

Hogan, J., Barrett, P., & Hogan, R. (2007). Personality measurement, faking, and employment selection. *Journal of Applied Psychology, 92*, 1270–1285. https://doi.org/10.1037/0021-9010.92.5.1270

Hogan, R., & Hogan, J. (2001). Assessing leadership: A view from the dark side. *International Journal of Selection and Assessment, 9*, https://doi.org/10.1111/1468-2389.00162-51. 40

Hogan, R., & Hogan, J. (2007). *Hogan Personality Inventory (HPI). Manual* (3rd ed.). Hogan Assessment Systems.

Hogan, R., & Hogan, J. (2009). *Hogan Development Survey (HDS). Manual* (2nd ed.). Hogan Assessment Systems.

Holland, J.L. (1997). *Making vocational choices: A theory of vocational personalities and work environments*. Psychological Assessment Resources.

Holtzman, N.S. (2011). Facing a psychopath: Detecting the Dark Triad from emotionally-neutral faces, using prototypes from the Personality Faceaurus. *Journal of Research in Personality, 45*, 648–654. https://doi.org/10.1016/j.jrp.2011.09.002

Horney, K. (1950). *Neurosis and human growth*. Norton.

Howe, J., Falkenbach, D., & Massey, C. (2014). The relationship among psychopathy, emotional intelligence, and professional success in finance. *International Journal of Forensic Mental Health, 13*, 337–347. https://doi.org/10.1080/14999013.2014.951103

Hu, L., & Bentler, P.M. (1999). Cutoff criteria for fit indexes in covariance structure analysis: Conventional criteria vs. new alternatives. *Structural Equation Modeling, 6*, 1–55. https://doi.org/10.1080/10705519909540118

Hudek-Knežević, J., Kardum, I., & Mehić, N. (2016). Dark Triad traits and health outcomes: An exploratory study. *Psychological Topics, 25*, 129–156.

Hunt, S.D., & Chonko, L.B. (1984). Marketing and Machiavellianism. *Journal of Marketing, 48*, 30–42. https://doi.org/10.1177/002224298404800304

Hurst, C., Simon, L., Jung, Y., & Pirouz, D. (2017). Are "bad" employees happier under bad bosses? Differing effects of abusive supervision on low and high primary psychopathy employees. *Journal of Business Ethics, 158*, 1149–1164. https://doi.org/10.1007/s10551-017-3770-5

International Organization for Standardization (ISO). (2020). *ISO 10667-1:2020. Assessment service delivery: Procedures and methods to assess people in work and organizational settings*. Author.

Jackson, D.J. (2014). Can maladaptive personality be assessed in organizations? *Industrial and Organizational Psychology, 7*, 110–113. https://doi.org/10.1111/iops.12116

Jeske, D., & Shultz, K.S. (2016). Using social media content for screening in recruitment and selection: Pros and cons. *Work, Employment & Society, 30*, 535–546. https://doi.org/10.1177/0950017015613746

Jonason, P.K., Abboud, R., Tomé, J., Dummett, M., & Hazer, A. (2017). The Dark Triad traits and individual differences in self-reported and other-rated creativity. *Personality and Individual Differences, 117*, 150–154. https://doi.org/10.1016/j.paid.2017.06.005

Jonason, P.K., Baughman, H.M., Carter, G.L., & Parker, P. (2015). Dorian Gray without his portrait: Psychological, social, and physical health costs associated with the Dark Triad. *Personality and Individual Differences, 78*, 5–13. https://doi.org/10.1016/j.paid.2015.01.008

Jonason, P.K., & Buss, D.M. (2012). Avoiding entangling commitments: Tactics for implementing a short-term mating strategy. *Personality and Individual Differences, 52*, 606–610. https://doi.org/10.1016/j.paid.2011.12.015

Jonason, P.K., Foster, J.D., Egorova, M.S., Parshikova, O., Csathó, Á., Oshio, A., & Gouveia, V.V. (2017). The Dark Triad traits from a life history perspective in six countries. *Frontiers in Psychology: Evolutionary Psychology, 8*, Article 1476. https://doi.org/10.3389/fpsyg.2017.01476

Jonason, P.K., Icho, A., & Ireland, K. (2016). Resources, harshness, and unpredictability: The socioeconomic conditions associated with the Dark Triad traits. *Evolutionary Psychology, 14*, 1–11. https://doi.org/10.1177/1474704915623699

Jonason, P.K., Kavanagh, P.S., Webster, G.D., & Fitzgerald, D. (2011). Comparing the measured and latent Dark Triad: Are three measures better than one? *Journal of Methods and Measurement in the Social Sciences, 2*, 28–44. https://doi.org/10.2458/jmm.v2i1.12363

Jonason, P.K., Koehn, M., Okan, C., & O'Connor, P.J. (2018). The role of personality in individual differences in yearly earnings. *Personality and Individual Differences, 121*, 170–172. https://doi.org/10.1016/j.paid.2017.09.038

Jonason, P.K., & Krause, L. (2013). The emotional deficits associated with the Dark Triad traits: Cognitive empathy, affective empathy, and alexithymia. *Personality and Individual Differences, 55*, 532–537. https://doi.org/10.1016/j.paid.2013.04.027

Jonason, P.K., & Kroll, C.H. (2015). A multidimensional view of the relationship between empathy and the Dark Triad. *Journal of Individual Differences, 36*, 150–156. https://doi.org/10.1027/1614-0001/a000166

Jonason, P.K., & Lavertu, A.N. (2017). The reproductive costs and benefits associated with the Dark Triad traits in women. *Personality and Individual Differences, 110*, 38–40. https://doi.org/10.1016/j.paid.2017.01.024

Jonason, P.K., Li, N.P., & Buss, D.M. (2010). The costs and benefits of the Dark Triad: Implications for mate poaching and mate retention tactics. *Personality and Individual Differences, 48*, 373–378. https://doi.org/10.1016/j.paid.2009.11.003

Jonason, P.K., Li, N.P., Webster, G.D., & Schmitt, D.P. (2009). The Dark Triad: Facilitating a short-term mating strategy in men. *European Journal of Personality, 23*, 5–18. https://doi.org/10.1002/per.698

Jonason, P.K., Luevano, V.X., & Adams, H.M. (2012). How the Dark Triad traits predict relationship choices. *Personality and Individual Differences, 53*, 180–184. https://doi.org/10.1016/j.paid.2012.03.007

Jonason, P.K., Lyons, M., Baughman, H.M., & Vernon, P.A. (2014). What a tangled web we weave: The Dark Triad and deception. *Personality and Individual Differences, 70*, 117–119. https://doi.org/10.1016/j.paid.2014.06.038

Jonason, P.K., Lyons, M., Bethell, E., & Ross, R. (2013). Different routes to limited empathy in the sexes: Examining the links between the Dark Triad and empathy. *Personality and Individual Differences, 54*, 572–576. https://doi.org/10.1016/j.paid.2012.11.009

Jonason, P.K., & O'Connor, P.J. (2017). Cutting corners at work: An individual differences perspective. *Personality and Individual Differences, 107*, 146–153. https://doi.org/10.1016/j.paid.2016.11.045

Jonason, P.K., & Tost, J. (2010). I just cannot control myself: The Dark Triad and self-control. *Personality and Individual Differences, 49*, 611–615. https://doi.org/10.1016/j.paid.2010.05.031

Jonason, P.K., Valentine, K.A., Li, N.P., & Harbeson, C.L. (2011). Mate-selection and the Dark Triad: Facilitating a short-term mating strategy and creating a volatile environment. *Personality and Individual Differences, 51*, 759–763. https://doi.org/10.1016/j.paid.2011.06.025

Jonason, P.K., & Webster, G.D. (2010). The Dirty Dozen: A concise measure of the Dark Triad. *Psychological Assessment, 22*, 420–432. https://doi.org/10.1037/a0019265

Jonason, P.K., & Webster, G.D. (2012). A protean approach to social influence: Dark Triad personalities and social influence tactics. *Personality and Individual Differences, 52*, 521–526. https://doi.org/10.1016/j.paid.2011.11.023

Jonason, P.K., Wee, S., & Li, N.P. (2015). Competition, autonomy, and prestige: Mechanisms through which the Dark Triad predict job satisfaction. *Personality and Individual Differences, 72*, 112–116. https://doi.org/10.1016/j.paid.2014.08.026

Jonason, P.K., Wee, S., Li, N.P., & Jackson, C. (2014). Occupational niches and the Dark Triad traits. *Personality and Individual Differences, 69*, 119–123. https://doi.org/10.1016/j.paid.2014.05.024

Jones, D.N. (2014). Risk in the face of retribution: Psychopathic individuals persist in financial misbehavior among the Dark Triad. *Personality and Individual Differences, 67*, 109–113. https://doi.org/10.1016/j.paid.2014.01.030

Jones, D.N., & Figueredo, A.J. (2013). The core of darkness: Uncovering the heart of the Dark Triad. *European Journal of Personality, 27*, 521–531. https://doi.org/10.1002/per.1893

Jones, D.N., & Hare, R.D. (2016). The mismeasure of psychopathy: A commentary on Boddy's PM-MRV. *Journal of Business Ethics, 138*, 579–588. https://doi.org/10.1007/s10551-015-2584-6

Jones, D.N., & Olderbak, S.G. (2014). The associations among dark personalities and sexual tactics across different scenarios. *Journal of Interpersonal Violence, 29*, 1050–1070. https://doi.org/10.1177/0886260513506053

Jones, D.N., & Paulhus, D.L. (2009). Machiavellianism. In M.R. Leary & R.H. Hoyle (Eds.), *Handbook of individual differences in social behavior* (pp. 93–108). Guilford.

Jones, D.N., & Paulhus, D.L. (2010). Different provocations trigger aggression in narcissists and psychopaths. *Social Psychological and Personality Science, 1*, 12–18. https://doi.org/10.1177/1948550609347591

Jones, D.N., & Paulhus, D.L. (2011). The role of impulsivity in the Dark Triad of personality. *Personality and Individual Differences, 51*, 679–682. https://doi.org/10.1016/j.paid.2011.04.011

Jones, D.N., & Paulhus, D.L. (2014). Introducing the short Dark Triad (SD 3): A brief measure of dark personality traits. *Assessment, 21*, 28–41. https://doi.org/10.1177/1073191113514105

Jones, D.N., & Paulhus, D.L. (2017). Duplicity among the Dark Triad: Three faces of deceit. *Journal of Personality and Social Psychology, 113*, 329–342. https://doi.org/10.1037/pspp0000139

Judge, T.A., LePine, J.A., & Rich, B.L. (2006). Loving yourself abundantly: relationship of the narcissistic personality to self-and other perceptions of workplace deviance, leadership, and task and contextual performance. *Journal of Applied Psychology, 91*, 762–776. https://doi.org/10.1037/0021-9010.91.4.762

Judge, T.A., Piccolo, R.F., & Kosalka, T. (2009). The bright and dark sides of leader traits: A review and theoretical extension of the leader trait paradigm. *The Leadership Quarterly, 20*, 855–875. https://doi.org/10.1016/j.leaqua.2009.09.004

Kaiser, R.B., LeBreton, J.M., & Hogan, J. (2015). The dark side of personality and extreme leader behavior. *Applied Psychology, 64*, 55–92. https://doi.org/10.1111/apps.12024

Kajonius, P.J., Persson, B.N., & Jonason, P.K. (2015). Hedonism, achievement, and power: Universal values that characterize the Dark Triad. *Personality and Individual Differences, 77*, 173–178. https://doi.org/10.1016/j.paid.2014.12.055

Kajonius, P.J., Persson, B.N., Rosenberg, P., & Garcia, D. (2016). The (mis)measurement of the Dark Triad Dirty Dozen: Exploitation at the core of the scale. *PeerJ, 4*, e1748. https://doi.org/10.7717/peerj.1748

Kanning, U.P. (2009). *Inventar sozialer Kompetenzen (ISK)* [Inventory of social competencies (ISK)]. Hogrefe.

Kanning, U.P. (2018). Digitalisierung in der Eignungsdiagnostik [Digitalization in aptitude diagnostics]. *Report Psychologie, 10*, 396–405.

Kapoor, H. (2015). The creative side of the Dark Triad. *Creativity Research Journal, 27*, 58–67. https://doi.org/10.1080/10400419.2014.961775

Kersting, M. (2005). *Fragebogen zur Messung der Akzeptanz diagnostischer Verfahren für Persönlichkeitstests (AKZEPT!-P)* [Questionnaire on the acceptance of diagnostic procedures for personnel selection (AKZEPT!-P)]. Institut für Psychologie, Lehrstuhl II für Betriebs- und Organizationspsychologie, RWTH.

Kessler, S.R., Bandelli, A.C., Spector, P.E., Borman, W.C., Nelson, C.E., & Penney, L.M. (2010). Re-examining Machiavelli: A three-dimensional model of machiavellianism in the workplace. *Journal of Applied Social Psychology, 40*, 1868–1896. https://doi.org/10.1111/j.1559-1816.2010.00643.x

Kiazad, K., Restubog, S.L.D., Zagenczyk, T.J., Kiewitz, C., & Tang, R.L. (2010). In pursuit of power: The role of authoritarian leadership in the relationship between supervisors' Machiavellianism and subordinates' perceptions of abusive supervisory behavior. *Journal of Research in Personality, 44*, 512–519. https://doi.org/10.1016/j.jrp.2010.06.004

Knight, N.M., Dahlen, E.R., Bullock-Yowell, E., & Madson, M.B. (2018). The HEXACO model of personality and Dark Triad in relational aggression. *Personality and Individual Differences, 122*, 109–114. https://doi.org/10.1016/j.paid.2017.10.016

Köchling, A.C., & Körner, S. (1996). Personalauswahl aus der Sicht der Betroffenen: Zur bewerberorientierten Gestaltung von Beurteilungssituationen [Personnel selection from the view of the affected: On the applicant-focused construction of assessment situations]. *Zeitschrift für Arbeits- und Organizationspsychologie, 40*, 22–37.

Kohlberg, L. (1984). *Philosophy of moral development*. Harper and Row.

Köhler, D., Müller, R., & Huchzermeier, C. (in preparation). *Das Kieler Psychopathie-Inventar (KPI).* [The Kiel Psychopathy Inventory (KPI)]. Hogrefe.

Korponay, C., Pujara, M., Deming, P., Philippi, C., Decety, J., Kosson, D.S., Kiehl, K.A., & Koenigs, M. (2017). Impulsive-antisocial dimension of psychopathy linked to enlargement and abnormal functional connectivity of the striatum. *Biological Psychiatry: Cognitive Neuroscience and Neuroimaging, 2*, 149–157. https://doi.org/10.1016/j.bpsc.2016.07.004

Kowalski, C.M., Rogoza, R., Vernon, P.A., & Schermer, J.A. (2018). The Dark Triad and the self-presentation variables of socially desirable responding and self-monitoring. *Personality and Individual Differences, 120*, 234–237. https://doi.org/10.1016/j.paid.2017.09.007

Kowalski, C.M., Vernon, P.A., & Schermer, J.A. (2016). The general factor of personality: the relationship between the Big One and the Dark Triad. *Personality and Individual Differences, 88*, 256–260. https://doi.org/10.1016/j.paid.2015.09.028

Kowalski, C.M., Vernon, P.A., & Schermer, J.A. (2017). Vocational interests and dark personality: Are there dark career choices? *Personality and Individual Differences, 104*, 43–47. https://doi.org/10.1016/j.paid.2016.07.029

Kramer, M., Cesinger, B., Schwarzinger, D., & Gelléri, P. (2011). Investigating entrepreneurs' dark personality: How narcissism, Machiavellianism, and psychopathy relate to entrepreneurial intention. *Proceedings of the 25th ANZAM Conference, Wellington, New Zealand.*

Krosnick, J.A. (1999). Survey research. *Annual Review of Psychology, 50*, 537–567. https://doi.org/10.1146/annurev.psych.50.1.537

Krueger, R.F., Derringer, J., Markon, K.E., Watson, D., & Skodol, A.E. (2012). Initial construction of a maladaptive personality trait model and inventory for DSM-5. *Psychological Medicine, 42*, 1879–1890. https://doi.org/10.1017/S0033291711002674

Krueger, R.F., & Eaton, N.R. (2010). Personality traits and the classification of mental disorders: Toward a more complete integration in DSM-5 and an empirical model of psychopathology. *Personality Disorders: Theory, Research, and Treatment, 1*, 97–118. https://doi.org/10.1037/a0018990

Küfner, A.C., Dufner, M., & Back, M.D. (2014). Das Dreckige Dutzend und die Niederträchtigen Neun [The Dirty Dozen and the Naughty Nine]. *Diagnostica, 61*, 76–91. https://doi.org/10.1026/0012-1924/a000124

Kuyumcu, D., & Dahling, J.J. (2014). Constraints for some, opportunities for others? Interactive and indirect effects of Machiavellianism and organizational constraints on task performance ratings. *Journal of Business and Psychology, 29*, 301–310. https://doi.org/10.1007/s10869-013-9314-9

Lais, M. (2013). *Silence is silver, voice is golden?* Verlag Dr. Kovač.

Lämmle, L., Nussbeck, F.W. & Ziegler, M. (2021). Hello from the other side: Can we perceive others' darkness? Observers' accuracy of the Dark Triad. *Journal of Personality Assessment*, *103*(1), 106–119. https://psycnet.apa.org/doi/10.1080/00223891.2019.1683020

LeBreton, J.M., Barksdale, C.D., Robin, J., & James, L.R. (2007). Measurement issues associated with conditional reasoning tests: Indirect measurement and test faking. *Journal of Applied Psychology, 92*, 1–16. https://doi.org/10.1037/0021-9010.92.1.1

LeBreton, J.M., Shiverdecker, L.K., & Grimaldi, E.M. (2018). The Dark Triad and workplace behavior. *Annual Review of Organizational Psychology and Organizational Behavior, 5*, 387–414. https://doi.org/10.1146/annurev-orgpsych-032117-104451

Lee, K., & Allen, N.J. (2002). Organizational citizenship behavior and workplace deviance: The role of affect and cognitions. *Journal of Applied Psychology, 87*, 131–142. https://doi.org/10.1037/0021-9010.87.1.131

Lee, K., & Ashton, M.C. (2005). Psychopathy, Machiavellianism, and narcissism in the Five-Factor model and the HEXACO model of personality structure. *Personality and Individual Differences, 38*, 1571–1582. https://doi.org/10.1016/j.paid.2004.09.016

Lee, K., & Ashton, M.C. (2006). Further assessment of the HEXACO Personality Inventory: Two new facet scales and an observer report form. *Psychological Assessment, 18*, 182–191. https://doi.org/10.1037/1040-3590.18.2.182

Lee, K., Ashton, M.C., & de Vries, R.E. (2005). Explaining workplace delinquency and integrity with the HEXACO and Five-Factor models of personality structure. *Human Performance, 18*, 179–197. https://doi.org/10.1207/s15327043hup1802_4

Lee, K., Ashton, M.C., Wiltshire, J., Bourdage, J.S., Visser, B.A., & Gallucci, A. (2013). Sex, power, and money: Prediction from the Dark Triad and honesty-humility. *European Journal of Personality, 27*, 169–184. https://doi.org/10.1002/per.1860

Lee, S.A., & Gibbons, J.A. (2017). The Dark Triad and compassion: Psychopathy and narcissism's unique connections to observed suffering. *Personality and Individual Differences, 116*, 336–342. https://doi.org/10.1016/j.paid.2017.05.010

Liem, C.S., Langer, M., Demetriou, A., Hiemstra, A.M.F., Wicaksana, A.S., Born, M.P., & König, C.J. (2018). Psychology meets machine learning: Interdisciplinary perspectives on algorithmic job candidate screening. In H.J. Escalante, S. Escalera, I. Guyon, X. Baró, Y. Güçlütürk, U. Güçlü, & M. Van Gerven (Eds.), *Explainable and interpretable models in computer vision and machine learning* (pp. 197–253). Springer. https://doi.org/10.1007/978-3-319-98131-4_9

Lienert, G., & Raatz, U. (1994). *Testaufbau und Testanalyse* [Test design and test analysis]. Beltz.

Lievens, F., De Corte, W., & Schollaert, E. (2008). A closer look at the frame-of-reference effect in personality scale scores and validity. *Journal of Applied Psychology, 93*, 268–279. https://doi.org/10.1037/0021-9010.93.2.268

Lilienfeld S. O., & Andrews, B. P. (1996). Development and preliminary validation of a self-report measure of psychopathic personality traits in noncriminal populations. *Journal of Personality Assessment*, 66, 488–524. https://doi.org/10.1207/s15327752jpa6603_3. PMID: 8667144.

Lilienfeld, S.O., & Fowler, K.A. (2006). The self-report assessment of psychopathy: Problems, pitfalls, and promises. In C.J. Patrick (Ed.), *Handbook of psychopathy* (pp. 107–132). Guilford.

Lohaus, D., & Schuler, H. (2014). Leistungsbeurteilung [Performance assessment]. In H. Schuler & U.P. Kanning (Eds.), *Lehrbuch der Personalpsychologie* (3rd ed., pp. 357–411). Hogrefe.

Lopes, B., & Yu, H. (2017). Who do you troll and Why: An investigation into the relationship between the Dark Triad personalities and online trolling behaviors toward popular and less popular Facebook profiles. *Computers in Human Behavior, 77*, 69–76. https://doi.org/10.1016/j.chb.2017.08.036

Lykken, D.T. (2006). Psychopathic personality: The scope of the problem. In C.J. Patrick (Ed.), *Handbook of psychopathy* (pp. 3–13). Guilford.

Lynam, D. (2011). Psychopathy and narcissism. In W.K. Campbell, & J. D Miller (Eds.), *The handbook of narcissism and narcissistic personality disorder: Theoretical approaches, empirical findings, and treatments* (pp. 272–282). Wiley.

Lyons, M. (2019). *The Dark Triad of personality: Narcissism, Machiavellianism, and psychopathy in everyday life*. Academic Press.

Lyons, M., & Brockman, C. (2017). The Dark Triad, emotional expressivity and appropriateness of emotional response: Fear and sadness when one should be happy? *Personality and Individual Differences, 104*, 466–469. https://doi.org/10.1016/j.paid.2016.08.038

MacNeil, B.M. (2008). *The Dark Triad and faking ability on self-report personality inventories and autobiographical accounts*. Unpublished doctoral dissertation, Queen's University, Canada.

MacNeil, B.M., Whaley, I., & Holden, R.R. (2007). *A confirmatory factor analysis of the Dark Triad screening measure.* Paper presented at the meeting of the Canadian Psychological Association, Ottawa.

Mai, C., Büttgen, M., & Schwarzinger, D. (2017). "Think-Manager-Consider-Female": Eine Analyse stereotypischer Ansichten über weibliche Führungskräfte und die empirische Überprüfung ihrer realen Persönlichkeit anhand der Big Five und Dunklen Triade ["Think-Manager-Consider-Female": An analysis of stereotypical views of female leaders and empirical testing of their real personality using the Big Five and Dark Triad]. *Schmalenbachs Zeitschrift für betriebswirtschaftliche Forschung, 69*, 119–152. https://doi.org/10.1007/s41471-016-0022-9

Malesza, M., & Kaczmarek, M.C. (2018). The convergent validity between self-and peer-ratings of the Dark Triad personality. *Current Psychology*, 1–8. https://doi.org/10.1007/s12144-018-9906-7

Malesza, M., & Ostaszewski, P. (2016). The utility of the Dark Triad model in the prediction of the self-reported and behavioral risk-taking behaviors among adolescents. *Personality and Individual Differences, 90*, 7–11. https://doi.org/10.1016/j.paid.2015.10.026

Maples, J.L., Lamkin, J., & Miller, J.D. (2014). A test of two brief measures of the Dark Triad: The Dirty Dozen and short Dark Triad. *Psychological Assessment, 26*, 326–331. https://doi.org/10.1037/a0035084

Marcus, B. (2000). *Kontraproduktives Verhalten im Betrieb: Eine individuumsbezogene Perspektive* [Counterproductive behavior in organizations: An individual-based perspective]. Hogrefe.

Marcus, B., & Schuler, H. (2004). Antecedents of counterproductive behavior at work: A general perspective. *Journal of Applied Psychology, 89*, 647–660. https://doi.org/10.1037/0021-9010.89.4.647

Marcus, B., Taylor, O.A., Hastings, S.E., Sturm, A., & Weigelt, O. (2016). The structure of counterproductive work behavior: A review, a structural meta-analysis, and a primary study. *Journal of Management, 42*, 203–233. https://doi.org/10.1177/0149206313503019

Marcus, D.K., Preszler, J., & Zeigler-Hill, V. (2018). A network of dark personality traits: What lies at the heart of darkness? *Journal of Research in Personality, 73*, 56–62. https://doi.org/10.1016/j.jrp.2017.11.003

Marcus, D.K., & Zeigler-Hill, V. (2015). A big tent of dark personality traits. *Social and Personality Psychology Compass, 9*, 434–446. https://doi.org/10.1111/spc3.12185

Markon, K.E., Krueger, R.F., & Watson, D. (2005). Delineating the structure of normal and abnormal personality: An integrative hierarchical approach. *Journal of Personality and Social Psychology, 88*, 139–157. https://doi.org/10.1037/0022-3514.88.1.139

Marsh, H.W., Hau, K.T., & Wen, Z. (2004). In search of golden rules: Comment on hypothesis-testing approaches to setting cutoff values for fit indexes and dangers in overgeneralizing Hu and Bentler's (1999) findings. *Structural Equation Modeling, 11*, 320–341. https://doi.org/10.1207/s15328007sem1103_2

Marshall, M.B., De Fruyt, F., Rolland, J.P., & Bagby, R.M. (2005). Socially desirable responding and the factorial stability of the NEO PI-R. *Psychological Assessment, 17*, 379–384. https://doi.org/10.1037/1040-3590.17.3.379

Mathieu, C. (2013). Personality and job satisfaction: The role of narcissism. *Personality and Individual Differences, 55*, 650–654. https://doi.org/10.1016/j.paid.2013.05.012

Mathieu, C., & Babiak, P. (2016a). Validating the B-Scan Self: A self-report measure of psychopathy in the workplace. *International Journal of Selection and Assessment, 24*, 272–284. https://doi.org/10.1111/ijsa.12146

Mathieu, C., & Babiak, P. (2016b). Corporate psychopathy and abusive supervision: Their influence on employees' job satisfaction and turnover intentions. *Personality and Individual Differences, 91*, 102–106. https://doi.org/10.1016/j.paid.2015.12.002

Mathieu, C., Hare, R.D., Jones, D.N., Babiak, P., & Neumann, C.S. (2013). Factor structure of the B-Scan 360: A measure of corporate psychopathy. *Psychological Assessment, 25*, 288–293. https://doi.org/10.1037/a0029262

Mathieu, C., Neumann, C.S., Hare, R.D., & Babiak, P. (2014). A dark side of leadership: Corporate psychopathy and its influence on employee well-being and job satisfaction. *Personality and Individual Differences, 59*, 83–88. https://doi.org/10.1016/j.paid.2013.11.010

Matz, S.C., Kosinski, M., Nave, G., & Stillwell, D.J. (2017). Psychological targeting as an effective approach to digital mass persuasion. *Proceedings of the National Academy of Sciences, 14*, 1214–1219. https://doi.org/10.1073/pnas.1710966114

Mayer, J.D., Salovey, P., & Caruso, D.R. (2002). *Mayer-Salovey-Caruso Emotional Intelligence Test* (MSCEIT). Multi-Health Systems.

Maynard, D.C., Brondolo, E.M., Connelly, C.E., & Sauer, C.E. (2015). I'm too good for this job: Narcissism's role in the experience of overqualification. *Applied Psychology, 64*, 208–232. https://doi.org/10.1111/apps.12031

McCord, M.A., Joseph, D.L., & Grijalva, E. (2014). Blinded by the light: The dark side of traditionally desirable personality traits. *Industrial and Organizational Psychology, 7*, 130–137. https://doi.org/10.1111/iops.12121

McFarland, L.A., & Ployhart, R.E. (2015). Social media: A contextual framework to guide research and practice. *Journal of Applied Psychology, 100*, 1653–1677. https://doi.org/10.1037/a0039244

McHoskey, J.W. (1995). Narcissism and Machiavellianism. *Psychological Reports, 77*, 755–759. https://doi.org/10.2466/pr0.1995.77.3.755

McHoskey, J.W., Worzel, W., & Szyarto, C. (1998). Machiavellianism and psychopathy. *Journal of Personality and Social Psychology, 74*, 192–210. https://doi.org/10.1037/0022-3514.74.1.192

McLarnon, M.J., & Tarraf, R.C. (2017). The Dark Triad: Specific or general sources of variance? A bifactor exploratory structural equation modeling approach. *Personality and Individual Differences, 112*, 67–73. https://doi.org/10.1016/j.paid.2017.02.049

Melson-Silimon, A., Harris, A. M., Shoenfelt, E. L., Miller, J. D., & Carter, N. T. (2019). Personality testing and the Americans with Disabilities Act: Cause for concern as normal and abnormal personality models are integrated. *Industrial and Organizational Psychology, 12*, 119–132. https://doi.org/10.1017/iop.2018.156

Mershon, B., & Gorsuch, R.L. (1988). Number of factors in the personality sphere: Does increase in factors increase predictability of real-life criteria? *Journal of Personality and Social Psychology, 55*, 675–680. https://doi.org/10.1037/0022-3514.55.4.675

Miao, C., Humphrey, R.H., Qian, S., & Pollack, J.M. (2019). The relationship between emotional intelligence and the Dark Triad personality traits: A meta-analytic review. *Journal of Research in Personality, 78*, 189–197. https://doi.org/10.1016/j.jrp.2018.12.004

Michel, J.S., & Bowling, N.A. (2013). Does dispositional aggression feed the narcissistic response? The role of narcissism and aggression in the prediction of job attitudes and counterproductive work behaviors. *Journal of Business and Psychology, 28*, 93–105. https://doi.org/10.1007/s10869-012-9265-6

Miller, J.D., Bagby, R.M., Pilkonis, P.A., Reynolds, S.K., & Lynam, D.R. (2005). A simplified technique for scoring DSM-IV personality disorders with the five-factor model. *Assessment, 12*, 404–415. https://doi.org/10.1177/1073191105280987

Miller, J.D., Dir, A., Gentile, B., Wilson, L., Pryor, L.R., & Campbell, W.K. (2010). Searching for a vulnerable Dark Triad: Comparing factor 2 psychopathy, vulnerable narcissism, and borderline personality disorder. *Journal of Personality, 78*, 1529–1564. https://doi.org/10.1111/j.1467-6494.2010.00660.x

Miller, J. D., Few, L. R., Seibert, L. A., Watts, A., Zeichner, A., & Lynam, D. R. (2012). An examination of the Dirty Dozen measure of psychopathy: A cautionary tale about the costs of brief measures. *Psychological Assessment, 24*, 1048–1053. https://doi.org/10.1037/a0028583

Miller, J. D., Hyatt, C. S., Maples-Keller, J. L., Carter, N. T., & Lynam, D. R. (2017). Psychopathy and Machiavellianism: A distinction without a difference? *Journal of Personality, 85*, 439–453. https://doi.org/10.1111/jopy.12251

Miller, J. D., Vize, C., Crowe, M. L., & Lynam, D. (2019). A critical appraisal of the Dark Triad literature and suggestions for moving forward. *Current Directions in Psychological Science, 28*, 353-360. https://doi.org/10.1177/0963721419838233

Mischel, W. (1968). *Personality and assessment*. Wiley.

Mörzinger, D. (2012). *Die Entwicklung eines impliziten Verfahrens zur Erfassung der Dunklen Tetrade* [Development of an implicit measure of the Dark Tetrad]. Unpublished diploma thesis, University of Vienna, Austria.

Moscoso, S., & Salgado, J. F. (2004). "Dark side" personality styles as predictors of task, contextual, and job performance. *International Journal of Selection and Assessment, 12*, 356–362. https://doi.org/10.1111/j.0965-075X.2004.00290.x

Moshagen, M., Hilbig, B. E., & Zettler, I. (2018). The dark core of personality. *Psychological Review, 125*, 656–688. https://doi.org/10.1037/rev0000111

Motowidlo, S. J. (2003). Job performance. In W. Borman, D. Ilgen, & R. Klimoski (Eds.), *Handbook of psychology, Volume 12: Industrial and Organizational Psychology* (pp. 39–54). Wiley.

Mumford, M. D., Connelly, M. S., Helton, W. B., Strange, J. M., & Osburn, H. K. (2001). On the construct validity of integrity tests: Individual and situational factors as predictors of test performance. *International Journal of Selection and Assessment, 9*, 240–257. https://doi.org/10.1111/1468-2389.00177

Muris, P., Merckelbach, H., Otgaar, H., & Meijer, E. (2017). The malevolent side of human nature: A meta-analysis and critical review of the literature on the Dark Triad (narcissism, Machiavellianism, and psychopathy). *Perspectives on Psychological Science, 12*, 183–204. https://doi.org/10.1177/1745691616666070

Murphy, K. R. (Ed.). (2014). Special Issue with responses to focal article: "Maladaptive personality at work: Exploring the darkness" of Guenole (2014). *Industrial and Organizational Psychology, 7*(1).

Musek, J. (2007). A general factor of personality: Evidence for the Big One in the five-factor model. *Journal of Research in Personality, 41*, 1213–1233. https://doi.org/10.1016/j.jrp.2007.02.003

Mussel, P. (2003). Persönlichkeitsinventar zur Integritätsabschätzung (PIA) [Personality Inventory for Integrity Assessment]. In J. Erpenbeck & L. von Rosenstiel (Eds.), *Handbuch Kompetenzmessung* (pp. 3–18). Schäffer-Poeschel.

Mussel, P. (2013). Intellect: A theoretical framework for personality traits related to intellectual achievements. *Journal of Personality and Social Psychology, 104*, 885–906. https://doi.org/10.1037/a0031918

Mussel, P., Gatzka, T., & Hewig, J. (2018). Situational judgment tests as an alternative measure for personality assessment. *European Journal of Psychological Assessment, 34*, 328–335. https://doi.org/10.1027/1015-5759/a000346

Mussel, P., Spengler, M., Litman, J. A., & Schuler, H. (2012). Development and validation of the German work-related curiosity scale. *European Journal of Psychological Assessment, 28*, 109–117. https://doi.org/10.1027/1015-5759/a000098

Mussel, P., Winter, C., Gelléri, P., & Schuler, H. (2011). Explicating the openness to experience construct and its subdimensions and facets in a work setting. *International Journal of Selection and Assessment, 19*, 145–156. https://doi.org/10.1111/j.1468-2389.2011.00542.x

Nagler, U. K., Reiter, K. J., Furtner, M. R., & Rauthmann, J. F. (2014). Is there a "dark intelligence"? Emotional intelligence is used by dark personalities to emotionally manipulate others. *Personality and Individual Differences, 65*, 47–52. https://doi.org/10.1016/j.paid.2014.01.025

Nathanson, C., Paulhus, D. L., & Williams, K. M. (2006). Personality and misconduct correlates of body modification and other cultural deviance markers. *Journal of Research in Personality, 40*, 779–802. https://doi.org/10.1016/j.jrp.2005.09.002

Neider, L. L., & Schriesheim, C. A. (Eds.). (2010). *The dark side of management*. Information Age.

Nerdinger, F. W. (2008). *Unternehmensschädigendes Verhalten erkennen und verhindern* [Detecting and preventing organization-harming behavior]. Hogrefe.

Nevicka, B., De Hoogh, A.H., Van Vianen, A.E., Beersma, B., & McIlwain, D. (2011). All I need is a stage to shine: Narcissists' leader emergence and performance. *The Leadership Quarterly, 22*, 910–925. https://doi.org/10.1016/j.leaqua.2011.07.011

Nicholls, A.R., Madigan, D.J., Backhouse, S.H., & Levy, A.R. (2017). Personality traits and performance enhancing drugs: The Dark Triad and doping attitudes among competitive athletes. *Personality and Individual Differences, 112*, 113–116. https://doi.org/10.1016/j.paid.2017.02.062

O'Boyle, E.H. Jr., Forsyth, D.R., Banks, G.C., & McDaniel, M.A. (2012). A meta-analysis of the Dark Triad and work behavior: A social exchange perspective. *Journal of Applied Psychology, 97*, 557–579. https://doi.org/10.1037/a0025679

O'Boyle, E.H. Jr., Forsyth, D., Banks, G.C., & Story, P.A. (2013). A meta-analytic review of the Dark Triad-Intelligence connection. *Journal of Research in Personality, 47*, 789–794. https://doi.org/10.1016/j.jrp.2013.08.001

O'Boyle, E.H., Forsyth, D.R., Banks, G.C., Story, P.A., & White, C.D. (2015). A meta-analytic test of redundancy and relative importance of the Dark Triad and five-factor model of personality. *Journal of Personality, 83*, 644–664. https://doi.org/10.1111/jopy.12126

Ogloff, J.R., Campbell, R.E., & Shepherd, S.M. (2016). Disentangling psychopathy from antisocial personality disorder: An Australian analysis. *Journal of Forensic Psychology Practice, 16*, 198–215. https://doi.org/10.1080/15228932.2016.1177281

Ones, D.S., & Viswesvaran, C. (1998). The effects of social desirability and faking on personality and integrity assessment for personnel selection. *Human Performance, 11*, 245–269. https://doi.org/10.1207/s15327043hup1102&3_7

Ones, D.S., & Viswesvaran, C. (2001). Personality at work. Criterion-focused occupational personality scales used in personnel selection. In B.W. Roberts & R. Hogan (Eds.), *Personality psychology in the workplace* (pp. 63–92). American Psychological Association.

Ones, D.S., Viswesvaran, C., & Schmidt, F.L. (1993). Comprehensive meta-analysis of integrity test validities: Findings and implications for personnel selection and theories of job performance. *Journal of Applied Psychology, 78*, 679–703. https://doi.org/10.1037/0021-9010.78.4.679

Ong, C.W., Roberts, R., Arthur, C.A., Woodman, T., & Akehurst, S. (2016). The leader ship is sinking: A temporal investigation of narcissistic leadership. *Journal of Personality, 84*, 237–247. https://doi.org/10.1111/jopy.12155

O'Reilly III, C.A., Doerr, B., Caldwell, D.F., & Chatman, J.A. (2014). Narcissistic CEOs and executive compensation. *The Leadership Quarterly, 25*, 218–231. https://doi.org/10.1016/j.leaqua.2013.08.002

O'Reilly III, C.A., Doerr, B., & Chatman, J.A. (2018). "See you in court": How CEO narcissism increases firms' vulnerability to lawsuits. *The Leadership Quarterly, 29*, 365–378. https://doi.org/10.1016/j.leaqua.2017.08.001

Owens, B.P., Wallace, A.S., & Waldman, D.A. (2015). Leader narcissism and follower outcomes: The counterbalancing effect of leader humility. *Journal of Applied Psychology, 100*, 1203–1213. https://doi.org/10.1037/a0038698

Paleczek, D., Bergner, S., & Rybnicek, R. (2018). Predicting career success: Is the dark side of personality worth considering? *Journal of Managerial Psychology, 33*, 437–456. https://doi.org/10.1108/JMP-11-2017-0402

Palmer, J.C., Komarraju, M., Carter, M.Z., & Karau, S.J. (2017). Angel on one shoulder: Can perceived organizational support moderate the relationship between the Dark Triad traits and counterproductive work behavior? *Personality and Individual Differences, 110*, 31–37. https://doi.org/10.1016/j.paid.2017.01.018

Paracelsus, T. (1965). Septem Defensiones (1538). In W.-E. Peukert (Ed.), *Theophrast Paracelsus: Werke.* Wissenschaftliche Buchgesellschaft.

Patrick, C.J. (2006a). *Handbook of psychopathy*. Guilford.

Patrick, C.J. (2006b). Back to the future: Cleckley as a guide to the next generation of psychopathy research. In C.J. Patrick (Ed.), *Handbook of psychopathy* (pp. 605–617). Guilford.

Patrick, C.J. (2018a). *Handbook of psychopathy* (2nd ed.). Guilford.

Patrick, C.J. (2018b). Preface. In C.J. Patrick (Ed.), *Handbook of psychopathy* (2nd ed., pp. xi–xvi). Guilford.

Paulhus, D. L. (2001). Normal narcissism: Two minimalist accounts. *Psychological Inquiry, 12*, 228–230.

Paulhus, D. L. (2014). Toward a taxonomy of dark personalities. *Current Directions in Psychological Science, 23*, 421–426. https://doi.org/10.1177/0963721414547737

Paulhus, D. L., & Jones, D. N. (2015). Measures of Dark Personalities. In G. Boyle, D. Saklofske, & G. Matthews (Eds.), *Measures of personality and social psychological constructs* (pp. 562–594). Academic Press. https://doi.org/10.1016/B978-0-12-386915-9.00020-6

Paulhus, D. L., Neumann, C. S., & Hare, R. D. (2016). *Self-Report Psychopathy Scale-Fourth edition* (SRP 4). Multi-Health Systems.

Paulhus, D. L., Westlake, B. G., Calvez, S. S., & Harms, P. D. (2013). Self-presentation style in job interviews: The role of personality and culture. *Journal of Applied Social Psychology, 43*, 2042–2059. https://doi.org/10.1111/jasp.12157

Paulhus, D. L., & Williams, K. M. (2002). The Dark Triad of personality: Narcissism, Machiavellianism, and psychopathy. *Journal of Research in Personality, 36*, 556–563. https://doi.org/10.1016/S0092-6566(02)00505-6

Paulhus, D., Williams, K., & Harms, P. (2001). *Shedding light on the Dark Triad of personality: Narcissism, Machiavellianism, and psychopathy.* Paper presented at the SPSP Convention, San Antonio, TX.

Paunonen, S. V. (1998). Hierarchical organization of personality and prediction of behavior. *Journal of Personality and Social Psychology, 74*, 538–556. https://doi.org/10.1037/0022-3514.74.2.538

Paunonen, S. V. (2002). *Design and construction of the Supernumerary Personality Inventory*. Research Bulletin 763, University of Western Ontario.

Pelt, D. H., van der Linden, D., Dunkel, C. S., & Born, M. P. (2017). The general factor of personality and job performance: Revisiting previous meta-analyses. *International Journal of Selection and Assessment, 25*, 333–346. https://doi.org/10.1111/ijsa.12188

Penney, L. M., & Spector, P. E. (2002). Narcissism and counterproductive work behavior: Do bigger egos mean bigger problems? *International Journal of Selection and Assessment, 10*, 126–134. https://doi.org/10.1111/1468-2389.00199

Perri, F. S., & Brody, R. G. (2011). The Dark Triad: Organized crime, terror and fraud. *Journal of Money Laundering Control, 14*, 44–59. https://doi.org/10.1108/13685201111098879

Peterson, S. J., Galvin, B. M., & Lange, D. (2012). CEO servant leadership: Exploring executive characteristics and firm performance. *Personnel Psychology, 65*, 565–596. https://doi.org/10.1111/j.1744-6570.2012.01253.x

Petrides, K. V., & Furnham, A. (2006). The role of trait emotional intelligence in a gender-specific model of organizational variables. *Journal of Applied Social Psychology, 36*, 552–569. https://doi.org/10.1111/j.0021-9029.2006.00019.x

Petrides, K. V., Vernon, P. A., Schermer, J. A., & Veselka, L. (2011). Trait emotional intelligence and the Dark Triad traits of personality. *Twin Research and Human Genetics, 14*, 35–41. https://doi.org/10.1375/twin.14.1.35

Pierce, J. R., & Aguinis, H. (2013). The too-much-of-a-good-thing effect in management. *Journal of Management, 39*, 313–338. https://doi.org/10.1177/0149206311410060

Pina, A., Holland, J., & James, M. (2017). The malevolent side of revenge porn proclivity: Dark personality traits and sexist ideology. *International Journal of Technoethics, 8*, 30–43. https://doi.org/10.4018/IJT.2017010103

Podsakoff, P. M., MacKenzie, S. B., Lee, J. Y., & Podsakoff, N. P. (2003). Common method biases in behavioral research: A critical review of the literature and recommended remedies. *Journal of Applied Psychology, 88*, 879–903. https://doi.org/10.1037/0021-9010.88.5.879

Ragatz, L. L., Fremouw, W., & Baker, E. (2012). The psychological profile of white-collar offenders: Demographics, criminal thinking, psychopathic traits, and psychopathology. *Criminal Justice and Behavior, 39*, 978–997. https://doi.org/10.1177/0093854812437846

Raskin, R. N., & Hall, C. S. (1979). A narcissistic personality inventory. *Psychological Reports, 45*, 590. https://doi.org/10.2466/pr0.1979.45.2.590

Raskin, R., & Terry, H. (1988). A principal-components analysis of the Narcissistic Personality Inventory and further evidence of its construct validity. *Journal of Personality and Social Psychology, 54*, 890–902. https://doi.org/10.1037/0022-3514.54.5.890

Rauthmann, J.F. (2013). Investigating the MACH-IV with item response theory and proposing the trimmed MACH. *Journal of Personality Assessment, 95*, 388–397. https://doi.org/10.1080/00223891.2012.742905

Rauthmann, J.F., & Kolar, G.P. (2012). How "dark" are the Dark Triad traits? Examining the perceived darkness of narcissism, Machiavellianism, and psychopathy. *Personality and Individual Differences, 53*, 884–889. https://doi.org/10.1016/j.paid.2012.06.020

Rauthmann, J.F., & Kolar, G.P. (2013). The perceived attractiveness and traits of the Dark Triad: Narcissists are perceived as hot, Machiavellians and psychopaths not. *Personality and Individual Differences, 54*, 582–586. https://doi.org/10.1016/j.paid.2012.11.005

Rauthmann, J.F., & Will, T. (2011). Proposing a multidimensional Machiavellianism conceptualization. *Social Behavior and Personality, 39*, 391–403. https://doi.org/10.2224/sbp.2011.39.3.391

Ray, J. (2007). *Psychopathy, attitudinal beliefs, and white collar crime*. Unpublished master's thesis, University of South Florida.

Ray, J.V., & Jones, S. (2011). Self-reported psychopathic traits and their relation to intentions to engage in environmental offending. *International Journal of Offender Therapy and Comparative Criminology, 55*, 370–391. https://doi.org/10.1177/0306624X10361582

Reichin, S.L., Grimaldi, E.M., & LeBreton, J.M. (2019). Critically evaluating the use of dark trait measurement in selection. *Industrial and Organizational Psychology, 12*, 163–166. https://doi.org/10.1017/iop.2019.32

Resick, C.J., Whitman, D.S., Weingarden, S.M., & Hiller, N.J. (2009). The bright-side and the dark-side of CEO personality: Examining core self-evaluations, narcissism, transformational leadership, and strategic influence. *Journal of Applied Psychology, 94*, 1365–1381. https://doi.org/10.1037/a0016238

Ricks, J., & Fraedrich, J. (1999). The paradox of Machiavellianism: Machiavellianism may make for productive sales but poor management reviews. *Journal of Business Ethics, 20*, 197–205. https://doi.org/10.1023/A:1005956311600

Ricks, J., & Sterrett, J. (2002). An empirical examination of Machiavellianism on adaptive sales performance. *Academy of Marketing Studies Journal, 6*, 15–23.

Roberts, B.W., Edmonds, G., & Grijalva, E. (2010). It is developmental me, not generation me: Developmental changes are more important than generational changes in narcissism–Commentary on Trzesniewski & Donnellan (2010). *Perspectives on Psychological Science, 5*, 97–102. https://doi.org/10.1177/1745691609357019

Roczniewska, M., & Bakker, A.B. (2016). Who seeks job resources, and who avoids job demands? The link between dark personality traits and job crafting. *The Journal of Psychology, 150*, 1026–1045. https://doi.org/10.1080/00223980.2016.1235537

Roeser, K., McGregor, V.E., Stegmaier, S., Mathew, J., Kübler, A., & Meule, A. (2016). The Dark Triad of personality and unethical behavior at different times of day. *Personality and Individual Differences, 88*, 73–77. https://doi.org/10.1016/j.paid.2015.09.002

Rogoza, R., & Cieciuch, J. (2020). Dark Triad traits and their structure: An empirical approach. *Current Psychology, 39*, 1287–1302. https://doi.org/10.1007/s12144-018-9834-6

Ross, S.R., & Rausch, M.K. (2001). Psychopathic attributes and achievement dispositions in a college sample. *Personality and Individual Differences, 30*, 471–480. https://doi.org/10.1016/S0191-8869(00)00038-6

Roulin, N., & Bourdage, J.S. (2017). Once an impression manager, always an impression manager? Antecedents of honest and deceptive impression management use and variability across multiple job interviews. *Frontiers in Psychology, 8*, Article 29. https://doi.org/10.3389/fpsyg.2017.00029

Rubin, R.S., Dierdorff, E.C., & Bachrach, D.G. (2013). Boundaries of citizenship behavior: Curvilinearity and context in the citizenship and task performance relationship. *Personnel Psychology, 66*, 377–406. https://doi.org/10.1111/peps.12018

Sackett, P.R. (2002). The structure of counterproductive work behaviors: Dimensionality and relationships with facets of job performance. *International Journal of Selection and Assessment, 10*, 5–11. https://doi.org/10.1111/1468-2389.00189

Sackett, P.R. (2011). Integrating and prioritizing theoretical perspectives on applicant faking of personality measures. *Human Performance, 24*, 379–385. https://doi.org/10.1080/08959285.2011.597478

Sackett, P.R., Berry, C.M., Wiemann, S.A., & Laczo, R.M. (2006). Citizenship and counterproductive behavior: Clarifying relations between the two domains. *Human Performance, 19*, 441–464. https://doi.org/10.1207/s15327043hup1904_7

Sackett, P.R., Lievens, F., Van Iddekinge, C.H., & Kuncel, N.R. (2017). Individual differences and their measurement: A review of 100 years of research. *Journal of Applied Psychology, 102*, 254–273. https://doi.org/10.1037/apl0000151

Sackett, P.R., & Wanek, J.E. (1996). New developments in the use of measures of honesty, integrity, Conscientiousness, dependability, trustworthiness, and reliability for personnel selection. *Personnel Psychology, 49*, 787–829. https://doi.org/10.1111/j.1744-6570.1996.tb02450.x

Salgado, J.F. (2000). *Manual técnico del cuestionario de estilos de personalidad* (CEP) [Technical manual of the personality styles questionnaire]. Metis.

Samuel, D.B., & Widiger, T.A. (2008a). A meta-analytic review of the relationships between the five-factor model and DSM-IV-TR personality disorders: A facet level analysis. *Clinical Psychology Review, 28*, 1326–1342. https://doi.org/10.1016/j.cpr.2008.07.002

Samuel, D.B., & Widiger, T.A. (2008b). Convergence of narcissism measures from the perspective of general personality functioning. *Assessment, 15*, 364–374. https://doi.org/10.1177/1073191108314278

Sanecka, E. (2013). The effects of supervisors' subclinical psychopathy on subordinates organizational commitment, job satisfaction and satisfaction with supervisor. *The Journal of Education Culture and Society, 2*, 172–191.

Saucier, G. (2019). On the curious history of the big six. Variable selection and "moral exclusion" in the formation of fundamental personality models. *Zeitschrift für Psychologie, 227*, 166–173. https://doi.org/10.1027/2151-2604/a000375

Schaufeli, W., & Bakker, A. (2003). *Utrecht Work Engagement Scale: Preliminary manual*. Occupational Health Psychology Unit, Utrecht University.

Scherer, K.T., Baysinger, M., Zolynsky, D., & LeBreton, J.M. (2013). Predicting counterproductive work behaviors with sub-clinical psychopathy: Beyond the Five Factor Model of personality. *Personality and Individual Differences, 55*, 300–305. https://doi.org/10.1016/j.paid.2013.03.007

Schlenker, B.R. (2008). Integrity and character: Implications of principled and expedient ethical ideologies. *Journal of Social and Clinical Psychology, 27*, 1078–1125. https://doi.org/10.1521/jscp.2008.27.10.1078

Schmidt, F.L., & Hunter, J.E. (1998). The validity and utility of selection methods in personnel psychology: Practical and theoretical implications of 85 years of research findings. *Psychological Bulletin, 124*, 262–274. https://doi.org/10.1037/0033-2909.124.2.262

Schmitt, N. (1996). Uses and abuses of coefficient alpha. *Psychological Assessment, 8*, 350–353. https://doi.org/10.1037/1040-3590.8.4.350

Schneider, B. (1987). The people make the place. *Personnel Psychology, 40*, 437–453. https://doi.org/10.1111/j.1744-6570.1987.tb00609.x

Schneider, T.J., McLarnon, M.J., & Carswell, J.J. (2017). Career interests, personality, and the Dark Triad. *Journal of Career Assessment, 25*, 338–351. https://doi.org/10.1177/1069072715616128

Schröder, P. (2004). *Niccolò Machiavelli*. Campus.

Schuler, H. (2004). Leistungsbeurteilung – Gegenstand, Funktionen und Formen [Performance assessment – subject, functions, and forms]. In H. Schuler (Ed.), *Beurteilung und Förderung beruflicher Leistung* (2nd ed., pp. 1–24). Hogrefe.

Schuler, H. (2008). Improving assessment centers by the trimodal concept of personnel assessment. *Industrial and Organizational Psychology, 1*, 128–130. https://doi.org/10.1111/j.1754-9434.2007.00024.x

Schuler, H. (2014a). *Psychologische Personalauswahl* (4th ed.) [Psychological personnel selection]. Hogrefe.

Schuler, H. (2014b). Gegenstand und Aufgaben der Personalpsychologie [Subject and tasks of personnel psychology]. In H. Schuler & U.P. Kanning (Eds.), *Lehrbuch der Personalpsychologie* (3rd ed., pp. 13–23). Hogrefe.

Schuler, H. (2018). Wie passen Menschen und Berufe zusammen? Rede zur Entgegennahme des Deutschen Psychologiepreises 2017 [How do people and jobs fit together? Address given on the occasion of receiving the German Psychology Award 2017]. *Report Psychologie, 43*, 10–17.

Schuler, H., & Höft, S. (2006). Konstruktorientierte Verfahren der Personalauswahl [Construct-oriented methods of personnel selection]. In H. Schuler (Ed.), *Lehrbuch der Personalpsychologie* (2nd ed., pp. 101–144). Hogrefe.

Schuler, H., Höft, S., & Hell, B. (2014). Eigenschaftsorientierte Verfahren der Personalauswahl [Trait-oriented methods of personnel selection]. In H. Schuler & U.P. Kanning (Eds.), *Lehrbuch der Personalpsychologie* (3rd ed., pp. 149–213). Hogrefe.

Schuler, H., & Prochaska, M. (2001). *Leistungsmotivationsinventar* (LMI) [Achievement Motivation Inventory]. Hogrefe.

Schuler, H., & Stehle, W. (1983). Neuere Entwicklungen des Assessment-Center-Ansatzes – beurteilt unter dem Aspekt der sozialen Validität [Developments of the Assessment Center approach – assessed by the aspect of social validity]. *Psychologie und Praxis, 27*, 33–44.

Schütte, N., Blickle, G., Frieder, R.E., Wihler, A., Schnitzler, F., Heupel, J., & Zettler, I. (2018). The role of interpersonal influence in counterbalancing psychopathic personality trait facets at work. *Journal of Management, 44*, 1338–1368. https://doi.org/10.1177/0149206315607967

Schütz, A., Marcus, B., & Sellin, I. (2004). Die Messung von Narzissmus als Persönlichkeitskonstrukt [The measurement of narcissism as a personality construct]. *Diagnostica, 50*, 202–218. https://doi.org/10.1026/0012-1924.50.4.202

Schwarzinger, D. (2009). *Die Dunkle Triade der Persönlichkeit im eignungsdiagnostischen Kontext: Eine empirische Untersuchung des Zusammenhangs von Integrität, Narzissmus, Machiavellismus und Psychopathie* [The Dark Triad of personality in the context of aptitude diagnostics: An empirical investigation of the relationship between integrity, narcissism, Machiavellianism, and psychopathy]. Unpublished diploma thesis, University of Hohenheim.

Schwarzinger, D. (2020). *Die Dunkle Triade der Persönlichkeit in der Personalauswahl. Narzissmus, Machiavellismus und subklinische Psychopathie am Arbeitsplatz* [Dark Triad of personality in personnel selection]. (German original). Hogrefe.

Schwarzinger, D., & Schuler, H. (2016). *Dark Triad of Personality at Work* (TOP; German original version). Hogrefe.

Schwarzinger, D., & Schuler, H. (2019). *Dark Triad of Personality at Work* (TOP; UK/US Adaptation). Hogrefe Ltd.

Schwarzinger, D., & Schuler, H. (2020). *Dark Triad of Personality at Work* (TOP; Finnish Adaptation). Hogrefe Psykologien Kustannus Oy.

Schwarzinger, D., & Schuler, H. (2021a). *TOP – Temná triáda osobnosti v pracovním prostředí* (TOP; Czech Adaptation). Hogrefe – Testcentrum s.r.o.

Schwarzinger, D., & Schuler, H. (2021b). *TOP Werkgerelateerde persoonlijkheidsvragenlijst over de 'dark triad'* (TOP; Dutch Adaptation). Hogrefe Uitgevers.

Schwarzinger, D., & Schuler, H. (2021c). *Dark Triad of Personality at Work* (TOP; Italian Adaptation). Hogrefe Editore.

Schwarzinger, D., & Schuler, H. (2022a). *Dark Triad of Personality at Work* (TOP; Swedish Adaptation). Hogrefe Psykologiförlaget AB.

Schwarzinger, D., & Schuler, H. (2022b). *Dark Triad of Personality at Work* (TOP; Norwegian Adaptation). Hogrefe Psykologiförlaget AB.

Schwarzinger, D., Schuler, H., Gelléri, P., Mussel, P., & Winter, C. (2010). *Shedding light from the dark side: Integrity from the perspective of the Dark Triad.* Poster contribution at the Congress of the German Society of Psychology, Bremen.

Schyns, B. (2015). Dark personality in the workplace: Introduction to the special issue. *Applied Psychology, Special Issue, 64*, 1–14. https://doi.org/10.1111/apps.12041

Semenyna, S.W., Belu, C.F., Vasey, P.L., & Honey, P.L. (2017). Not straight and not straightforward: The relationships between sexual orientation, sociosexuality, and Dark Triad traits in women. *Evolutionary Psychological Science, 4*, 1–14.

Shaffer, J.A., & Postlethwaite, B.E. (2012). A matter of context: A meta-analytic investigation of the relative validity of contextualized and noncontextualized personality measures. *Personnel Psychology, 65*, 445–494. https://doi.org/10.1111/j.1744-6570.2012.01250.x

Shiramizu, V.K.M., Kozma, L., DeBruine, L.M., & Jones, B.C. (2019). Are Dark Triad cues really visible in faces? *Personality and Individual Differences, 139*, 214–216. https://doi.org/10.1016/j.paid.2018.11.011

Shotland, A., Alliger, G.M., & Sales, T. (1998). Face validity in the context of personnel selection: A multimedia approach. *International Journal of Selection and Assessment, 6*, 124–130. https://doi.org/10.1111/1468-2389.00081

Shultz, C.J. (1993). Situational and dispositional predictors of performance: A test of the hypothesized Machiavellianism x structure interaction among sales persons. *Journal of Applied Social Psychology, 23*, 478–498. https://doi.org/10.1111/j.1559-1816.1993.tb01099.x

Simonet, D.V., Tett, R.P., Foster, J., Angelback, A.I., & Bartlett, J.M. (2018). Dark-side personality trait interactions: Amplifying negative predictions of leadership performance. *Journal of Leadership & Organizational Studies, 25*, 233–250. https://doi.org/10.1177/1548051817727703

Sitser, T., van der Linden, D., & Born, M.P. (2013). Predicting sales performance criteria with personality measures: The use of the general factor of personality, the Big Five and narrow traits. *Human Performance, 26*, 126–149. https://doi.org/10.1080/08959285.2013.765877

Skeem, J.L., & Cooke, D.J. (2010). Is criminal behavior a central component of psychopathy? Conceptual directions for resolving the debate. *Psychological Assessment, 22*, 433–445. https://doi.org/10.1037/a0008512

Skeem, J.L., Polaschek, D.L., Patrick, C.J., & Lilienfeld, S.O. (2011). Psychopathic personality: Bridging the gap between scientific evidence and public policy. *Psychological Science in the Public Interest, 12*, 95–162. https://doi.org/10.1177/1529100611426706

Sleep, C.E., Lynam, D.R., Hyatt, C.S., & Miller, J.D. (2017). Perils of partialing redux: The case of the Dark Triad. *Journal of Abnormal Psychology, 126*, 939–950. https://doi.org/10.1037/abn0000278

Smith, C.A., Organ, D.W., & Near, J.P. (1983). Organizational citizenship behavior: Its nature and antecedents. *Journal of Applied Psychology, 68*, 653–663. https://doi.org/10.1037/0021-9010.68.4.653

Smith, D.B., & Ellingson, J.E. (2002). Substance versus style: A new look at social desirability in motivating contexts. *Journal of Applied Psychology, 87*, 211–219. https://doi.org/10.1037/0021-9010.87.2.211

Smith, M.B., Hill, A.D., Wallace, J.C., Recendes, T., & Judge, T.A. (2018). Upsides to dark and downsides to bright personality: A multidomain review and future research agenda. *Journal of Management, 44*, 191–217. https://doi.org/10.1177/0149206317733511

Smith, M.B., Wallace, C.J., & Jordan, P. (2016). When the dark ones become darker: How promotion focus moderates the effects of the Dark Triad on supervisor performance ratings. *Journal of Organizational Behavior, 37*, 236–254. https://doi.org/10.1002/job.2038

Smith, M.B., & Webster, B.D. (2017). A moderated mediation model of Machiavellianism, social undermining, political skill, and supervisor-rated job performance. *Personality and Individual Differences, 104*, 453–459. https://doi.org/10.1016/j.paid.2016.09.010

Smith, S.F., & Lilienfeld, S.O. (2013). Psychopathy in the workplace: The knowns and unknowns. *Aggression and Violent Behavior, 18*, 204–218. https://doi.org/10.1016/j.avb.2012.11.007

Society for Industrial and Organizational Psychology (SIOP). (2018). *Principles for the validation and use of personnel-selection procedures* (5th ed.). Author. https://www.apa.org/ed/accreditation/about/policies/personnel-selection-procedures.pdf

Southard, A.C., & Zeigler-Hill, V. (2016). The Dark Triad traits and fame interest: Do dark personalities desire stardom? *Current Psychology: A Journal for Diverse Perspectives on Diverse Psychological Issues, 35*, 255–267. https://doi.org/10.1007/s12144-016-9416-4

Soyer, R.B., Rovenpor, J.L., & Kopelman, R.E. (1999). Narcissism and achievement motivation as related to three facets of the sales role: Attraction, satisfaction and performance. *Journal of Business and Psychology, 14*, 285–304. https://doi.org/10.1023/A:1022147326001

Spain, S.M. (2019). *Leadership, work, and the dark side of personality*. Academic Press.

Spain, S.M., Harms, P., & LeBreton, J.M. (2014). The dark side of personality at work. *Journal of Organizational Behavior, 35*, 41–60. https://doi.org/10.1002/job.1894

Sparks, J.R. (1994). Machiavellianism and personal success in marketing: The moderating role of latitude for improvisation. *Journal of the Academy of Marketing Science, 22*, 393-400. https://doi.org/10.1177/0092070394224008-400.393

Spezzaferri, M.R., Collins, G., Aguilar, J.E., & Larsen, A.M. (2017). Moral depravity: Going beyond just an attribute of psychopathy. *Journal of Forensic Psychology, 2*, 1000122. https://doi.org/10.4172/2475-319X.1000122

Spurk, D., Keller, A.C., & Hirschi, A. (2016). Do bad guys get ahead or fall behind? Relationships of the Dark Triad of personality with objective and subjective career success. *Social Psychological and Personality Science, 7*, 113–https://doi.org/10.1177/1948550615609735. 121

Staufenbiel, T., & Hartz, C. (2000). Organizational citizenship behavior: Entwicklung und Validierung eines Messinstruments [Organizational citizenship behavior: Development and validation of an instrument]. *Diagnostica, 46*, 73–83. https://doi.org/10.1026//0012-1924.46.2.73

Stephan, U. (Ed.). (2015). Beyond the bright side: Dark personality in the workplace [Special Issue]. *Applied Psychology*, 64.

Steyer, R., & Eid, M. (2001). *Messen und Testen* [Measuring and testing] (2nd ed.). Springer. https://doi.org/10.1007/978-3-642-56924-1

Stucke, T.S. (2003). Who's to blame? Narcissism and self-serving attributions following feedback. *European Journal of Personality, 17*, 465–478. https://doi.org/10.1002/per.497

Sumner, C., Byers, A., Boochever, R., & Park, G.J. (2012). Predicting Dark Triad personality traits from twitter usage and a linguistic analysis of tweets. In IEEE. (Eds.), *Proceedings at the IEEE 11th International Conference on Machine Learning and Applications* (pp. 386–393). IEEE. https://doi.org/10.1109/ICMLA.2012.218

Sutton, A., Roche, M., Stapleton, M., & Roemer, A. (2020). Can psychopathy be adaptive at work? Development and application of a work focused self-and other-report measure of the triarchic psychopathy model. *International Journal of Environmental Research and Public Health, 17*, Article 3938. https://doi.org/10.3390/ijerph17113938

S & F Personalpsychologie (Ed.). (n.d.a). *Selbsteinschätzungsskala der Intelligenz* [Self-assessment scale of intelligence] (Self-IQ). S & F Personalpsychologie.

S & F Personalpsychologie (Ed.). (n.d.b). *Kurzskala der allgemeinen Intelligenz* [Short scale of general intelligence] (KAPPA). S & F Personalpsychologie.

S & F Personalpsychologie (Ed.). (n.d.c). *Beruflicher Interessentest* [Occupational interests test] (INTEREST). S & F Personalpsychologie.

S & F Personalpsychologie (Ed.). (n.d.d). *Beruflicher Motivationstest* [Occupational motivation test] (BMT). S & F Personalpsychologie.

S & F Personalpsychologie (Ed.). (n.d.e). *Persönlichkeitsinventar zur Integritätsabschätzung* [Personality inventory to assess integrity] (PIA). S & F Personalpsychologie.

Tellegen, A. (1993). Folk concepts and psychological concepts of personality and personality disorder. *Psychological Inquiry, 4*, 122–130. https://doi.org/10.1207/s15327965pli0402_12

Templer, K.J. (2018). Dark personality, job performance ratings, and the role of political skill: An indication of why toxic people may get ahead at work. *Personality and Individual Differences, 124*, 209–214. https://doi.org/10.1016/j.paid.2017.11.030

ten Brinke, L., Black, P.J., Porter, S., & Carney, D.R. (2015). Psychopathic personality traits predict competitive wins and cooperative losses in negotiation. *Personality and Individual Differences, 79*, 116–122. https://doi.org/10.1016/j.paid.2015.02.001

ten Brinke, L., Kish, A., & Keltner, D. (2018). Hedge fund managers with psychopathic tendencies make for worse investors. *Personality and Social Psychology Bulletin, 44*, 214–223. https://doi.org/10.1177/0146167217733080

Tikkanen, R., Auvinen-Lintunen, L., Ducci, F., Sjöberg, R.L., Goldman, D., Tiihonen, J., Ojansuu, I., & Virkkunen, M. (2011). Psychopathy, PCL-R, and MAOA genotype as predictors of violent reconvictions. *Psychiatry Research, 185*, 382–386. https://doi.org/10.1016/j.psychres.2010.08.026

Titze, J., Blickle, G., & Wihler, A. (2017). Fearless dominance and performance in field sales: A predictive study. *International Journal of Selection and Assessment, 25*, 299–310. https://doi.org/10.1111/ijsa.12181

Tokarev, A., Phillips, A.R., Hughes, D.J., & Irwing, P. (2017). Leader dark traits, workplace bullying, and employee depression: Exploring mediation and the role of the dark core. *Journal of Abnormal Psychology, 126*, 911–920. https://doi.org/10.1037/abn0000299

Touhey, J.C. (1973). Intelligence, Machiavellianism and social mobility. *British Journal of Clinical Psychology, 12*, 34–37. https://doi.org/10.1111/j.2044-8260.1973.tb00842.x

Trzesniewski, K.H., Donnellan, M.B., & Robins, R.W. (2008). Is "Generation Me" really more narcissistic than previous generations? *Journal of Personality, 76*, 903–918. https://doi.org/10.1111/j.1467-6494.2008.00508.x

Tupes, E.C., & Christal, R.E. (1958). *Stability of personality trait ratings obtained under diverse conditions* (USAF WADC techn. Note. No. 58-61, AD-151 041). Personnel Research Laboratory, Wright Air Development Center, Lackland Air Force Base. https://doi.org/10.21236/AD0151041

Tupes, E.C., & Christal, R.E. (1961). *Recurrent personality factors based on trait ratings* (USAF ASD Tech. Rep. No. 61-97). U.S. Government Printing Office. https://doi.org/10.21236/AD0267778

Turner, C.F., & Martinez, D.C. (1977). Socioeconomic achievement and the Machiavellian personality. *Sociometry, 40*, 325–336. https://doi.org/10.2307/3033481

Twenge, J.M., & Campbell, S.M. (2008). Generational differences in psychological traits and their impact on the workplace. *Journal of Managerial Psychology, 23*, 862–877. https://doi.org/10.1108/02683940810904367

Twenge, J.M., & Campbell, W.K. (2009). *The narcissism epidemic: Living in the age of entitlement*. Simon and Schuster.

Twenge, J.M., & Foster, J.D. (2010). *Birth cohort increases in narcissistic personality traits among American college students*, 1982-2009. *Social Psychological and Personality Science, 1*, 99–106. https://doi.org/10.1177/1948550609355719

Twenge, J.M., Konrath, S., Foster, J.D., Campbell, W.K., & Bushman, B.J. (2008). Egos inflating over time: A cross-temporal meta-analysis of the Narcissistic Personality Inventory. *Journal of Personality, 76*, 875–902. https://doi.org/10.1111/j.1467-6494.2008.00507.x

Ullrich, S., Farrington, D.P., & Coid, J.W. (2008). Psychopathic personality traits and life-success. *Personality and Individual Differences, 44*, 1162–1171. https://doi.org/10.1016/j.paid.2007.11.008

Van Geel, M., Goemans, A., Toprak, F., & Vedder, P. (2017). Which personality traits are related to traditional bullying and cyberbullying? A study with the Big Five, Dark Triad and sadism. *Personality and Individual Differences, 106*, 231–235. https://doi.org/10.1016/j.paid.2016.10.063

Van Iddekinge, C.H., Lanivich, S.E., Roth, P.L., & Junco, E. (2013). Social media for selection? Validity and adverse impact potential of a Facebook-based assessment. *Journal of Management, 42*, 1811–1835. https://doi.org/10.1177/0149206313515524

Van Iddekinge, C.H., Roth, P.L., Raymark, P.H., & Odle-Dusseau, H.N. (2012). The criterion-related validity of integrity tests: An updated meta-analysis. *Journal of Applied Psychology, 97*, 499–530. https://doi.org/10.1037/a0021196

Vander Molen, R.J., Kaplan, S., Choi, E., & Montoya, D. (2018). Judgments of the Dark Triad based on Facebook profiles. *Journal of Research in Personality, 73*, 150–163. https://doi.org/10.1016/j.jrp.2017.11.010

Van Scotter, J. R. (2020). Narcissism in CEO research: A review and replication of the archival approach. *Management Review Quarterly, 70*, 629–674. https://doi.org/10.1007/s11301-019-00178-1

van Someren, G., Livesey, A., Gutierrez, S., & Khabo, N. (2019). There is no "ab" in "normal": Bridging the gap between adaptive and maladaptive personality. *Industrial and Organizational Psychology, 12*, 184–189. https://doi.org/10.1017/iop.2019.36

Vedel, A., & Thomsen, D.K. (2017). The Dark Triad across academic majors. *Personality and Individual Differences, 116*, 86–91. https://doi.org/10.1016/j.paid.2017.04.030

Vernon, P.A., Villani, V.C., Vickers, L.C., & Harris, J.A. (2008). A behavioral genetic investigation of the Dark Triad and the Big 5. *Personality and Individual Differences, 44*, 445–452. https://doi.org/10.1016/j.paid.2007.09.007

Veselka, L., Giammarco, E.A., & Vernon, P.A. (2014). The Dark Triad and the seven deadly sins. *Personality and Individual Differences, 67*, 75–80. https://doi.org/10.1016/j.paid.2014.01.055

Veselka, L., Schermer, J.A., & Vernon, P.A. (2011). Beyond the Big Five: The Dark Triad and the supernumerary personality inventory. *Twin Research and Human Genetics, 14*, 158–168. https://doi.org/10.1375/twin.14.2.158

Veselka, L., Schermer, J.A., & Vernon, P.A. (2012). The Dark Triad and an expanded framework of personality. *Personality and Individual Differences, 53*, 417–425. https://doi.org/10.1016/j.paid.2012.01.002

Viswesvaran, C., & Ones, D.S. (1999). Meta-analyses of fakeability estimates: Implications for personality measurement. *Educational and Psychological Measurement, 59*, 197–210. https://doi.org/10.1177/00131649921969802

Viswesvaran, C., Schmidt, F.L., & Ones, D.S. (2005). Is there a general factor in ratings of job performance? A meta-analytic framework for disentangling substantive and error influences. *Journal of Applied Psychology, 90*, 108–131. https://doi.org/10.1037/0021-9010.90.1.108

Vize, C.E., Collison, K.L., Miller, J.D., & Lynam, D.R. (2018). Examining the effects of controlling for shared variance among the Dark Triad using meta-analytic structural equation modeling. *European Journal of Personality, 32*, 46–61. https://doi.org/10.1002/per.2137

Vize, C.E., Lynam, D.R., Collison, K.L., & Miller, J.D. (2018). Differences among Dark Triad components: A meta-analytic investigation. *Personality Disorders: Theory, Research, and Treatment, 9*, 101–111. https://doi.org/10.1037/per0000222

Volmer, J., Koch, I.K., & Göritz, A.S. (2016). The bright and dark sides of leaders' Dark Triad traits: Effects on subordinates' career success and well-being. *Personality and Individual Differences, 101*, 413–418. https://doi.org/10.1016/j.paid.2016.06.046

Volmer, J., Koch, I.K., & Wolff, C. (2019). Illuminating the "dark core": Mapping global versus specific sources of variance across multiple measures of the Dark Triad. *Personality and Individual Differences, 145*, 97–102. https://doi.org/10.1016/j.paid.2019.03.024

Wai, M., & Tiliopoulos, N. (2012). The affective and cognitive empathic nature of the Dark Triad of personality. *Personality and Individual Differences, 52*, 794–799. https://doi.org/10.1016/j.paid.2012.01.008799. 794

Wallace, H.M., & Baumeister, R.F. (2002). The performance of narcissists rises and falls with perceived opportunity for glory. *Journal of Personality and Social Psychology, 82*, 819–834. https://doi.org/10.1037/0022-3514.82.5.819

Waller, N.G., & Zavala, J.D. (1993). Evaluating the Big Five. *Psychological Inquiry, 4*, 131–134. https://doi.org/10.1207/s15327965pli0402_13

Watts, A.L., Lilienfeld, S.O., Smith, S.F., Miller, J.D., Campbell, W.K., Waldman, I.D., Rubenzer, S.J., & Faschingbauer, T.J. (2013). The double-edged sword of grandiose narcissism: Implications for successful and unsuccessful leadership among US presidents. *Psychological Science, 24*, 2379–2389. https://doi.org/10.1177/0956797613491970

Watts, A.L., Waldman, I.D., Smith, S.F., Poore, H.E., & Lilienfeld, S.O. (2017). The nature and correlates of the Dark Triad: The answers depend on the questions. *Journal of Abnormal Psychology, 126*, 951–968. https://doi.org/10.1037/abn0000296

Webster, G.D., & Jonason, P.K. (2013). Putting the "IRT" in "Dirty": Item response theory analyses of the Dark Triad Dirty Dozen – An efficient measure of narcissism, psychopathy, and Machiavellianism. *Personality and Individual Differences, 54*, 302–306. https://doi.org/10.1016/j.paid.2012.08.027

Wetzel, E., Brown, A., Hill, P.L., Chung, J.M., Robins, R.W., & Roberts, B.W. (2017). The narcissism epidemic is dead; long live the narcissism epidemic. *Psychological Science, 28*, 1833–1847. https://doi.org/10.1177/0956797617724208

Widiger, T.A., Trull, T.J., Clarkin, J.F., Sanderson, C., & Costa, P.T., Jr. (2002). A description of the DSM-IV personality disorders with the five-factor model of personality. In P.T. Costa, Jr. & T.A. Widiger (Eds.), *Personality disorders and the five-factor model of personality* (pp. 89–99). American Psychological Association. https://doi.org/10.1037/10423-006

Wiggins, J.S., & Trapnell, P.D. (1997). Personality structure: The return of the Big Five. In R. Hogan, J.A. Johnson, & S.R. Briggs (Eds.), *Handbook of personality psychology* (pp. 737–765). Academic Press.

Wille, B., De Fruyt, F., & De Clercq, B. (2013). Expanding and reconceptualizing aberrant personality at work: Validity of five-factor model aberrant personality tendencies to predict career outcomes. *Personnel Psychology, 66*, 173–223. https://doi.org/10.1111/peps.12016

Williams, K.M., McAndrew, A., Learn, T., Harms, P.D., & Paulhus, D.L. (2001). *The Dark Triad returns: Entertainment preferences and antisocial behavior among narcissists, Machiavellians, and psychopaths.* Paper presented at the Annual Meeting of the American Psychological Association, San Francisco.

Williams, K.M., Orpen, S., Hutchinson, L.R., Walker, L.J., & Zumbo, B.D. (2006). *Personality, empathy, and moral development: Examining ethical reasoning in relation to the Big Five and the Dark Triad*. Paper presented at the Annual Meeting of the Canadian Psychological Association, Calgary, Alberta.

Williams, K.M., Paulhus, D.L., & Hare, R.D. (2007). Capturing the four-factor structure of psychopathy in college students via self-report. *Journal of Personality Assessment, 88*, 205–219. https://doi.org/10.1080/00223890701268074

Winterberg, C. A., Tapia, M. A., Nei, K. S., & Brummel, B. J. (2019). A clarification of ADA jurisprudence for personality-based selection. *Industrial and Organizational Psychology, 12*, 172–176. https://doi.org/10.1017/iop.2019.34

Wisse, B., Barelds, D.P., & Rietzschel, E.F. (2015). How innovative is your employee? The role of employee and supervisor Dark Triad personality traits in supervisor perceptions of employee innovative behavior. *Personality and Individual Differences, 82*, 158–162. https://doi.org/10.1016/j.paid.2015.03.020

Wisse, B., & Sleebos, E. (2016). When the dark ones gain power: Perceived position power strengthens the effect of supervisor Machiavellianism on abusive supervision in work teams. *Personality and Individual Differences, 99*, 122–126. https://doi.org/10.1016/j.paid.2016.05.019

Wissing, B.G., & Reinhard, M.A. (2017). The Dark Triad and the PID-5 maladaptive personality traits: Accuracy, confidence and response bias in judgments of veracity. *Frontiers in Psychology, 8*, Article 1549. https://doi.org/10.3389/fpsyg.2017.01549

World Health Organization (WHO). (2019). *International classification of diseases for mortality and morbidity statistics. Eleventh revision (ICD-11)*. Author. https://icd.who.int/icd11refguide/en/index.html

Wright, J.P., Morgan, M.A., Almeida, P.R., Almosaed, N.F., Moghrabi, S.S., & Bashatah, F.S. (2017). Malevolent forces: Self-control, the Dark Triad, and crime. *Youth Violence and Juvenile Justice, 15*, 191–215. https://doi.org/10.1177/1541204016667995

Wu, J., & LeBreton, J.M. (2011). Reconsidering the dispositional basis of counterproductive work behavior: The role of aberrant personality. *Personnel Psychology, 64*, 593–626. https://doi.org/10.1111/j.1744-6570.2011.01220.x

Yang, Y., & Raine, A. (2009). Prefrontal structural and functional brain imaging findings in antisocial, violent, and psychopathic individuals: A meta-analysis. *Psychiatry Research: Neuroimaging, 174*, 81–88. https://doi.org/10.1016/j.pscychresns.2009.03.012

Yang, Y., Raine, A., Colletti, P., Toga, A.W., & Narr, K.L. (2010). Morphological alterations in the prefrontal cortex and the amygdala in unsuccessful psychopaths. *Journal of Abnormal Psychology, 119*, 546–554. https://doi.org/10.1037/a0019611

Yildirim, B.O., & Derksen, J.J. (2013). Systematic review, structural analysis, and new theoretical perspectives on the role of serotonin and associated genes in the etiology of psychopathy and sociopathy. *Neuroscience & Biobehavioral Reviews, 37*, 1254–1296. https://doi.org/10.1016/j.neubiorev.2013.04.009

Zeigler-Hill, V.E., Besser, A., Morag, J., & Campbell, W.K. (2016). The Dark Triad and sexual harassment proclivity. *Personality and Individual Differences, 89*, 75–79. https://doi.org/10.1016/j.paid.2015.09.048

Zeigler-Hill, V.E., & Marcus, D.K. (2016). *The dark side of personality: Science and practice in social, personality, and clinical psychology*. American Psychological Association. https://doi.org/10.1037/14854-000

Zettler, I., Friedrich, N., & Hilbig, B.E. (2011). Dissecting work commitment: The role of Machiavellianism. *Career Development International, 16*, 20–35. https://doi.org/10.1108/13620431111107793

Zettler, I., & Solga, M. (2013). Not enough of a "dark" trait? Linking Machiavellianism to job performance. *European Journal of Personality, 27*, 545–554. https://doi.org/10.1002/per.1912

Zhang, I.Y., & Goffin, R.D. (2018). *Evil geniuses at work: Does intelligence interact with the Dark Triad to predict workplace deviance?* Undergraduate Honors Theses, Psychology Department, University of Western Ontario.

Zhu, D.H., & Chen, G. (2015). Narcissism, director selection, and risk-taking spending. *Strategic Management Journal, 36*, 2075–2098. https://doi.org/10.1002/smj.2322

Ziegler, M., & Bühner, M. (2009). Modeling socially desirable responding and its effects. *Educational and Psychological Measurement, 69*, 548–565. https://doi.org/10.1177/0013164408324469

Ziegler, M., Danay, E., Heene, M., & Bühner, M. (2011). *Faking in Persönlichkeitsinventaren: Ein potemkinsches Dorf?* [Faking in personality inventories: A Potemkin village?] Lecture at the conference of the working group Differential Psychology, Personality Psychology and Psychological Diagnostics, Saarbrücken.

Zimmermann, J., Altenstein, D., Krieger, T., Grosse Holtforth, M. G., Pretsch, J., Alexopoulos, J., Spitzer, C., Benecke, C., Krueger, R. F., Markon, K. E., & Leising, D. (2014). The structure and correlates of self-reported DSM-5 maladaptive personality traits: Findings from two German-speaking samples. *Journal of Personality Disorders, 28*, 518–540. https://doi.org/10.1521/pedi_2014_28_130

Zimmermann, J., Brakemeier, E. L., & Benecke, C. (2015). Alternatives DSM-5-Modell zur Klassifikation von Persönlichkeitsstörungen [Alternative DSM-5-model for the classification of personality disorders]. *Psychotherapeut, 60*, 269–227. https://doi.org/10.1007/s00278-015-0033-8

Peer Commentaries

This book offers an excellent overview of the theoretical foundations of the Dark Triad and its relation to other personality constructs, especially the Big Five. Readers learn about the history of the underlying research and assessment related aspects, and are provided with practical recommendations. I was very impressed by the comprehensive approach and the easy-to-understand presentation. This is a book that much can be taken from.

Matthias Ziegler, PhD, Department of Psychology, Humboldt-Universität zu Berlin, Germany

This book is an excellent starting point for everyone interested in learning about the Dark Triad traits and their relationships to a variety of social and workplace outcomes. It provides a comprehensive history of the Dark Triad concept, critical commentary on the current standing of this literature, and helpful suggestions for how an understanding of the Dark Triad traits in the workplace could be enhanced through the development of better measures and more robust research designs. In short, it is an accessible, engaging, and informative introductory text for those who may be interested in exploring the ways in which the Dark Triad may be relevant for understanding the world of work.

Peter D. Harms, PhD, Department of Management, The University of Alabama, Tuscaloosa, AL, USA

Dr. Schwarzinger has produced an organized and accessible collection of research related to the Dark Triad traits at work. It is a great resource for scholars and practitioners who seek to explore the research on the Dark Triad. It takes the reader through the foundational steps of what the Dark Triad is, how these traits affect the workplace, and the steps that need to be taken to address future challenges. Thus, it not only covers the basics, but goes beyond to propose applied solutions. In doing so, Dr. Schwarzinger takes the Dark Triad research out of the abstract and into the applied with a comprehensive volume on a badly needed topic.

Daniel N. Jones, PhD, Management and Interdisciplinary Social Psychology, University of Nevada, Reno, NV, USA